Energy Psychology Interactive

Energy Psychology Interactive
Rapid Interventions for Lasting Change

David Feinstein, Ph.D.

In consultation with Fred P. Gallo, Ph.D., Donna Eden, and the
Energy Psychology Interactive Advisory Board

Foreword by Candace Pert, Ph.D.

Keyed to the
Energy Psychology Interactive CD Training Program
for Health Care Professionals

Innersource
Ashland, OR

INNERSOURCE, 777 East Main Street, Ashland, OR 97520
541-482-1800
www.innersource.net

Cover design by Tracy Baldwin

Printed in Canada

Library of Congress Control Number 2002114994

Catalog Information:

    Feinstein, David
        Energy Psychology Interactive: Rapid Interventions for
        Lasting Change – First edition
                Includes bibliographic references and index
                ISBN 0-9725207-7-5 (Pbk)
                1. Energy Psychology–Tutorial and Reference
                2. Mind and body therapies
                3. Acupressure 4. Mental Healing
                I.Title   2004
                616.89'1 – dc 21

Dedication

To Peg Elliott Mayo, mentor, favorite living novelist, forever friend . . .

Join the Free Online *Energy Psychology Interactive* e-Group

http://groups.yahoo.com/group/EnergyPsychology

For information about Continuing Education Credit or about the *Energy Psychology Interactive* CD Training Program and the *Self-Help Guide*, both keyed to this text, visit

www.EnergyPsychologyInteractive.com.

Energy Psychology Interactive Advisory Board

Contents

Acknowledgments   xi

Foreword   xiii

Introduction   1

1. The *Basic* Basics   15

2. Energy Checking   37

3. Neurological Disorganization   57

4. Psychological Reversals   75

5. The Opening Phases of Treatment   93

6. Meridian Treatment Basics   109

7. Formulating Energy Interventions   127

8. Advanced Meridian Treatments   137

9. Closing Phases   151

10. The State of the Art   165

Epilogue: Subtle Energy—Psychology's Missing Link   187

Postscript: A Skeptic's Journey   191

Appendix I: Articles, Lists, and Resources   195

Appendix II: Meridian Charts   257

Links   277

References   279

Index   283

Acknowledgments

GRATITUDE TO FRED GALLO AND DONNA EDEN for their dedicated, pioneering work with energy methods and their direct support and contributions to this program, cannot be overstated.

George Goodheart, Alan Beardall, David Walther, Sheldon Deal, and John Thie, by bringing the energy perspective of ancient Eastern healing arts into the Western and thoroughly modern form called Applied Kinesiology, provided the foundation upon which this program rests.

The pioneering work of Roger Callahan and John Diamond in applying the principles of Applied Kinesiology for treating psychological problems is respectfully acknowledged.

The contributions of the *Energy Psychology Interactive* Advisory Board, in setting a high clinical and academic standard for this program, have been immense.

In addition to the Advisory Board, the following practitioners of energy psychology also reviewed earlier versions of this program. Their comments were exceedingly valuable and are gratefully acknowledged: Bill Beckett, Patricia Butler, Gary Craig, Stephanie J. Eldringhoff, Sue Fraser, Marian Jerry, Wayne McCleskey, and Ronda Mau.

The following practitioners of energy psychology have provided some of the case material that appears on the CD: Dan Benor, Robin Bilazarian, Patricia Carrington, Asha Nahoma Clinton, Gary Craig, John Diepold, Donna Eden, Fred Gallo, Wayne McCleskey, Deborah Mitnick, Gary Peterson, Larry Stoler, and some who preferred to remain anonymous to further insure client confidentiality.

As any author who has taken a book into publication fully appreciates, the contributions of the production people who work behind the scenes are incalculable. Special thanks go to Martha Meyer, who designed this book as well as the *Self-Help Guide*, Anne Hellman, who has been a dream of a copyeditor, and Tracy Baldwin, who conceived of and created the cover design. Deborah Malmud, Director of Norton Professional Books, has supported *Energy Psychology Interactive* from the beginning and lent prestige and visibility by arranging for Norton to distribute the program.

The following individuals provided substantial technical and computer assistance: Catherine Christopher, Lori Kats, Patrick Russell, Amy Walinsky, and especially Judith Allgood and David Alvarez. Judith Allgood was responsible for the final design of the CD.

While the influences of each of these individuals are gratefully acknowledged, responsibility for the program's content rests solely with its author.

Foreword

OUR ABILITY TO HELP PEOPLE overcome self-defeating emotional patterns, achieve higher levels of psychological well-being, and open their spiritual sensibilities is accelerating at an extraordinary pace. This program introduces you to a powerful development within this unfolding story.

The biochemical underpinnings of awareness—of sensations such as pleasure and pain, drives such as hunger and thirst, emotions such as anger and joy, and "higher" states such as awe and spiritual inspiration—have been identified. "Informational substances" such as hormones, peptides, and neurotransmitters find their way—in one of nature's most stunning designs—to receptor molecules that are on the surface of every cell in the body.

Even though the "molecules of emotion" have been precisely mapped throughout the brain and body, their actions are highly dynamic, not at all static. When emotions flow, informational substances move to receptor molecules, learning occurs. A person's mental and emotional state can also be influenced by synthetic informational substances—medications designed to target specific receptors. Whether natural or synthetic, the molecules of emotion shape mood and thought. Significantly, it is a two-way process. Emotions and thoughts initiate a series of cascading chemical events—including the formation of new neurons!—that are the basis of other emotions and thoughts. Some studies suggest, in fact, that meditation may be as effective as medication in alleviating anxiety and depression.

Energy Psychology Interactive is a synthesis of practices designed to deliberately shift the molecules of emotion. These practices have four distinct advantages over psychiatric medications. They are non-invasive, highly specific, have no side effects, and they are free. Energy interventions are rooted in an emerging paradigm that is still just outside the embrace of Western science, though it has long been central to the worldview of Eastern medicine and spiritual disciplines.

These practices focus on the body's "energy system," which includes the familiar electromagnetic spectrum and is also believed to encompass so-called subtle energies. While not well understood, subtle energies can be operationally defined as energies that cannot be measured using existing instrumentation but which, like gravity, are known for their effects. Energy is also involved, it is becoming abundantly clear, in the link between chemistry and emotion. There is much interest now in understanding this connection in Western scientific terms. One hypothesis, for example, emphasizes the rate of the molecular vibration of receptors and their ligands as a key to understanding emotional energy. The program you are about to begin teaches you how to influence these energies to shift patterns of emotion, thought, and behavior that are blatantly dysfunctional, or simply limiting.

Energy Psychology Interactive is designed for psychotherapists and other health practitioners who are interested in psychological issues. It is an early formulation of a new field, bringing unfamiliar methods into the therapist's office, using tapping as much as talk, aiming for energy integration as much as insight. The procedures, as you will see, can look quite strange. The range of appropriate clinical and other applications is still being debated, but my personal impression, based on my own experience, is that it is enormous.

The "state of the art" within energy psychology is characterized by four contradictions. First, a flood of reports coming from reputable, well-credentialed psychotherapists claiming clinical results that are unusual in their speed and in their effectiveness, even with recalcitrant problems, raises both interest and suspicion. Second, this substantial body of anecdotal evidence is not yet backed by controlled clinical investigations. Third, if research were to verify the clinical outcomes claimed by the field's proponents, some of the mechanisms involved may well lie outside of established explanatory models. Fourth, the enthusiasm of the field's proponents has been met with the strong misgivings of authoritative credentialing bodies.

Enter *Energy Psychology Interactive*. David Feinstein was conducting research on psychotherapeutic innovations at the Department of Psychiatry of the Johns Hopkins University Medical School in the 1970s, the same time I was there doing my early work on the opiate receptor. Thirty years later his focus has turned to the intersection of psychotherapy and energy medicine. While he has practiced as a clinical psychologist during the intervening decades and in fact pioneered a powerful system for helping people transform their guiding myths, he has also accumulated some unusual credentials for a psychologist, not the least of which is that he is married to one of the world's most renowned energy healers, Donna Eden.

With *Energy Psychology Interactive*, Dr. Feinstein has culled through the wide range of practices being used by at least 5,000 psychotherapists whose work explicitly focuses on the body's energy systems. In consultation with Dr. Fred Gallo, author of several of the pioneering professional books on energy psychology, and Donna Eden, who provided the perspective of energy medicine, he identified the procedures that seemed the most promising, and he organized them into a systematic approach for introducing the field's basic methods to clinicians who are new to energy psychology. He then submitted this formulation to an advisory board of 24 of the field's leading thinkers and acknowledged innovators with the question, "Does this program cover the essential methods that clinicians who are new to energy psychology would need to learn in order to incorporate its methods into their practices?" Because the field, new as it is, already has many factions, the critiques of the 24 people who form the advisory board led to literally hundreds of changes in the program, large and small, until the presentation represented a consensus of techniques and explanations.

Energy psychology is a leading-edge therapy and *Energy Psychology Interactive* is a leading-edge way to learn it, combining print and electronic media to provide a thoroughly engaging, self-paced experience. Its teaching style includes a Socratic question-and-answer format, video demonstrations that appear with the click of a mouse, multiple practice sessions, and hundreds of links to other parts of the program and to auxiliary papers, charts, diagrams, and relevant websites.

Energy psychology has rapidly become one of the hottest areas of what I call "New Paradigm Medicine." Research is accumulating which suggests that healing the emotions is not only a gateway to a happier and more fulfilling life, it is a gateway to healing the body of virtually any physical illness. Based on the meticulous process by which it was developed, *Energy Psychology Interactive* is the most authoritative introduction available to clinicians who wish to incorporate this highly significant set of innovations into their practices. I am personally committed to conducting research in this important area, but as with so many effective treatments in medicine, the current lack of understanding of its mechanisms should not prevent people from benefiting now by applying the procedures presented in this program.

—Candace Pert, Ph.D.
Research Professor
Georgetown University School of Medicine

Introduction

Energy Psychology applies principles and techniques for working with the body's physical energies to facilitate desired changes in emotions, thought, and behavior. Energy psychology has been used interchangeably with "energy-based psychotherapy," or simply "energy therapy," and it is also an umbrella term for numerous specific formulations, such as Thought Field Therapy, Emotional Freedom Techniques, Energy Diagnostic and Treatment Methods, and more than a dozen others.

Case Examples

While applications of energy psychology are being pioneered with clients suffering from a wide range of diagnoses, its methods have received the most attention for their purported speed and effectiveness with anxiety-related disorders, such as phobias, generalized anxiety, and post-traumatic stress disorder (PTSD). A case that illustrates its use with PTSD introduces you to the approach.

A Vietnam veteran who had been in therapy for 17 years for PTSD suffered from over 100 haunting, recurrent war memories, a major height phobia (related to having made more than 50 parachute jumps), and severe insomnia. The energy treatment initially focused on the height phobia. In a protocol that has some similarities to systematic desensitization, the client imagined a fear-provoking situation involving heights. At the same time, several acupuncture points (or, acupoints) were stimulated by having the client tap them. Within 15 minutes of this treatment, the client had no subjective sense of fear when imagining situations involving heights. To test this in vivo, the client walked up several stories in the building, climbed onto the fire escape, and looked down. He expressed amazement when he had no phobic reaction whatsoever.

The treatment then focused on several of the client's most intense war memories. They were similarly "neutralized" within an hour. He still remembered them, of course, but they had lost their debilitating emotional charge. The therapist taught him a technique for stimulating acupoints that he could apply to his remaining memories outside the treatment setting. He complied with this back-home assignment. Within a few days his insomnia had cleared. At a two-month follow-up, he was still free of the height phobia, the insomnia, and the intrusion of disturbing war memories. The treatment, administered at the Veteran's Administration Hospital in Los Angeles by Gary Craig, one of the pioneers of energy psychology, is documented on videotape and available through www.emofree.com. Another video showing the rapid cure of a height phobia can be found on the CD that supplements this book (access from "Video Clip Index").

Energy interventions have been successfully applied with a wide range of psychological disorders, but phobia treatments (as in the above case and the video on the CD) lend themselves particularly well to demonstrations because the results can be immediately tested. In the video, you will see the subject begin to shake, perspire, and fight back a sense of being pulled forward as she approaches the edge of a balcony. Thirty minutes later, you see her calmly walk up to the railing, lean over, and with some shock and disbelief, say about her longstanding fear of heights, "It's gone!!!"

I was recently scheduled to co-teach a week-long class on complementary medicine, but my arrival was delayed for several days. My co-instructor decided to introduce me to the class by having me demonstrate a phobia treatment. The volunteer was a 37-year-old woman who had had a debilitating stroke at age 30. When she was placed in an MRI machine, she became fearful, began to panic, and then terror took over. She had been claustrophobic ever since, to the point that she could not sleep with the lights out or even under a blanket, could not drive through a tunnel, or get into an elevator. Besides being enormously inconvenient, this was confidence-shattering as she worked to regain her speech. So there we were, her and me in front of the group. Within 20 minutes of reprogramming her meridian energy response to enclosed places (using techniques you will learn in this program for stimulating selected acupuncture points while having her mentally activate the fear-inducing stimulus), her anxiety when thinking about taking an MRI went from 10+, on a scale of 10, down to 0.

The only way I could think to test it was to have her go back into her room and get into the closet. During the break, she did just that. She went into the closet and her partner then turned out the lights. She stayed there five minutes with no anxiety. When she returned to report what happened to the group, she said the only problem was that she found it "boring." The rest of the group was amazed. That evening she slept with the lights out and under the covers for the first time in seven years. Her partner was elated.

Six weeks after this single session, the following e-mail arrived: "You are not going to believe this! The test of all claustrophobia tests happened to me. I got stuck in an elevator by myself for nearly an hour. In the past I would have gone nuts and clawed the door off, but I was calm and sat down on the floor and waited patiently for the repair men to arrive. . . . It was an amazing confirmation that I am no longer claustrophobic!!!!!!! Thank you. Thank you."

Based upon a growing body of clinical evidence, her phobia is not likely to return unless bad fortune retraumatizes her in a situation that involves an enclosed space. While I would not have attempted such a single-session demonstration unless my initial interactions and questions led to a sense that the person was relatively stable and that the phobia was specific to a particular context rather than a symptom of deeper psycho- logical issues, the basic techniques can be used in a wide range of clinical situations. This program will show you how to apply them, and it will give you a context for determining when they are and are not indicated.

3

How Can This Be?

You just read descriptions of three long-standing phobias being decisively cured within 15 to 30 minutes each. Some had not responded to years of treatment. Experienced therapists, on hearing of such near-instant cures for long-standing problems, are understandably skeptical. Therapy is not that rapid. Time is needed for building rapport, examining the antecedents of the problem, exploring the meaning of the symptoms in the person's life, assessing which therapeutic modalities are most appropriate for this unique situation, and applying them. What is going on? Are these stories falsified or are they the three most impressive outcomes from many thou- sands of cases, selectively exhibited to dramatize and embellish? Surely they do not represent the typical course of treatment.

They do and they don't. For an uncomplicated phobia—an irrational fear that is not enmeshed with other significant emotional issues—the results reported are neither unusual nor extraordinary. If we try to understand these reports in terms of insight, cognitive restructuring, reward and punishment, or even the curative powers of the therapeutic relationship, the treatment outcomes make no sense. If we examine electrochemical shifts in brain chemistry that are brought about by stimulating acupuncture points, however, a coherent hypothesis begins to emerge. The neurological basis of the reported clinical outcomes of stimulating acupuncture points in the treatment of anxiety can be summarized as follows:

> Stimulating acupuncture points while simultaneously activating an anxiety-provoking image changes the neurological connections to the amygdala and other brain structures in a manner that reduces the anxious response to that image.

This summary of the actions of stimulating acupuncture points is based on three empirically demonstrated principles:

1. Brain wave patterns that are markers of anxiety have been identified and are generally accepted (Amen, 2003).
2. Stimulating a given acupuncture point sends signals to given parts of the brain (Cho, 1998). A study coming out of Harvard Medical School concludes: "These preliminary results [based upon functional MRI readings] suggest that acupuncture needle manipulation modulates the activity of the limbic system and subcortical structures. We hypothesize that modulation of subcortical structures may be an important mechanism by which acupuncture exerts its complex multi-system effects" (Hui et al., 2000).
3. Reactivating a memory makes it vulnerable to events that can change the connections to and from the amygdala that are implicated in conditioned fear (Nader, Schafe, & LeDoux, 2000).

Brain wave studies conducted by Joaquín Andrade, M.D. (a member of the *EPI* Advisory Board), demonstrate how these principles converge so that stimulating certain acupuncture points while an anxiety-evoking image has been activated sends signals that normalize the affected wave patterns (see brain scan images accessed from the Embedded Topics Index of the CD). Early clinical trials suggest that neutralizing an anxiety-evoking thought, image, or memory in this manner is rapid and tends to be permanent, and this has become one of the core procedures being advanced within energy psychology. Acupuncture points, charted thousands of years ago, have low electrical resistance as well as high concentrations of receptors that are responsive to mechanical stimulation of the skin. Tapping, massaging, or holding them, as well as more invasive procedures like the use of needles or electrical impulses, activates signals that go to various brain centers and appear potent in shifting brain wave patterns, often bringing disturbed patterns, as seen on brain scans, to within normal range.

These electrochemical shifts correlate with the reduction of fear in the treatment of a simple phobia. While most clients do not present with a simple phobia, the procedure can be adapted to a wide range of other problems and therapeutic goals. As problems become more complex, the modalities a therapist might use need to expand, focusing on cognitive, affective, behavioral, and interpersonal dimensions of the problem. But the psychological difficulties people bring into therapy can often be traced to dysfunctional emotional responses within specific situations. And working with acupuncture points can be surprisingly effective in reprogramming such responses.

The *Energy* of Energy Psychology

Stimulating an acupuncture point in the toe affects blood activity in the brain (Cho, 1998). No nerve, vascular, or other physical connections are known to exist, but somehow an electrical impulse has been transmitted that reliably sets certain events into motion. Such signals, and the brain wave frequencies they affect, are energies that are targeted within energy psychology, but they are not the only energies that are of concern. Still, they explain a great deal about the sequence by which 1) a phobia is mentally evoked, 2) certain points on the skin that send impulses to the brain when they are stimulated are tapped, and 3) the symptoms rapidly diminish.

Other kinds of energy are also worked with within energy psychology (see p. 215 for a brief overview of the body's electrical, electromagnetic, and subtle energy systems), but introducing them brings us ever further from established paradigms. While the "signal and brain wave" hypothesis provides a fair mechanical explanation for the actions of some of the basic procedures within energy psychology, many practitioners of energy interventions feel that other kinds of energy are also involved. They believe that other cultures have been more astute than ours in exploring the energies that are the very foundation of life. In non-technological societies, for instance, healers are often far more attuned to the forces that surge through the body and employ natural means to influence them to increase health, from suggestion and hypnosis to herbs and healing touch. *Chi*, the basis of acupuncture, is among the most well-known terms in the West for describing energies that cannot be experienced directly through the senses, yet which are believed to influence people's lives. Most cultures, however, have analogous concepts, such as *ki* (in Japan), *prana* (in India and Tibet), *baraka* (in Sufism), *waken* (in the Lakota Sioux tradition), *megbe* (in the Ituri pygmy culture of the northeastern Congo forests), and *yesod* (in Jewish Kabalistic tradition).

Another kind of energy, the "biofield," can readily be measured by existing instrumentation, but it also exhibits some unusual properties. The electromagnetic field produced by the heart, for instance, can be detected anywhere on the surface of the body using an electrocardiogram (ECG). This field also extends a number of feet away from the body, radiating in all directions, as can be measured by an instrument called a SQUID-based magnetometer. When two people are within conversational distance, fluctuations in the heart signal of one correspond with fluctuations in the brain waves of the other (McCraty, in press). Far more than just electrical fluctuations, your heart's energies carry information that influences a person's mood, personality, and preferences. The body's "brain" is not just in the brain. Cells throughout the body receive and transmit informational molecules that impact mental states (Pert, 1977). The degree to which organs besides the brain carry psychologically relevant information is vividly evidenced in transplant patients. Documented reports on dozens of people who have received a donor heart have revealed unanticipated shifts in the recipient toward tastes and behavioral patterns that were characteristic of the donor (Pearsall, 1998).

A fourth kind of energy field referred to in energy psychology, and this one is far outside established paradigms, is the thought field. Thought affects not only the neurons in our brain, it can affect physical events outside our body. Studies at a variety of centers, from the Department of Engineering at Princeton (Radin, 1997) to the Department of Physical Sciences at Stanford (Tiller, 1997) to the Heartmath Institute in California (www.heartmath.com), have provided impressive empirical evidence that human intention can alter the activity of material, electrical, and biological processes. Some concept of subtle energy or of a "thought field" is often posited to explain these observed phenomena.

Subtle Energy

While it is not necessary to accept the subtle energy hypothesis to understand how stimulating an acupuncture point can send electrochemical signals that affect brain wave patterns, it is not possible to introduce energy psychology without addressing the concept of subtle energy. The term is often used if vaguely defined ("energies that cannot be measured by existing instrumentation but which are known for their effects"). Subtle energy hypotheses keep being introduced in attempting to account for phenomena that elude established understanding. And it is the phenomena we cannot explain, the anomalies, that cause us to expand our paradigms.

For instance, the physical impact, from a distance, of visualization and prayer on people, animals, plants, organs, blood, and cells is well established (Benor, 2001), suggesting that some form of energy is activated by the mind that affects physical matter. Hundreds of controlled studies, in fact, now document the beneficial effects of prayer, from making geraniums grow faster to decreasing the risk of complications in cardiac patients (Dossey, 1993; Harris et al., 1999).

Various mechanical methods can also detect the effects of mental activity on the physical world. Researchers at several independent centers, for instance, have found that readings of a random event generator (an electronic device that uses a random physical process such as radioactive decay to generate random events or random numbers) reveal different patterns when in the presence of a group of people whose attention is focused (as when watching a touchdown during a football game) than with a group whose attention is scattered (Radin, 1997). Attempts to explain this often replicated phenomenon tend to require some concept of subtle energy or organizing field (a field is a "region of influence") to account for the way the attention of the individuals in the group appears to produce patterns in the output of a random number generator.

The two photos on the next page provide a vivid demonstration of the possible impact of mental activity on physical matter.[1] The first is a microscope's magnification of an ice crystal. The second is the magnification of an ice crystal after a prayer was offered in the presence of water from the same source. The water was subsequently frozen and photographed.

---

[1] From *Messages from Water* by Japanese researcher Masaru Emoto, 1999, pp. 135 and 137, respectively. Reprinted with permission. For further information, visit www.hado.net.

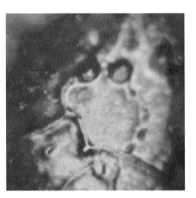 

Water from Fujiwara Dam, frozen before offering a prayer and magnified.

Water from Fujiwara Dam, frozen after offering a prayer and magnified.

These images are taken from a provocative two-volume study of the effects of various conditions on water crystals, including the source of the water (crystals derived from a spring in Saijo, Japan, do not resemble crystals taken from a polluted section of the Yodo River in Japan), the effects of music (crystals derived from water that was exposed to Bach do not resemble crystals from water that was exposed to heavy metal music), and exposure to different emotions (appreciation leads to beautiful symmetrical crystals, hatred to disfigured patterns). Although these findings have so far not been replicated, if subsequent research does show the procedures to be sound and the findings to be reliable, the series of photos would constitute a vivid demonstration of the impact of thought on physical matter. Given that the human body is over 70 percent water, these demonstrations have caused many people to think twice about what they think.

What possible mechanism could account for these dramatic effects of mental activity? An explanation favored among practitioners of energy psychology is that subtle energies or energy fields, influenced by the mind, operate in concert with the firing of the neurons. Mental activities such as prayer and focused intention, along with the corresponding brain activity, produce or influence energy fields that are capable of impacting physical events, such as the crystal structure of water or the output of "random" number generators. Increased attention to the presumed effects of subtle energy is, in fact, leading to new models within the healing arts.

These "new" models echo, however, the insights of healers, seers, mystics, and spiritual adepts throughout the ages. While the notion that the physical body is coupled with an energy field, a subtle body, or energy body, is not new, what is new is that these energies are being examined scientifically (see research summaries in Becker, 1990; Collinge, 1998; Gerber, 2001; Oschman, 2000; and Tiller, 1997). In energy-based psychotherapy, dysfunctional patterns of thought and behavior are understood as being coded or carried in the client's energy field. They are treated in part by shifting the electromagnetic and other more subtle energies that are maintaining them. As with Chinese medicine, to which some of its roots trace, the theoretical core of energy psychology is simple:

> *Whatever the presenting problem, it has a counterpart in the client's energy system and can be treated at that level.*

The Field of Energy Psychology

Energy psychology, as such, is a relatively new discipline. The first national professional meeting in the United States was held in 1999. Although research evidence is still limited, systematic investigation does support claims regarding energy treatments in related areas, such as acupuncture (see, for example, the journal *Clinical Acupuncture and Oriental Medicine*) and Therapeutic Touch (Hover-Kramer, 2001).

9

Anesthesia through acupuncture, for instance, is now used throughout the world and has been widely documented in procedures from appendectomies to heart surgery (and brought to public attention in the U.S. when Bill Moyers televised a brain operation in which acupuncture was the primary anesthetic and the patient was alert and in dialogue during the procedure). While this is challenging for many Westerners to assimilate into their worldviews, once this well-established phenomenon is accepted, it is a relatively small conceptual step to entertain the possibility that stimulating a set of acupuncture points can reduce anxiety. Empirical demonstrations of energy fields and associated phenomena date back at least to Harold Burr's work at Yale in the 1930s (Gerber, 2001).

Evidence bearing upon the efficacy of energy psychology itself is also accumulating. Anecdotal reports are numerous. Clinical accounts describing the successful application of energy psychology with phobias, generalized anxiety, PTSD, obsessive-compulsive disorders, psychogenic illnesses, and other psychiatric disorders are being offered by clinicians from a wide range of backgrounds. Thousands of clinical records in the files of the 24 members of the *Energy Psychology Interactive* Advisory Board alone suggest that both therapist-assisted and back-home applications of energy psychology have led to rapid improvement, often in situations where traditional psychotherapy has had little effect. Some of these cases are on videotape, along with follow-up interviews, and are readily available for examination (sources for obtaining such videos are listed in Chapter 1).

Systematic research supporting the field's claims is beginning to be conducted. Some 31,400 patients received energy therapy treatments over a 14-year period at 11 allied treatment centers in Argentina and Uruguay (see p. 197). Records of the intake evaluation (the most prevalent diagnosis was anxiety disorder), procedures used, and clinical outcomes were all maintained, and the patients were followed at 1 month, 3 months, 6 months, and 12 months after treatment. While these are very preliminary pilot studies, the clinical success rates exceeded what would be expected from the established treatment of choice for anxiety disorders—the coordinated use of cognitive-behavior therapy (CBT) and medication. Beyond this large-scale clinical trial, which had no control group, randomized, controlled pilot studies were also conducted. One of these compared approximately 2,500 patients receiving energy therapy treatment with 2,500 receiving CBT and medication. The energy therapy was superior to the CBT/medication protocol in the proportion of patients showing some improvement (90% vs. 63%) and the proportion of patients showing complete remission of symptoms (76% vs. 51%). In another pilot study by the same team, the length of treatment was significantly shorter with energy therapy than with CBT (mean = 3 sessions vs. mean = 15 sessions).

A small but rapidly expanding circle within the psychotherapeutic profession considers the ability to work directly with the energies underlying a client's presenting problem to be an essential clinical tool. While at this point there is still a lack of consensus about the essential mechanisms that might explain the favorable treatment outcomes, virtually all of the energy-based psychotherapies share two essential components:

1. They all have the client mentally access a "problem state."
2. They simultaneously introduce an intervention designed to balance energies that become disturbed when that problem state is accessed.

There is also general agreement among practitioners that energy interventions retrain the body so that a stimulus which had triggered a disturbed emotional response no longer evokes that response.

What You Will Learn in *Energy Psychology Interactive*

As in any other form of treatment, energy psychology sessions vary widely from practitioner to practitioner, client to client, and session to session. However, certain features distinguish energy-based psychotherapy from other treatment approaches, and in this program you will gain skill and understanding about each of these components. Along with developing rapport and gathering information about the client's background and treatment goals, the major elements of energy-based psychotherapy include:

1. Explaining the nature of an energy-oriented approach to psychological problems, discussing its relevance to the client's concerns, and obtaining *informed consent* about proceeding.
2. Introducing procedures such as *energy checking* for assessing the body's energies as they impact and are impacted by psychological problems.
3. Checking for and correcting specific forms of *neurological disorganization* that tend to interfere with the outcome of energy-based treatment techniques.
4. Checking for and correcting a specific variation of cognitive dissonance, called a *psychological reversal*, which also tends to interfere with treatment outcomes if left unchecked.
5. Identifying an initial *target problem*, often within a more comprehensive treatment plan, and formulating that problem in a manner that is appropriate for energy interventions.
6. Assessing the client's *subjective level of distress* in relationship to the target problem as well as the level of distress in the body's energetic response to the target problem.
7. *Energetically "locking"* the problem into the body (for the purposes of the treatment session).
8. Proceeding with a series of procedures designed to *reprogram energy responses* that are involved with the target problem.
9. *Anchoring the gains* by pairing energy methods with mental projections of positive back-home outcomes and teaching energy techniques for use in the back-home setting.

11

You will gain basic skills and knowledge in each of these areas by working through this book or the corresponding modules in the CD. The program provides both an entry point for the clinician with little or no experience in energy-based approaches to psychotherapy and a resource for experienced practitioners. It takes you step by step through many of the fundamentals of energy psychology.

The Relationship of This Book to the CD

Compared to the CD, the book is *Energy Psychology Interactive Lite*. The CD is a highly interactive course, using a Socratic question-and-answer format, integrated practice sessions, art, color, videotaped instruction for many of the techniques, and hundreds of hyperlinks for moving within the program as well as to related websites. The CD also includes many more topics. The book, however, is more convenient. It can be read wherever you wish. Its diagrams, charts, and summaries, printed from the CD, are readily accessible. It includes the basic instructions given in each of the CD's nine modules on the "elements of treatment," translated from the CD's interactive format into a text presentation. Many people prefer reading a book to a computer screen, and the book/CD program is intended to accommodate as wide a range of personal preferences and learning styles as possible.

So, depending on your preferences, you can move from here to Chapter 1 *or* to the first module of the CD. You can, in fact, go through the entire program on the CD and use the book only for reference and review. Everything in the book is on the CD. But you can also begin with the book and later pursue the CD for greater depth. Because the material in the book is presented in normal text format and the same material is presented on the CD in an interactive question-and-answer format, you can master the concepts quite readily by first reading a chapter in the book and then going through the corresponding module on the CD for review and greater depth. The CD, which works much like a website, is very user-friendly, and it can be fun to jump to wherever you feel drawn. The book, used alone, will still provide a solid introduction to the fundamental concepts and procedures of energy-based psychotherapy.

Getting Started

The CD is comprised of 17 Basic Modules: 9 covering the elements of energy-oriented psychotherapy (each corresponding to a chapter in this book) and 8 additional units that are designed to broaden your knowledge and skill base after you have mastered the basic elements of treatment. Numerous figures, flow charts, tables, client handouts, instruction sheets, and monographs on topics of interest that are accessed directly from the CD's 17 Basic Modules are also listed in the CD's Embedded Topics Index, so that you can study them independently as you wish (some of these are also printed in the book's Appendices).

Wherever you see the ⛶ symbol in the book, a video clip illustrating the procedure being presented can be found in the corresponding module of the CD. You can also access the video clips directly through the CD's Video Clip Index. If you begin with the CD, you will find that each of its 17 Basic Modules opens with a brief introduction to the topic you are about to explore and is then comprised primarily of interactive questions and answers. These questions, rather than reviewing material you have already studied, are ways of introducing you to each new idea that will follow. They are to stimulate your interest and curiosity. They are not to test you—you are not expected to know the answers—though if you have already read the corresponding chapter in the book, you can use them to review the program and to gain a sense of the degree to which you have mastered the material. Also placed within many of the modules, as well as the corresponding book chapters, are suggestions for "practice sessions." While not essential for continuing through the module or the chapter, they serve as an early bridge across the divide between theory and practice.

The program is designed for self-study. It also lends itself well to an ongoing study group. An excellent way to learn the materials is for two or more individuals to independently go through the program, a module or chapter at a time, and then meet to discuss the principles described and practice the techniques it presents. This is also the way in which the program is typically used as a text for graduate classes in psychology and related fields.

The first chapter of the book (and the first module of the CD), "The *Basic* Basics," is designed to provide you with an experience of how energy psychology works and feels. It introduces you to some of the discipline's more fundamental methods and invites you to experience them with relatively little explanation. The remainder of the program builds upon these "*basic* basics" and provides theory and rationale for each additional procedure that is introduced. The six "use considerations" listed below frame the designers' intentions regarding the relationship between the program and its user, and specify important disclaimers.

Use Considerations

1. *Energy Psychology Interactive* is based on the premise that those who apply the methods it teaches will do so in contexts appropriate to their level of clinical training, experience, and licensing. Also please see the discussion of ethical considerations on pp. 97–98.

2. The program systematically develops in the user a knowledge base and a set of skills for bringing an energy perspective to the treatment of psychological problems. It provides you with concepts, formulas, and techniques. To use a musical analogy, mastering them is like mastering the notes of a scale. In the hands of a seasoned practitioner, the formulas and techniques fall away into the moment-by-moment inspiration of a jazz player who excels at improvisation.

3. Face-to-face training, personal therapy that utilizes an energy-based approach, and supervised clinical experience will help you advance the skills offered by this program into their seasoned application.

4. While rooted in a 5,000-year-old tradition, energy psychology as such is a relatively new field of practice. The treatments presented in this program are still considered "experimental." Research on their effectiveness is underway, successful clinical outcomes have been reported by a wide range of practitioners, and a handful of preliminary studies appear promising. The efficacy of these methods, however, has not yet been established through a body of published, replicated, peer-reviewed studies.

5. The material in this program is intended as a training resource for psychotherapists and other professionals in the healing arts. It is not a substitute for psychological treatment.

6. While many clinical reports describe successful treatments using energy psychology with multiple-trauma patients, borderline personality, and other serious psychiatric disorders, these uses are often adjuncts to more established treatment approaches. Energy-oriented interventions should be used with serious mental disorders only by clinicians already trained and experienced in working with these disorders.

—1—

The Basic *Basics*

AFTER INTRODUCING YOU to a few of the field's basic concepts, this chapter will lead you through an experience with some of the most basic tools used in energy psychology. It offers a subjective introduction to the methods from a client's perspective.

Thousands of anecdotal reports (this program is based in part on interviews with more than 30 practitioners of energy psychology) suggest that a broad spectrum of emotional, psychological, and behavioral problems or goals lend themselves to energy-based interventions. These interventions often complement more traditional treatment methods, but energy techniques alone can be effective with numerous conditions. In the 11 treatment centers in South America mentioned in the Introduction, where 31,400 patients received energy psychology treatments, several preliminary clinical trials were conducted to determine the indications and contraindications for energy interventions.

Based on this preliminary systematic observation (see p. 197), energy-based procedures that focus on the meridian system seem to be particularly effective with anxiety-related conditions—panic disorders, generalized anxiety, PTSD, phobias, separation anxiety disorders, and acute distress disorders—as well as with delimited emotional problems (not involving personality disorders) related to fear, grief, guilt, anger, shame, jealousy, rejection, painful memories, loneliness, frustration, love pain, procrastination, and impulse control. An energy-based approach may be effective as an adjunct to more conventional therapies for personality disorders, depressive disorders, dissociative disorders, addictions, and eating disorders, but probably should not be the primary treatment for these conditions. There is some preliminary evidence that a meridian-oriented approach is ineffective or contraindicated with psychotic disorders, bipolar disorders, delirium, and dementia, but the integration of energy interventions with other treatments in working with even these disorders is now being reported.

Because much of the evidence within energy psychology is still anecdotal, any conclusions regarding the clinical efficacy of energy-based interventions are highly tentative at this time. The body of clinical reports published by energy-based psychotherapists is rapidly expanding, however, and a variety of case treatments are documented on videotape and available for review and critique. You may at this point wish to view the clip mentioned earlier on the CD 📼 , demonstrating one of the "single-session phobia cures" that have brought so much popular attention to energy psychology while at the same time sparking so much understandable skepticism within the psychotherapy profession. It is from an expanding base of documented outcomes such as this one, however—certainly not from early extravagant claims, odd-looking procedures, or contradictory theoretical explanations—that so many seasoned clinicians are being drawn to incorporate energy-based techniques into their practices.

Videotaped treatment sessions and follow-up interviews conducted by many of the leaders within energy psychology are available through their respective websites (see "Links," p. 247) and are often instructive as well as persuasive. Two videotaped treatments, for instance, showing rapid symptom relief with women who had been raped, are available from www.tat-intl.com/tat-materials.htm. In a poignant videotaped energy-based treatment, a crime victim who had been decompensating for six months despite medication and periods of hospitalization, attained rapid relief in a single session and returned to normal functioning within three sessions. The video is available through msise3@aol.com.

A compelling series of sessions, presented on video and audio tape, is part of the Emotional Freedom Techniques (EFT) home study course (available through www.emofree.com). Several dozen people are treated for a wide range of physical and psychological problems. Some of the outcomes are starkly illustrated, as when a woman with a fear of rats, after

16

a brief treatment, allows a pet rat to lick her fingers as she says, "I don't believe I'm doing this. I am doing this!" The treatment of the Vietnam veteran described in the Introduction is part of this series, which also shows work with several other men suffering from years of PTSD who are relieved of intense symptoms in the space of a single session.

By the end of this chapter, you will have identified a troubling memory and worked with it using one of the simplest, most fundamental energy-based treatment protocols that have been formulated. Proponents of this method claim, nonetheless, that it is effective more than 80 percent of the time for certain well-delimited problems, such as uncomplicated phobias.

Tapping Techniques

The strategies for intervening in the body's energy system by tapping energy gateway points on the surface of the skin are collectively called "tapping techniques." The rationale for this approach, and for related techniques that massage, hold, pinch, circle, or trace over certain areas of the body, will be addressed in the following chapters.

Several systems for tapping energy points have been developed and taught widely. It is likely that a number of your clients will have been exposed to them. Protocols from Thought Field Therapy (TFT), Energy Diagnostic and Treatment Methods (EDxTM) Emotional Freedom Techniques (EFT), Be Set Free Fast (BSFF), the Tapas Acupressure Technique (TAT), and Thought Energy Synchronization Therapies (TEST), to name a few, have been taught to hundreds of thousands of people, and the numbers are growing. Each is based on the underlying principle emphasized earlier: *Psychological problems have a counterpart in the client's energy system and can be treated at that level.*

The treatments focus on the body's energy responses in relationship to psychological problems and have both a *psychological* component and a *mechanical/energetic* component. Energy psychology gained notoriety based on widely publicized claims of its effectiveness in bringing about rapid symptomatic relief, and you will see in this chapter that the most basic techniques are quite mechanical and symptom oriented. While its methods have also been applied to psychodynamic and archetypal dimensions of experience, this program focuses on more circumscribed problems. Once you have learned the mechanics, you can apply the techniques to broader psychodynamic, existential, and spiritual concerns and integrate them with virtually any other system of psychotherapy for the purpose of making that system more effective. This program teaches you those mechanics.

What Do I Need to Learn to Begin to Incorporate an Energy-Based Approach into My Own Clinical Practice?

This chapter presents a basic, "one-size-fits-all" approach to formulating energy interventions. It appears, however, based on thousands of anecdotal reports and very preliminary research findings, to produce the desired outcome with some frequency. The self-experiments presented in this chapter will give you a more direct basis for evaluating the methods.

The approach you will learn here traces back to methods from traditional Chinese medicine as popularized in the U.S. through Roger Callahan's Thought Field Therapy. Many variations of this approach, both shortcuts and elaborations, have been formulated. Gary Craig's Emotional Freedom Techniques is probably the most widely known of these, notable for being accessible, effective (based on preliminary evidence), and easily learned. We will begin by providing you with enough instruction in EFT[1] so that you can apply it to a personal issue.

After this rudimentary introduction to EFT, the program provides an overview of the range of ways energy psychology is practiced and a broader set of tools that can be adapted to a spectrum of clinical situations. Specifically, it adds a series of layers to the basic treatment protocol presented in this chapter. These additional methods will give you greater flexibility and power to pursue increasingly complex and recalcitrant psychological problems. When the most basic basics you are about to learn do not produce the desired outcome, the more advanced procedures presented in the remainder of the program can be applied.

A Preliminary Step: The Three Thumps/Three Navel Touch

Even before focusing on a psychological issue, a variety of techniques can be used to balance the energies in the nervous system and optimize their flow. While a more complete set of procedures is presented in Chapter 3

18

---

[1] This presentation of EFT was written with generous consultation from Gary Craig.

(Neurological Disorganization), a brief sequence of six simple techniques (all six can be completed within 90 seconds) is taught here. It will in many instances improve the energetic balance of the nervous system and increase the effectiveness of subsequent energy interventions. It is called the Three Thumps/Three Navel Touch :

The Three Thumps

Certain points on your body, when tapped with your fingers, will affect your nervous system in predictable ways, sending electrochemical impulses to targeted regions of your brain and releasing neurotransmitters. By tapping three specific sets of points, a sequence called the Three Thumps, you can activate a series of internal responses that will help restore you when you are tired, increase your vitality, and keep your immune system stronger amidst stress. The three thumps include the K-27 points, the thymus, and the spleen points. Tap each for 15–20 seconds. You can tap these points any time you need a boost.

19

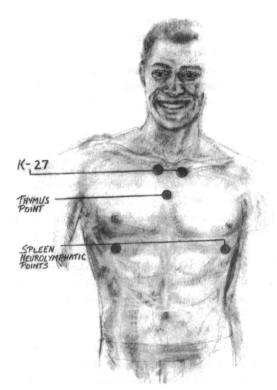

FIGURE 1.1
Do not be too concerned about finding the precise location of each point. If you use several fingers to tap in the vicinity shown on the drawing, you will hit the right spots. Tap hard enough that you hear the tap, but never so hard as to risk bruising yourself.

Drawing by Brooks Garten reproduced, with permission, from Donna Eden's *Energy Medicine*.

Thump	Approximate Time
K-27 Points	15–20 seconds
Thymus Gland	15–20 seconds
Spleen Points	15–20 seconds

1—K-27

20

2—THYMUS

3—SPLEEN POINTS

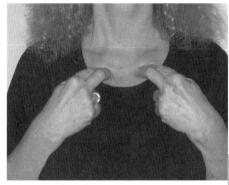

The Three Navel Touch

Following the Three Thumps, breathe deeply as you perform the:

1. Navel/Skull-Base Hold.

- Find the soft area where the back of your neck merges with the base of your skull.
- Place your thumb and forefinger into this area with a bit of pressure.
- Place the middle finger of your other hand into your navel, push in, pull up.
- Hold for about 12 seconds.

2. Navel/Tailbone Massage.

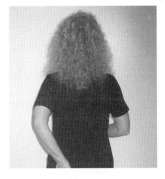

- Simultaneously hold or rub the tailbone and the navel for about 12 seconds.

21

3. Navel/Third-Eye Hook-Up.

- Place the middle finger of one hand on the third eye (between the eyebrows above the bridge of the nose).
- Place the middle finger of the other hand in the navel.
- Gently push in and pull both fingers upwards and hold for about 12 seconds.

A principle illustrated by this set of procedures is that many energy interventions require very little time to obtain the desired effect. Some, such as these, are more like flipping a switch; others, which are more like dredging a river, are more time consuming. This brief sequence is worth memorizing and using whenever you are not functioning at your best, physically or mentally. It will jumpstart your own energy system. And it can help prepare your clients, energetically and neurologically, for subsequent energy interventions.

An Overview of the Basic EFT Sequence

EFT is among the most streamlined approaches available, which is another reason we begin with it. After steps to optimize the energy flow in the nervous system, three additional preliminaries include:

> **PRELIMINARIES:**
> **A target problem** is *identified*.
> **This problem** is *rated* on a scale from 0 to 10 for the amount of distress it causes.
> **A reminder phrase** (a few words that bring the problem to mind) is *selected*.

Target problems can range from daily concerns to serious disorders. Emotional and physical reactions, habits of thought, or patterns of behavior that get in a person's way can all be shifted using energy-based interventions. Examples of day-to-day problems that lend themselves to this approach include:

- *Emotional reactions*, such as: "Every time I see a large dog, I feel fear that traces back to having been bitten as a child."
- *Physical reactions*, such as: "When I think of confronting my boss, I get a headache."
- *Habits of thought*, such as: "I worry obsessively that my daughter will not start a family until it is too late for her to have children."
- *Patterns of behavior*, such as: "I promise myself, over and over, that I will stop interrupting people when they are speaking with me, yet all my relationships continue to suffer from this habit."

Once a problem area has been identified, rated in terms of the amount of distress it causes, and associated with a reminder phrase, the steps are then as follows (familiarize yourself with them here; you will be applying them to a personal issue later in the chapter):

> TREATMENT
>   1. **Set-up affirmation**
>   2. **Tapping sequence**
>   3. **Bridging technique**
>   4. **Tapping sequence** (again)
>   5. **Subsequent rounds**

Step 1: The Set-Up Affirmation

The **set-up affirmation** is designed to resolve a specific form of internal conflict about a desired change, called a *psychological reversal*. Psychological reversals involve unconscious resistance to the treatment goal, as well as a resistance within the body's energy system. Until they are resolved, no other therapeutic intervention is likely to have a deep or lasting effect. While psychological reversals may operate on many different levels (and an entire chapter is devoted to them), practitioners of energy-based psychotherapy have developed some deceptively simple yet apparently effective methods for working with psychological reversals.

EFT offers one of the simplest of these methods for addressing psychological reversals. It accomplishes this with a blanket intervention rather than formulating the treatment around assessments of the specific type of psychological reversal, as you will learn to do in Chapter 4. EFT is a self-help program whose training manual freely acknowledges the importance of assessment and diagnosis in clinical settings, but it offers instead *generic* treatment strategies that it claims are, nonetheless, effective with a high proportion of individuals and their problems.

The two parts to the set-up affirmation are the *affirmation* and an *energy intervention* that involves rubbing a specific point on the body. 🔊

The Affirmation

The **affirmation** includes a few words that are "filled in" based on the target problem. The form of the affirmation is as follows:

23

*"Even though I have this _____, I deeply love
and accept myself."*

The blank is filled in with a brief description of the problem being addressed. For example:

- *"Even though I have this fear of dogs, I deeply love and accept myself."*
- *"Even though I get a headache when I think of confronting my boss, I deeply love and accept myself."*
- *"Even though I have this obsession about my daughter's biological clock, I deeply love and accept myself."*
- *"Even though I have this habit of interrupting people, I deeply love and accept myself."*

This is, of course, only a partial list keyed to the earlier examples. Any psychological or behavioral problem or goal can be inserted into this format.

The affirmation is best stated out loud and with feeling and emphasis. It does not matter whether or not you believe it to be a true statement, it is a self-suggestion that becomes more true in the process of saying it and stimulating specific energy points. While the phrase "I deeply love and accept myself" may seem like an overly simple and pat self-affirmation, it actually penetrates to the heart of the psychological reversal (reasons for this are discussed in Chapter 4). Various alternative wordings are possible within this general format, acknowledging the problem and creating an affirmation of self-acceptance despite the existence of the problem. The format shown here, however, is easy to memorize and has been used widely with good reports. An alternative to the phrase, "I deeply love and accept myself," when working with children, might be along the lines of "I know I'm a great kid deep inside."

Other formats have also been used. A popular one emphasizes choice and opportunity (access an overview of psychologist Patricia Carrington's Choices Method from the Embedded Topics Index of the CD) rather than self-acceptance, e.g., "Even though I have neglected my body, I choose to know that I deserve to have the time for regular, enjoyable exercise," or "Even though I still focus on my son's shortcomings, I choose to know that I deeply love and accept him." The strategy is to stimulate energy points that help pair a negative self-evaluation with a positive cognition or recog-

24

nition of an opportunity. In essence, this programs the negative thought to become a trigger for a positive choice.

This method can be used even in situations that are bleak or overwhelming. A depressed client in his first psychotherapy session developed the affirmation, "Even though my life feels hopeless, I choose to find unexpected help in this therapy." Writing to her colleagues the day after September 11, 2001, on how to help people deal with the psychological aftermath of the attack, Dr. Carrington suggested phrasings such as: "Even though I am stunned and bewildered by this terrible happening, I choose to learn something absolutely essential for my own life from this event" (or ". . . , I choose to be a still point amidst all the chaos"; or ". . . , I choose to have this dreadful event open my heart"; or ". . . , I choose to sense the Divine intent for a greater good in all this").

The Energy Intervention

An **energy intervention** is the second part of the set-up affirmation. As you will be learning throughout this program, the body's energy system can be affected by rubbing, tapping, stretching, holding, or tracing specific points or areas on the surface of the body. The effectiveness of the set-up affirmation can be increased substantially by rubbing points referred to as the "sore spots." Located in the upper left and right portions of the chest, you can find them by pressing in on various points until you find one or more that are sore. This is the area you will rub while stating the affirmation three times. You may want to rub an area on each side simultaneously.

25

The sore spots are lymphatic points where toxins tend to accumulate, thus blocking the flow of the body's energies. Soreness is felt as clusters of toxins are broken apart by rubbing the points, dispersing them for elimination and opening a flow of energy to the heart, chest cavity, and entire body. You may want to rub both sides simultaneously.

SORE SPOTS

Rubbing a sore spot should not cause more than a little discomfort. If it does, apply less pressure. Also, if you have had an operation in that area of the chest or if there is any medical reason that you should not be probing in that specific area, switch to the other side (or see alternative energy interventions for working with psychological reversals in Chapter 4).

You will later be putting together each of the elements of this basic protocol and focusing them on a personal issue.

Step 2: The Tapping Sequence

The EFT tapping sequence is concerned with the flow of energy through the body's *meridians*, or energy pathways. There are 14 major meridians and each is associated with points on the surface of the skin that, when tapped or otherwise stimulated, move the energy through the entire meridian system. As reported in EFT, only a subset of these points is usually necessary because the meridians are interconnected and stimulating one meridian can affect others. Various subsets have been used. The protocol you will learn here teaches eight points that are used in both EFT and TFT ⏚ . The abbreviations for the eight tapping points are summarized below in the same order as they are presented on the chart.

1. EB (for "Beginning of the Eyebrow") is at the beginning of the eyebrow, just above and to one side of the nose.

2. SE (for "Side of the Eye") is on the bone bordering the outside corner of the eye.

3. UE (for "Under the Eye") is on the bone under either eye, about one inch below the pupil.

4. UN (for "Under the Nose") is on the small area between the bottom of the nose and the top of the upper lip.

5. Ch (for "Chin") is midway between the point of the chin and the bottom of the lower lip (while not exactly on the point of the chin, the term "chin point" is descriptive enough for people to understand and remember easily).

6. CB (for "Collarbone") is the junction where the sternum (breastbone), collarbone, and the first rib meet (you learned this point earlier as "K-27").

7. UA (for "Under the Arm") is about four inches below the armpit, about even with the nipple for men, or in the middle of the bra strap for women.

8. KC (for "Karate Chop" points) are in the middle of the fleshy part on the outside of either hand, between the top of the wrist bone and the base of the baby finger (the part of your hand you would use to deliver a karate chop).

FIGURE 1.2
EFT EIGHT–POINT TREATMENT CHART

TAP EACH
POINT ABOUT
7 TIMES
(either side
or both
simultaneously)

EB: Beginning
of Eyebrow

SE: Side of Eye

UE: Under Eye

UN: Under Nose

Ch: Above Chin

CB: Collarbone
(indent
beneath CB)

UA: 4" Under
Arm

KC: Karate
Chop Points

Bacchus by Michelangelo (detail)

Two Additional Useful Points:
Thymus Thump ("Tarzan Spot")
Outside of Leg (midway between hip and knee)

27

These points are based on the Chinese acupuncture system (for one of the best popular introductions to the meridians and acupuncture points, see Gach, 1990). Each point has a name within that system, and a trend has begun within energy psychology to use the traditional names because almost every distinct approach has developed its own trademark nomenclature for the same points. Returning to the traditional names (generally an abbreviation for the meridian on which the point falls, followed by a number representing which acupuncture point it is on that meridian) will give the field a common language.

EB (Beginning of the Eyebrow) = BL-2 (Bladder Meridian)
SE (Side of the Eye) = GB-1 (Gallbladder Meridian)
UE (Under the Eye) = ST-1 (Stomach Meridian)
UN (Under the Nose) = GV-26 (Governing Vessel/Meridian)
Ch (Between Chin and Lower Lip) = CV-24 (Central Vessel/Meridian)
CB (Collarbone) = K-27 (Kidney Meridian)
UA (Under the Arm) = SP-21 (Spleen Meridian)
KC (Karate Chop) = SI-3 (Small Intestine Meridian)

The tapping points proceed down the body. Each is below the one before it. This makes them easy to memorize. A few trips through the sequence, Gary Craig tells his students, and it should be yours forever.

How to Tap. Tapping can be done with either hand, or both hands simultaneously, or in sequence. You can tap with the fingertips of your index finger and middle finger or make a "three-finger notch" by including your thumb. Tap solidly but never so hard as to hurt or risk bruising yourself.

Tap about seven times on each of the tapping points or, alternatively, for the length of a deep inhalation and exhalation. You will be repeating a *reminder phrase* (see below) while you are tapping, so you will not be counting, and it does not matter if you tap a few more or a few less than seven times.

Most of the tapping points exist on both sides of the body. It does not matter which side you use. And there may be some benefits to tapping both sides simultaneously. It might also be beneficial to alternate between the sides, tapping the left point once, then the right, then the left, etc. For the last area—the karate chop points—tap the entire length of the fleshy part of the side of the hand with all four fingers of the other hand.

28

Notes on the Reminder Phrase. Specific memories, thoughts, or circumstances cause disruptions in the energy system and elicit related negative emotions. If the problem from which you want relief is a fear of heights, that fear is not present while you are thinking about what to have for lunch. For an energy treatment to impact your target problem, that problem must be "activated" within your energy system.

A *problem state* can be activated by simply thinking about it. Bringing the problem to mind disrupts the meridian energies, which can then be re-established by applying the treatment. Balancing the meridian energy while thinking about the problem retrains the body to be able to hold the thought, or be in the circumstance, without creating the energy disruption that then impacts thoughts, feelings, and behavior. *When the energy is not disturbed, the problematic emotion associated with that energy disturbance is not triggered.*

You may, however, find it a bit difficult to consciously think about the problem while you are performing the other treatment procedures. By continually repeating a reminder phrase while doing the procedures, you keep yourself attuned to the situation that has been triggering the disruption in your energy system. This has been compared to keeping a radio dialed to the right station. The reminder phrase is a word or short phrase describing the problem. Repeat it out loud each time you tap one of the points in the tapping sequence. This activates the psychological, neurological, and energetic components of your problem.

The reminder phrase is often identical with or very close to the phrase used in the set-up affirmation. For example, if you were focusing on a memory in which you were humiliated as a child while performing in front of an audience, the set-up affirmation might be:

> "Even though I feel *humiliated by what happened at the eighth-grade play*, I deeply love and accept myself."

Within this affirmation, the words "humiliated by what happened at the eighth-grade play" can be used as the reminder phrase. Abbreviated versions of the statement, such as "humiliated at the play" or just "humiliated" will also suffice as long as their full meaning is clear to you. The reminder phrase may be as simple as (referencing the earlier examples):

- fear of large dogs (or simply "fear" or "large dogs")
- headaches about confronting my boss (or simply "headaches" or "confronting my boss")
- obsession about Mary's biological clock (or simply "obsession" or "biological clock")
- habit of interrupting people (or simply "habit" or "interrupting people")

The following additional reminder phrases suggest the range of possible areas for energy interventions: craving for sweets, my role in the accident, lower-back pain, anger toward my sister, appearing in court, ambivalence about my boyfriend, fired, fear of elevators, depression, stock losses, terrorist attack, divorce. The more specific the reminder phrase, or at least the more specific the problem it stands for is in your mind, the more effective it will be.

Step 3: The Bridging Technique

For reasons that are not entirely understood, though several hypotheses have been offered, activities that stimulate certain areas of the brain increase the effectiveness of the tapping techniques. Specific parts of the brain are stimulated when the eyes are moved, and various therapies, such as EMDR (www.emdr.com), utilize this principle. The most widely used eye movement technique within energy psychology is Roger Callahan's Nine Gamut

Procedure. It is introduced here with the comment that it is one of the more strange-looking procedures in energy psychology, with the tapping, eye movements, humming, and counting all designed to stimulate specific parts of the brain. While not directly targeting the problem with a reminder phrase, the Nine Gamut Procedure bridges two tapping sequences that do.

In the Nine Gamut Procedure,  one of the body's energy spots, the "gamut point," is continuously tapped while nine simple steps are carried out. The gamut point is on the back of either hand, 1/2 inch below the knuckles (toward the wrist), and in line with the midpoint between the little finger and the ring finger. While tapping the gamut point continuously, perform the following nine actions:

NINE GAMUT PROCEDURE

1. Close eyes.
2. Open eyes.
3. Move eyes to lower left.
4. Move eyes to lower right.
5. Rotate eyes clockwise 360 degrees (alternative: Move in a figure-eight).
6. Rotate eyes counter-clockwise 360 degrees (alternative: Reverse direction of the eight).
7. Hum a tune for a few seconds (e.g., "Happy Birthday," "Row, Row Your Boat," "Zipadee Doo Dah").
8. Count to five.
9. Hum again.

Step 4: The Tapping Sequence Repeated

EFT speaks of the treatment "sandwich":

Tapping sequence (with reminder phrase) 📇

Nine Gamut Procedure 📇

Tapping sequence (with reminder phrase) 📇

In step 4, you repeat the tapping sequence exactly as you did it in step 2. When you have completed these four steps, you again assess the intensity of the problem: Close your eyes, vividly bring the original problem to mind, and give it a rating from 0 to 10 on the amount of distress it causes you *now*, as you think about it.

If you can get no trace whatsoever of your previous emotional intensity, then your work with this issue is completed. If, on the other hand, you go down to, let's say, a 4, you would perform subsequent rounds until, ideally, 0 is reached (2 is often all that is required for the problem to essentially be resolved). Each round requires just over a minute.

Step 5: Subsequent Rounds

Sometimes a problem will be resolved after a single round of treatment. More often, only partial relief is obtained and additional rounds are necessary. Two simple adjustments need to be made for these subsequent rounds.

Psychological Reversals. A possible obstacle to success during the first round of treatment is the re-emergence of psychological reversals, those internal conflicts the set-up affirmation is designed to resolve. After treatment has begun and some progress has been made, the psychological reversal takes on a somewhat different quality. It is no longer preventing any change in the condition being treated, but it may be interfering with further progress. Its wording needs to reflect this. The set-up affirmation is a self-suggestion targeting the unconscious mind, which can be highly responsive to the literal meaning of a statement, so the wording should take into account the fact that some progress has been made. The addition of two words accomplishes this. The adjusted format for the set-up affirmation is:

31

> *"Even though I **still** have **some** of this _____, I deeply love and accept myself."*

The words "still" and "some" shift the emphasis of the affirmation toward a focus on the *remainder* of the problem. The affirmations below reflect adjustments to the affirmations listed earlier:

- *"Even though I **still** have **some** of this fear of dogs, I deeply love and accept myself."*
- *"Even though I **still** get a headache when I think of confronting my boss, I deeply love and accept myself."*
- *"Even though I **still** have **some** of this obsession about my daughter's biological clock, I deeply love and accept myself."*
- *"Even though I **still** have **some** of this impulse to interrupt people, I deeply love and accept myself."*

Reminder Phrase. The reminder phrase also needs a minor adjustment. Simply place the word "remaining" in front of the original reminder phrase. Here, as examples, are adjusted versions of the reminder phrases presented earlier:

- *remaining fear of large dogs* (or simply *"remaining fear"*)
- *remaining headaches about confronting my boss* (or simply *"remaining headaches"*)
- *remaining obsession about Mary's biological clock* (or simply *"remaining obsession"*)
- *remaining impulse to interrupt people* (or simply *"remaining impulse"*)

Following each round, do a new 0 to 10 assessment of the distress you now feel when you tune into the original problem. If the level of distress continues to decrease, do subsequent rounds until you reach 0, or until the distress stops decreasing. If the level of distress is more than 0 and will no longer decrease, you can apply the more advanced treatment methods that are taught in subsequent chapters.

32

Applying the EFT Protocol to a Personal Issue

To gain a fair sense of the effectiveness of these techniques, they must be experienced. Simply reading about them does not suffice. If you wish to do these personal experiments, please follow the steps precisely as they are written below. You may work out shortcuts and adjustments later, but the following is a good, tested, minimal routine to use while you learn the procedures.

Should you become dizzy, nauseous, or tearful during the process, stop, stretch your arms, legs, neck, and back. Take a break if you wish. When you feel rebalanced, consider returning to the steps, this time proceeding a bit more slowly. Alternatively, if the incident was more than you are ready to process at this time, note it for future attention and select an incident that does not hold as strong a charge.

The Preliminaries

1. Begin with the simple 90-second balancing procedure, the Three Thumps/Three Navel Touch 🎥 (p. 19).
2. Identify and clearly state a target problem. For this first personal experiment, identify a memory that brings you some discomfort or evokes in

you fear or anger that you consider to be inappropriate or dysfunctional. It should not be severely stressful or likely to evoke other highly troubling issues, but it can be substantial: a major failure, embarrassment, argument, loss, or betrayal. Memories that hold an emotional charge keep vital energies bound within them and make a person more reactive when analogous situations arise. The purpose of this experiment is to remove the emotional charge from the troubling memory.

3. Make a mental "movie" of this event or situation; replay it in your mind in detail; and rate its intensity. The focus for the rating is the intensity the movie creates for you now. Write down a number from 0 to 10, indicating the amount of distress you experience as you think about the problem, with 10 being extreme and 0 being none at all.

4. Give the movie a title. Based on this title, write down two to five words that will bring this memory to mind (reminder phrase). If your memory is of a time in your childhood when a dog bit you, you would recreate the scene in your imagination vividly enough to get a sense of the distress you feel when you think about the incident, but not so vividly as to emotionally retraumatize yourself. A way to keep some distance from the memory is to imagine it through a tunnel, or to simply ask yourself, "How much distress would I feel if I were to recreate the scene in my imagination?" Once a number comes to you, suppose it is 8, write that as the initial rating. Then give the movie or scene a title, such as "The Day Rocky Took a Bite out of My Innocence," and summarize it as a brief phrase that brings the scene to mind, such as "bit by Rocky."

The Basic Sequence (also summarized on p. 230):

1. Formulate and state three times a set-up affirmation while rubbing the chest sore spots (upper left and right portions of the chest) 🖐. The structure of the affirmation is as follows (replace the words in brackets with more specific wording when possible):

> "*Even though I* [am bothered by this memory], *I deeply love and accept myself.*"

With the dog bite example, the set-up affirmation, stated three times while rubbing the chest sore spots, might be:

> "*Even though* I feel terror when I think of Rocky biting me, *I deeply love and accept myself.*"

2. Do the tapping sequence (p. 26) while repeating the reminder phrase 🖬. In the dog bite example, the reminder phrase "bit by Rocky" would be stated out loud while tapping each of the eight points.
3. Do the 9 Gamut Procedure (p. 30) 🖬.
4. Repeat the tapping sequence, again using the reminder phrase 🖬.
5. Tune into the problem again and rate the amount of distress it causes. If it is not down to 0, repeat steps 1 through 4, this time modifying the set-up affirmation with the words "still" and "some," and modifying the reminder phrase with the word "remaining." Repeat for up to five rounds of the sandwich 🖬.

If the distress rating is not down to 0 or near 0 after five rounds of the sandwich, you may wish to store this scene for use in Chapter 8, Advanced Meridian Treatments. There are many possible reasons that improvement can become stalled:

- A small proportion of people do not respond to tapping the standard energy points.
- The problem may need to be formulated with more specific or altogether different wording.
- Other meridians or other energy systems may be involved with the problem and need special attention.
- Internal conflict about resolving the problem may need greater exploration.
- Aspects of the problem that are not being addressed may need to be identified and treated.

If after five rounds you were not able to significantly lower your distress around the issue, you may wish to consider chunking it down into its *aspects*, and use the earlier methods on each aspect.

Aspects of a Psychological Problem

The most common reason the distress rating will not go down to 0 or near 0 if you are following the instructions precisely is that an *aspect* of the problem that was not focused on in the energy intervention is involved. In the dog bite example, if the person who, as a child, was bitten by Rocky has now forgotten or repressed that experience and comes in for treatment for a fear of dogs, the tapping methods might reduce the fear a bit, but they probably won't be particularly effective until the experience with Rocky has been successfully processed. Actually, chances are that in doing the treatment around the current fear, memories of having been bitten as a child will emerge and the focus will be shifted to them. Being bitten by Rocky is an aspect of the "fear of dogs" and will probably require attention before the fear can fully be resolved.

Aspects can include earlier experiences involved in the current problem, but they can also slice in from other angles. An aspect can be a particular feeling or sensory experience that is involved with the problem, perhaps the feeling of being humiliated or blaming yourself for being bitten. Seeing your own blood could be an aspect of the problem. A vivid memory of how Rocky smelled might linger, or the helplessness of seeing Rocky baring his teeth, about to attack. This feeling might then tie into other memories of feeling helpless that must have their emotional charge neutralized before the original problem can be fully resolved. Most complex psychological goals and problems have numerous aspects and identifying the most relevant ones to focus on is part of the art of energy psychology.

Beyond the *Basic* Basics

You might be wondering how important it is to follow the sequence in the exact order in which it was presented. While the steps laid out here as the *basic protocol* have an internal logic that works, in actual practice there is a dance between the therapist and the client as the therapist stays attuned to the client's psychological and energetic responses to the treatment. The transcripts of two sessions conducted by EFT founder Gary Craig, included on the CD, illustrate how the basic procedures are continually attuned to the client in an actual treatment session.

In fact, every procedure in the sequence can be and often is modified, expanded, deleted, supplemented, or otherwise adapted according to the clinical situation and the therapist's personal style. For instance, while some use the same reminder phrase on every point as it is being stimulated, others will vary the statements, mixing the reminder phrase in its negative and positive forms (e.g., "this terrible craving," "free from this craving"), embedding suggestions as other points are tapped (e.g., "I will succeed here"), and addressing emotional issues related to overcoming the problem (e.g., "not having this addiction could make me feel empty").

Beyond the basic basics of bringing a problem to mind while tapping a pre-selected set of points, the following strategies will often increase the effectiveness of tapping in instances when the simplest approach does not lead to the desired result. These additional techniques comprise the remainder of this book. They include:

1. Establishing a more complete *electromagnetic and neurological receptiveness* for energy interventions.
2. Resolving a broader range of *psychological reversals*—internal conflicts about the treatment goal.
3. Identifying the *highest priority issue* for the next round of treatment.
4. Working with a *wider range of treatment points* than those presented in this chapter.
5. Identifying *specific treatment points* from within that wider range to focus on.
6. Using energy methods to instill *affirmations* and *images* tailored to the treatment goals.

Numerous other clinical issues that can arise when using energy-based interventions with psychological problems are also addressed later in the program.

The following chapter presents a technique called *energy checking.* Energy checking is used: 1) to assess how the ebbs and flows of the body's energies are involved in a psychological problem, and 2) to select interventions based on those assessments.

—2—

Energy Checking

ENERGY CHECKING IS A WAY OF ASSESSING the flow within the body's system of energy pathways. It is a fundamental tool used by many but not all practitioners of energy psychology. We emphasize it in this program because we believe it facilitates a relatively precise match between a client's unique energetic dynamics and the energy interventions that are formulated. Energy checking will be used throughout the remainder of the program.

What Does an "Energy Check" Check?

The *energy checks* you will learn in this chapter check whether the flow is optimal or disturbed in each of the body's major *meridians*. The meridians, the body's energy transportation system, need to flow properly in order to sustain physical and emotional health.[1] Disturbances in the meridian flow must be corrected to overcome the psychological as well as medical problems that result from such disturbances. While such corrections are a

---

[1] Unreferenced, declarative statements such as this one represent principles that are commonly accepted within the practice of acupuncture and other forms of energy medicine.

common though often unrecognized effect of any successful therapy, energy-based psychotherapy attempts to *directly* focus on and restore an optimal flow within the meridian system.

Disturbances in a meridian are generally thought to involve either a *lack* of energy or *too much* energy. Each is detrimental to health and well-being. Medical clairvoyants who are able to "see" the meridian flow also describe other potential forms of disturbed meridian energy, such as when the energy courses off the meridian lines, is sluggish, jumpy, blocked, bottlenecked, or moves in twists and other affected patterns.

How Many Meridians Are in the Body?

The meridian system consists of 14 major meridians, or energy pathways. Each runs deep into the body, bringing vital energy to at least one major organ or system. Each meridian also runs along a specific route on the surface of the skin, where its flow can be influenced by physical manipulation.

The use of the meridians in energy psychology traces to the practice of acupuncture. The acupuncture points (acupoints) are tiny areas of decreased electrical resistance (and therefore considered *openings* into the energy system—the correct translation from the Mandarin is actually not "point" but "hollow") that are situated on the surface of the skin along the meridian pathways. Stimulation of the acupoints through pressure, tapping, or more invasive means, such as needles or electrical current, affects the flow of energy within the meridian system.

Central to traditional Chinese medicine, currently the most widely practiced medical approach in the world, the meridians and the acupuncture points are described in texts dating back at least 4,500 years. The ancient Chinese diagrams illustrating the meridians on the body have been shown to correspond to modern scans of electrical patterns on the skin (Voll & Sarkisyanz, 1983).

While Western medicine tended to discount Eastern approaches, the situation began to shift after diplomatic relations improved between China and the United States. In 1980, one of the first groups of Western scientists invited to China included the renowned American psychologist Neal Miller. The group visited a mental hospital where a Chinese psychiatrist, trained in Western as well as Eastern medicine, described which acupuncture points to stimulate in treating a mental disorder. Dr. Miller, a pioneer in applying the scientific method to complex issues of personality and psychopathology, suggested, "You have an excellent opportunity for research here. You could stimulate the correct sites with one group and random sites with another and determine if there is a difference." The psychiatrist smiled and said, "We did that 5,000 years ago." According to Raymond Fowler (2002, p. 9), another psychologist in the group, "No one laughed harder than Neal Miller." The receptivity of Western medicine to acupuncture has been thawing ever since.

The Relationship of the Meridians to Psychological Problems

The energies transported by the meridians form a *bridge* between psychological states and their somatic counterparts. The firing of neurons, the feeling, the smile or frown, are all believed to be linked through the virtually instantaneous movement of the meridian energies. Assessing the energies that are involved with a psychological problem (e.g., with energy checking) and treating them (e.g., by stimulating appropriate acupoints) addresses the subtle infrastructure believed to maintain dysfunctional habits of emotion, thought, and behavior.

A maxim of energy-based approaches to healing is:

> *Matter follows energy.*

Laboratory studies corroborate this relationship. Both "medical intuitives" and instruments that measure the body's energies are able to detect changes in the energy field that *precede* physical changes. Energy healers, such as acupuncturists, focus on shifts in meridian activity to predict *and prevent* illness (in some provinces in ancient China, you paid the doctor when you were healthy, not when you were sick). Measured changes in the meridian system have been shown to match physical changes that occurred hours, days, sometimes even weeks later (Dumitrescu & Kenyon, 1983). When you change the energy flow, shifts in the body's physical structure, including patterns of neuron firing, follow.

Using techniques such as energy checking, the disturbed energies involved in a psychological problem can be more readily assessed than biochemical disturbances, and they can be treated using less invasive approaches. This is a primary reason so many psychotherapists are proposing that energy be added as another level of clinical focus, beyond psychological, behavioral, and pharmaceutical interventions.

To review, a **psychological problem** can be understood as:

> A *stimulus* (a recurring circumstance, memory, idea, or image) evokes a disturbed *response* within the body's energy system that *impairs* thought, emotion, or behavior.

A fundamental **treatment strategy** is:

> The conditioning of a new, *undisturbed* energy *response* to the problematic *stimulus*.

In brief, interventions into a person's *energy system* can catalyze desired changes in the person's *thoughts, emotions,* and *behavior.*

Altering a Conditioned Response in the Meridian System

Meridian energies that reflexively become disturbed in response to a recurring internal or external event play a role in maintaining psychological problems. The acupoints are a key to altering such conditioned responses in the meridian system. The procedures in energy psychology:

1. methodically identify external or internal stimuli (e.g., events, memories, or images) that trigger energy responses which impair feelings, thought, or behavior;
2. reprogram these responses by stimulating appropriate energy points while the problematic situation is psychologically activated, so that the stimulus becomes paired with a new, undisturbed response in the energy system.

Like systematic desensitization (Wolpe, 1958), the problematic response is extinguished by bonding the stimulus to a neutral or undisturbed physiological response (see the comparison of systematic desensitization to energy psychology techniques on p. 206). Unlike systematic desensitization, which is most effective with anxiety and phobias, the precision afforded by being able to target the specific response in any of the 14 meridians (each meridian is associated with a characteristic set of emotional and behavioral themes; see p. 234) allows the techniques of energy psychology to be applied to a wide range of psychological problems.

To precisely target and recondition the energies that underlie a psychological problem:

1. Determine the kind of energy disturbance that occurs when the problem state is activated.
2. Rebalance or realign the energies in the presence of the triggering stimulus.

These are the two fundamental skills you will learn in *Energy Psychology Interactive*. This chapter addresses the first.

An Overview of Energy Checking

Many healers, ancient and modern, register the body's energies through their senses, seeing them as colors of varying intensity, texture, and movement, palpably feeling them, sometimes even hearing, smelling, or tasting them. Various approaches have been developed for assisting practitioners who do not have this gift (a form of synesthesia—the phenomenon where, for instance, a person hears color or tastes sound) to nonetheless work with subtle energies. In traditional Chinese medicine, practitioners study many years to learn how to read the subtle pulses that reveal, in great detail, the condition of the body's energy system. Each meridian has its own pulsation. Reading the pulses accurately is an art that requires the development of an exquisite sensitivity.

Energy psychology is indebted to the field of applied kinesiology for having developed a method by which practitioners can readily learn how to assess the flow of meridian energy (visit www.icakusa.com for more information). The procedure is called *muscle testing* or *energy checking*. An energy check is a technique for evaluating the flow within a meridian by gauging the relative firmness when pressure is applied to a muscle that is affected by that meridian. Energy checking is based on the way the energies of specific meridians affect specific muscles. The terms *energy check* and *energy test* are interchangeable with the more popular term *muscle test*. *Energy checking* is used in this program because:

41

1. It is the flow of energy, not the muscle's strength, that is being examined.
2. A client's associations with the word "test," such as "pass or fail," "struggle to succeed," etc., can add another variable to the procedure.

At first glance, some therapists have assumed that energy checking picks up on unconscious processes rather than energy flow in the meridians. Energy checking has been likened, for instance, to the ideomotor response in hypnosis (Pulos, 2002), in which the muscle's reaction provides information that the conscious mind cannot access.

But energy checking appears to also detect the effects of stress and other factors on specific energy systems, independent of the person's conscious or unconscious beliefs. Distinctions between unconscious processes and the flow of the meridian energies are, ultimately, artificial. Just as the activities of the various organs are linked to unconscious processes (an increased heart rate might reflect underlying anger and it might also predispose a person toward anger), the meridian energies and unconscious processes are also integrally related.

42

Laboratory Studies of Energy Checking

A number of empirical investigations into the validity and reliability of energy checking support the efficacy of the procedure (see "Research on Energy Checking Studies," accessed from the Embedded Topics Index on the CD, for abstracts of 12 studies and references to 18 others). For instance, a well-controlled study comparing energy checking with measurements on computerized instruments has shown the difference in muscle firmness as the client made congruent or non-congruent statements to be significant at a .001 level of confidence (Monti et al., 1999).

The research evidence supporting energy checking, however, while growing, is still scientifically inconclusive. Another source of support for the efficacy of energy checking is found in the reports of a number of practitioners who are purportedly able to "see" or "feel" subtle energies. One of the two primary consultants to this program, Donna Eden, has this ability to clairvoyantly read the body's energies. She reports having "seen" exact correspondences between the meridian energies and the results of energy checks thousands of times while observing her students.

The claims of other healers and clairvoyants who offer medical and psychological diagnoses based on their reading of the body's energies have been validated in clinical and laboratory settings. In a study of one of the most famous modern "medical intuitives," Caroline Myss, for instance, Myss's diagnosis of 50 patients, with whom she had no physical contact (she was simply told their name and date of birth), matched a physician's diagnosis of the patient in 93 percent of the cases (Shealy, 1988). In research conducted over a 20-year period at UCLA by Valerie Hunt (1995), the reports of people sensitive to subtle energies corroborated one another, and also corresponded to readings from standard instruments for measuring galvanic skin response, brain waves, blood pressure, heartbeat, and muscle contraction.

What You Can Expect to Learn in this Chapter

This chapter reviews the basic principles of energy checking, and it provides enough fundamentals that you will be able to begin to practice and experiment with the technique. Because treatment choices are often based in part on the results of energy checking and the procedure requires a delicate sensitivity, hands-on training and/or supervised practice in this method is advised before applying energy checking in a professional setting. Both are readily available (see "Links," p. 273). Further instruction in energy checking can be found in *Energy Medicine* (Eden, 1999, pp. 29–59) and *Energy Diagnostic and Treatment Methods* (Gallo, 2000, pp. 35–58). The classic technical text is *Muscles: Testing and Function* by Florence Kendall and Elizabeth McCreary (1993).

43

You are now at a choice point in the program. While you have not yet learned how to perform an energy check, you do know enough about the procedure that you could proceed to the next chapter and return later to develop a facility in energy checking. Depending on your learning style and goals, particularly whether you are going for an overview or wishing to thoroughly learn how to conduct each of the component treatment procedures, you can either continue with this chapter or move on to the next, Neurological Disorganization.

The Postures for Three Energy Checks

Energy checking is a way to assess the flow within the meridians—the body's system of energy pathways. The results of an energy check are determined by the relative firmness of a *general indicator muscle*. A general indicator muscle is a muscle used in an energy check to gauge the overall state of the meridian system, based on the relative firmness of the muscle under different conditions. Although each muscle is associated with a specific meridian and can be used to check the energies of that meridian, a general indicator muscle is also sensitive to changes in the overall meridian system. You will learn three energy checks in this chapter that utilize general indicator muscles.

An Energy Check with the Arm Extended Out from the Body[2] 🖬

From *Energy Medicine*. Drawing by Brooks Garten

FIGURE 2.1
INDICATOR MUSCLE:
MIDDLE DELTOID

1. Stand facing the client with either of the client's arms extended and parallel to the floor, hand open, palm down.
2. Place yourself somewhat off to the client's side so as not to be in close contact with the client's "energy field."
3. Lightly rest your open hand just below (shoulder side of) the client's wrist.
4. Press gradually for approximately 1½ to 2 seconds to determine if there is a "bounce." Even if the arm gives in slightly to the pressure, if it immediately bounces back to its original position, the muscle has stayed firm.

The practitioner may place his or her other hand on the client's opposite shoulder to steady the client as pressure is applied. This can also create

---

[2] Before doing an energy check with a new person, obtain explicit permission and determine that there are no problems with the client's arm, neck, shoulder, or upper back that would make an application of pressure to the indicator muscle contraindicated.

a stronger energetic circuit between the client and the practitioner. If this seems intrusive or in any other way makes the client uncomfortable, it is not essential. Asking the client if it is okay to place your hand on his or her shoulder is, however, often enough to prevent discomfort.

An Energy Check with the Arm Down
and to the Side of the Body 📹

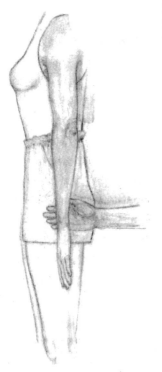

FIGURE 2.2
INDICATOR MUSCLE:
LATIMUS DORSI

1. Client stands with an arm firm against the side, elbow straight, and side of thumb against the side of the leg.

2. Practitioner places two or more fingers between the leg and the arm, just above the wrist.

3. Practitioner pulls away from the body gradually for approximately 1½ to 2 seconds to determine if there is a "bounce." Again, even if the arm gives in slightly to the pressure, if it immediately bounces back to its original position, the muscle has stayed firm.

45

From *Energy Medicine*. Drawing by Brooks Garten.

The practitioner may, when checking the latisimus dorsi muscle, place his or her other hand on the *same* shoulder as the arm being checked to steady the client as pressure is applied and to create a better energetic circuit. Again, if this feels intrusive or in any way makes the client uncomfortable, it is not essential, and asking the client's permission first is often enough to prevent discomfort.

An Energy Check That Does Not Use an Arm Muscle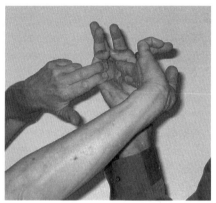

The O-Ring Test does not use an arm muscle. The subject makes an "O" with either hand by touching the tip of the thumb to the tip of the little finger.

O-RING TEST

The practitioner places the second and third fingers of each hand into the O and tries to separate the client's thumb and finger. A slight separation with a subsequent lock indicates that the muscle held firm.

If the thumb and little finger separate in situations in which the indicator muscle should stay firm (e.g., while the client says, "My name is [actual name]"), use the index finger instead of the little finger as the index finger has more strength.

46

Calibrating an Indicator Muscle

To *calibrate* an indicator muscle is to determine the optimal amount of pressure the practitioner should apply to distinguish whether the indicator muscle has remained firm or lost its firmness. You want to find the minimum amount of pressure to reliably make the distinction.

This can be done with a statement such as, "I am wearing a green shirt," where the truth of the statement is obvious to both parties. Immediately after the statement has been made, perform the energy check.

- If it is a true statement, the indicator muscle will generally stay firm and the pressure needed to determine the presence of that firmness can be gauged.
- If it is a false statement, the indicator muscle will generally lose its firmness, and the pressure needed to determine that the muscle has lost its firmness can similarly be gauged.

Several true and several false statements may be used to confirm the calibration. If the indicator muscle loses firmness after a true statement or stays firm after a false statement, additional steps are required. The primary reason for "false negatives" and "false positives" during an energy check in which both parties know the "correct response" is *neurological disorganization*, which is addressed in the following chapter. Another common reason, with inexperienced practitioners, is that pressure is applied before the client is ready. Don't jump the gun. Wait until the client has completed the statement and is clearly ready for you to begin applying pressure.

Practice Session 1: Gaining an Initial Feel for Energy Checking

A Note about Practice Sessions

Integrated throughout *Energy Psychology Interactive* are "practice sessions" that provide a space in which skills that have just been described can be practiced by applying them with a colleague. Depending on convenience, your learning preferences, and your goals for the program, these practice sessions can be completed:

- as they come up in the chapter
- after you have completed the chapter
- not until a second run through the program (the same practice sessions are also on the CD)

Energy Psychology Interactive also lends itself well to an ongoing study group. Two or more clinicians may go through the program independently, a chapter or CD module at a time, and then meet to discuss the principles presented in that unit and practice the techniques it presents.

If a partner is not available, there is still value in going through the practice sessions vividly in your imagination.

The reason to practice at this point is simply so you have an initial feel for performing an energy check as you learn more about the procedure. While in most of the practice sessions it is recommended that you do the session with a colleague, since psychological issues can arise that might put you into an unintended therapist role with a friend or family member, this is not a concern for the three practice sessions in this chapter. After you have chosen a practice partner:

1. Select one of the three energy checks to begin: a) arm parallel to the ground and out to the side  (p. 44); b) arm straight down side of body 🎥 (p. 45); or c) thumb and little finger or index finger forming a circle 🎥 (p. 46).

2. Make sure there is no contraindication for using the arm, such as an injury or sprain.

ENERGY CHECK/ARM EXTENDED

3. Gradually apply pressure for 1½ to 2 seconds to see if there is a "bounce."

4. If the muscle does not stay firm, have the person tap with all five fingers the center of his or her chest several times. This will usually make the muscle firm. If it does not, lead the person through the Three Thumps/Three Navel Touch (see pp.19–21). If after this the person's muscle still does not become firm, use one of the other two energy checks.

ENERGY CHECK/ARM AT SIDE

5. Once you have a firm indicator muscle, have the person say, "I am wearing [something actually being worn]." Energy check. The muscle should stay firm. Then have the person say, "I am wearing [something not being worn]." Energy check. This should give you a differential between the muscle staying firm and losing its firmness. If it does not, return to this practice session after you have corrected for neurological disorganization in the next chapter.

6. Reverse roles with your partner.

7. Repeat, using the other two energy checks.

48

Physical Considerations Prior to an Energy Check

In addition to insuring that there are no strains or injuries in the arm being used that might lead to further injury or interfere with the energy check, several other physical considerations should be observed:

1. Just as neurological disorganization can distort the results of an energy check, so can a lack of hydration. Water should be available so that neither the client nor the practitioner is even slightly thirsty.
2. Be sure the client does not hold his or her breath during the energy check.
3. If the practitioner and the client simultaneously take a deep breath and exhale just prior to the energy check, this tends to increase their energetic rapport.
4. Be sure jewelry such as metal necklaces, bracelets, metal-rimmed eyeglasses, metal belt buckles, and battery-operated devices including quartz watches, pagers, or cell phones do not interfere with the process. If you suspect that they are, you can either remove them altogether or confirm the suspicion with energy checks in their presence and their absence.
5. Be sure both the practitioner and the client are well grounded.

49

A Simple Grounding Technique 🔊

1. Stand with feet at shoulder width, knees slightly flexed, and hands at the tops of your thighs.
2. On the in-breath visualize bringing the energies of the earth in through your feet and up through your body.

3. As you do this, move your hands up your legs, over your stomach, heart, face, and off the top of your head, finally reaching to the sky.

4. On the out-breath, pull the energies from the heavens into the top of your head, over your face, through your heart, stomach, and down your legs.

5. Resting your hands again at the tops of your thighs, send the energy back into the earth.

6. Repeat one or two more times.

Considerations about Eye Contact during an Energy Check

1. Eye contact between client and practitioner can interfere with the energy check.

2. The client's eyes can be directed away from the practitioner, to the left or right, to avoid distraction, or the practitioner can step to the side while the client looks straight ahead. Although some practitioners have clients direct their gaze downward, if you are checking for emotions, having the eyes cast down can throw off the test, particularly with people who are highly kinesthetic.

3. The practitioner's eyes should not be directly on the client, as this may be inhibiting.

4. Smiling or laughing can also interfere with the outcome of the test.

Establishing Signals during an Energy Check

The practitioner might say:

- "Meet my pressure" the first few times immediately prior to applying pressure, or
- "Push up while I push down" (arm extending out from body), or
- "Hold in while I pull out" (arm by side or O-ring test).

After energy checking is established, simply saying "hold" before applying pressure is usually adequate.

The client might be instructed to say:

- "Ready" or "Okay," to signal that he or she is ready for the practitioner to check the muscle.

If unsure about the results of the energy check, the practitioner might ask the client what he or she experienced. Rather than invalidating the results, verbal feedback further involves the client while helping to calibrate the energy check.

51

Items to Address When Introducing Energy Checking to a Client

The energy dimension of psychological problems can be further discussed when introducing energy checking. Explain to the client that energy checking is a way of assessing how psychological problems impact people on an energetic level. It gives a way for both the therapist and the client to track changes as the treatment proceeds. The client will be asked to think about certain issues or events while touching specific points as the energies are checked. This helps to determine which energetic treatments are needed to address the psychological problem (see further discussion about orienting a new client on p. 220). Finally, obtain agreement before proceeding.

The issue of *touch* requires special consideration. Very little physical touch is actually required in the practice of energy-based psychotherapy, and practitioners vary widely in the amount of physical contact they use.

The client can be instructed to stimulate most of the treatment points. Some contact, however, is necessary to perform an energy check. Always obtain explicit verbal consent before touching a client and remain sensitive to and discuss any issues the client may have about physical touch. Simply asking permission is usually all that is necessary. Addressing the issue of touch in your informed consent form (see sample, p. 223) may be advisable for therapists who use an energy-based approach. Practitioners also need to look into any restrictions regarding physical contact that are imposed by their licensing board or insurance carrier.

Attitudes to Hold When Conducting an Energy Check

While you do an energy check, keep in mind that energy checking is a partnership, not a contest. You are accessing the innate intelligence of the body. Stay clear of opinions and expectations about what the outcome should be or will be. Let your curiosity lead you. Desire only to stay centered and obtain accurate information.

Beyond attitude, there is a simple acupressure technique for countering the effects of expectations or preconceived ideas the practitioner or client may hold:

1. Take the thumb and middle finger of one hand and place them with some pressure into the two indents where the back of the neck meets the head.
2. With the other hand, proceed with the energy check.

Practice Session 2: Preparing to Do an Energy Check

Imagine you are about to introduce energy checking to a new client (or have someone role-play the part):

1. What are five physical considerations you will attend to (p. 49)?
2. What will you do with your eyes during the energy check (p. 50)?
3. What signals will you use and ask the client to use during the energy check (p. 51)?
4. What attitudes will you keep in your awareness (p. 52)?
5. Vividly imagine a specific, unique client. Out loud, role-play what you will say to this person to introduce energy checking (p. 51).

Steps to Consider When an Indicator Muscle Stays Strong under Conditions That Should Weaken It

1. If the client is trying too hard, explain that together you are simply assessing whether the energy is flowing through the muscle, not testing muscle strength, and it is not necessary or desirable to engage other muscles or to put one's full strength into resisting.

2. The practitioner or the client *lightly* pinches the skin on the "belly" (center) of the indicator muscle, parallel with the length of the arm, several times  (this is called the *spindle cell releasing maneuver*). The pinch signals to the nervous system that the muscle is *overcontracted*, and a message is sent back to "switch off" the muscle, releasing the constriction.

   • For middle deltoid ("arm straight out" check), pinch at the top of the arm (just beyond shoulder curve).
   • For latisimus dorsi ("arm at side" check), pinch the back muscles about four inches above the waist.
   • For the O-ring test (thumb–little finger), pinch the bottom of the palm below the little finger.

3. Consider checking for neurological disorganization (see Chapter 3).

53

RELEASING MIDDLE DELTOID　　　**RELEASING LATISIMUS DORSI**

Steps to Consider When an Indicator Muscle Stays Weak under Conditions That Should Strengthen It

1. Have the client take a few deep breaths.
2. The practitioner or the client *stretches* the skin above and below the "belly" (center) of the indicator muscle, parallel with the length of the

arm, several times  (this is called the *spindle cell strengthening maneuver*). The stretch signals to the nervous system that the muscle is *undercontracted*, and a message is sent back to "switch on" the muscle, so it will hold firm.

STRENGTHENING MIDDLE DELTOID   STRENGTHENING LATISIMUS DORSI

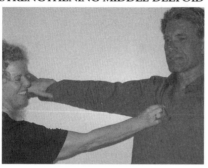 

- For middle deltoid, stretch at the top of the arm (just beyond shoulder curve).
- For latisimus dorsi, stretch back muscles about four inches above the waist.
- For the O-ring test (thumb–little finger), stretch the bottom of the palm below the little finger.

3. Have the client tap directly under the eyes (Stomach-1), four inches under the armpits (spleen-21), under the collarbones next to the chest bone (kidney-27), and over the thymus.
4. Hold one hand on the forehead while with the other hand rubbing any sore spots on the chest.
5. Consider checking for neurological disorganization (see Chapter 3).

Steps for Qualifying an Indicator Muscle with a New Client

1. After explaining the energy checking procedure and determining that there are no physical contraindications to using the indicator muscle, perform an energy check "in the clear" using the middle deltoid  , latisimus dorsi  , or O-ring  checks. Strengthen if weak (a simple procedure is to tap the "Tarzan spot" on the chest, over the thymus gland; more elaborate is the Three Thumps/Three Navel Hold) or find a different indicator muscle that checks strong.
2. Lightly pinch or have the client pinch the skin on the "belly" (center) of the indicator muscle several times (the *spindle cell releasing*

54

maneuver , p. 53). Energy check. This shows the client and the practitioner how the muscle responds when it has lost its strength. If the muscle stays firm, check for neurological disorganization (see Chapter 3).

3. Stretch or have the client stretch the skin above and below the "belly" (center) of the muscle several times (*spindle cell strengthening maneuver* , p. 54). This directs energy back to the muscle and shows the client and the practitioner how the muscle responds when it is maintaining its strength. If the muscle does not stay firm, check for neurological disorganization (see Chapter 3).

4. Just prior to an energy check, ask the client to relax, be open, and allow whatever physical response occurs when you say, "Show me, what is a 'yes.'" Energy check.

5. Repeat, this time saying, "Show me, what is a 'no.'"

6. Further calibrate the muscle by having the client make true statements and false statements where both practitioner and client know which is which (e.g., "The walls in this room are painted blue").

7. Ask, "Do I have permission to work with [client's name] today?"[3]

8. Ask, "Is there any reason I should not?"

55

These eight steps for qualifying an indicator muscle can act as guidelines while learning to do an energy check. As you become more experienced, you will begin to take shortcuts, using some of the procedures only when you sense they are necessary.

Practice Session 3: Doing an Energy Check

Now put it all together. With another person role-playing the client, go through the preparation phase (physical considerations, signals, eye position, internal attitudes, words you use to introduce the client to the energy checking) and qualify an indicator muscle. This is an "open book" practice session, so review liberally as you master each of these points.

---

[3] Asking a question of this nature is, like the ideomotor response in hypnosis, essentially an inquiry into the person's conscious and unconscious beliefs and attitudes; energy checks in the contexts you will be using later are believed to directly assess the effects of physical or emotional stress on specific energy systems, independent of the person's thoughts or attitudes. Some practitioners feel that the energy checking procedure should be limited to the latter kind of assessment, since introducing a verbal question so strongly engages the beliefs and expectations of the client as well as of the practitioner.

—3—

Neurological Disorganization

ENERGY TECHNIQUES FOR TREATING PSYCHOLOGICAL PROBLEMS will not be as effective if either of two conditions is present: neurological disorganization or psychological reversals.

- In *neurological disorganization*, the central nervous system scrambles and misinterprets nerve impulses.
- In a *psychological reversal*, a tendency toward unconsciously motivated outcomes that are the reverse of the client's consciously held goals undermines the treatment.

This chapter addresses neurological disorganization. The following chapter addresses psychological reversals.

Detecting Neurological Disorganization

Despite the sound of the term, neurological disorganization is not necessarily a serious medical or psychiatric condition. As used within energy psychology, neurological disorganization refers to subtle, pre-clinical disturbances as well as to more serious problems. Like a circuit board that picks up static electricity, the nervous system can, even in the course of normal functioning, lose its optimal organization and performance. Sleep is among nature's most effective "cures" for neurological disorganization. Exercise is another.

But when stress or other factors prevent the energies in the nervous system from reconstituting, day after day, year after year, the habitual disorganization detracts from a person's resilience, clarity of mind, and overall health. This chapter offers methods for providing the nervous system with energy-oriented adjustments that correct for neurological disorganization. You will learn how to energy check for several types of neurological disorganization and how to intervene with each type that is detected.

The energy checking procedure you learned in the previous chapter can be applied to assess neurological disorganization. The following signs should also alert you to the possibility of neurological disorganization:

- faltering when attempting to say what one means
- confusing left and right
- difficulties with spatial orientation
- reversing letters and numbers
- restricted arm swing or homolateral arm/leg movement (left arm moves with left leg, right with right) when walking
- significant awkwardness or clumsiness

Neurological Disorganization and Energy Interventions

Energy interventions for resolving psychological problems will be more effective if the energies that support brain functioning are in harmony and balance. Correcting for neurological disorganization, when present, is a routine procedure within energy psychology.

Neurological disorganization is triggered when certain electromagnetic and other more subtle energies that affect brain function have lost their optimal flow. These disturbances in the body's energies can trace to any of a wide range of causes, from the stresses of daily life to an accumulation of toxins in the body to actual brain damage. Electromagnetic disturbances in the nervous system are the common denominator. While the root cause might be chemical, electrical, structural, or psychological, each of these translates into an electromagnetic disturbance. Conditions within a client's *energy system* that can trigger neurological disorganization include:

- Meridians Running Backward
- Triple Warmer in Overwhelm
- Polarity Reversal
- Ocular Lock
- Homolateral Patterning

Later in this chapter, you will learn: a) the dynamics of each of these; b) a quick and simple energy check to determine if each is present; and c) simple treatment methods to correct each.

A Generic Correction for Neurological Disorganization

The Three Thumps/Three Navel Touch, which you learned in Chapter 1 📠 (pp. 19–21), is a simple 90-second sequence that generically corrects for neurological disorganization. Another generic routine requires about three minutes and casts a wider net. Clinical impressions are that this second sequence, or the two in succession, can provide enough of a correction that the therapy can proceed without interference from neurological disorganization in upwards of 80 percent of cases in which it was originally present. While these "touch and tap" treatments may all appear rather hocus-pocus, they are based upon the stimulation of carefully selected electrical points derived from the practice of acupuncture and other forms of energy medicine. Further explanation and rationale for many of them can be found in *Energy Medicine* (Eden, 1999).

59

The following sequence, like the Three Thumps/Three Navel Touch, may be applied without first having assessed whether neurological disorganization is present and, in any case, is likely to improve the client's mental acuity (as well as the therapist's if done simultaneously while guiding the client through the procedure). The steps in this three-part/three-minute sequence 📠 for improving mental acuity and at least temporarily correcting most simple forms of neurological disorganization include:

1. The Crown Pull
2. Connecting Heaven and Earth
3. The Wayne Cook Posture

Although these techniques can be used independently, they are particularly potent when used in combination. We suggest you perform each as you read the following instructions.

1. The Crown Pull

While doing the crown pull, breathe deeply, in through your nose and out through your mouth.

1. Place your thumbs at the side of your head on your temples. Curl your fingers and rest your fingertips just above the center of your eyebrows.
2. Slowly, and with some pressure, pull your fingers apart so the skin just above your eyebrows is stretched.
3. Rest your fingertips at the center of your forehead and repeat the stretch.
4. Rest your fingertips at your hairline and repeat the stretch.
5. Continue this pattern, moving back over your head, down to your neck, and finally resting on your shoulders and dragging your fingers over your shoulders.

FIGURE 3.1
THE CROWN PULL

60

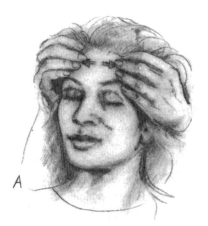
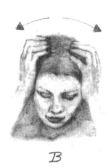

A

B

From *Energy Medicine*. Drawing by Brooks Garten.

2. Connecting Heaven and Earth

Stretching is one of the most natural ways to keep the body's energies moving, which is in turn one of the best ways to keep the mind clear. From watching cats and dogs upon waking to practicing disciplines that have made stretch into a science, such as yoga, many models are available. Versions of the following exercise have been found in numerous cultures, and it is not only an excellent way to get energy flowing throughout the body, it is formulated to help integrate the left and right brain hemispheres and activate the energy system known as the *radiant circuits* (see the module presenting the Radiant Energy System on the CD). Here are the instructions you would use to guide a client in Connecting Heaven and Earth.

CONNECTING HEAVEN AND EARTH

1. Rub your hands together and shake them out.
2. Stand with your hands on your thighs and fingers spread.
3. With a deep inhalation, circle your arms out.
4. On the exhalation, bring your hands together in a prayerful position.
5. Again with a deep inhalation, separate your arms from one another, stretching one high above your head and flattening your hand back, as if pushing something above you.
6. Stretch the other arm down, again flattening your hand as if pushing something toward the earth. Stay in this position for as long as is comfortable.
7. Release your breath through your mouth, returning your hands to the prayerful position.
8. Repeat, switching the arm that raises and the arm that lowers. Do one or more additional lifts on each side.
9. Coming out of this pose the final time, bring your arms down and allow your body to fold over at the waist. Hang there with your knees slightly bent as you take two deep breaths. Slowly return to a standing position with a backward roll of the shoulders.

61

3. The Wayne Cook Posture

1. While sitting, place your right foot over your left knee, wrap your left hand around your right ankle, and your right hand around the ball of your right foot (best done with shoes removed).
2. Breathe in slowly through your nose, allowing your breath to lift your body while breathing in. At the same time, pull your leg inward, creating a stretch. Exhale slowly out your mouth, letting your body relax. Repeat this slow breathing and stretching four or five times.
3. Switch to your other foot. Place your left foot over your right knee, wrap your right hand around your left ankle, and your left hand around the ball of your left foot. Use the same breathing.
4. Uncross your legs, place your fingertips together forming a pyramid, bring your thumbs to rest on your third eye, just above the bridge of your nose. Breathe slowly in through your nose and out through your mouth about five times.

Alternative to the Wayne Cook Posture

A simpler procedure with similar effects as the Wayne Cook Posture (although for some people it does not hold as long or impact the nervous system as strongly) is to:

1. While sitting, cross your ankles, left over right.
2. Place your hands in front of you, arms extended, with the backs of your hands touching.

3. Bring your right hand over your left hand and bring your palms together.
4. Clasp your fingers.
5. Fold your hands and arms inward and rest them on your chest underneath the chin.
6. Breathe deeply in this position for up to a minute.

63

Not only will the three-part/three-minute sequence help your clients overcome neurological disorganization, it is a powerful routine to use any time you have been concentrating intensely and want to "refresh your screen." It is easy to memorize and worth remembering.

You are again at a choice point. While you have not yet learned the more sophisticated ways of assessing and correcting for neurological disorganization, you do know enough about the topic that you can proceed to the next chapter and return later to develop more advanced skills for working with the perhaps 20 percent of instances of neurological disorganization that cannot be resolved by the treatments you have already learned. Depending on your learning style and goals at this point, particularly whether you are going for an overview or wishing to thoroughly learn how to conduct each of the component treatment procedures, you may continue with this chapter or proceed to the chapter on psychological reversals.

TABLE 3.1
NEUROLOGICAL DISORGANIZATION:
TRIGGERS, CHECKS, AND CORRECTIONS

ENERGY TRIGGER	ENERGY CHECK	CORRECTION
1. Meridians Running Backward	Reverse Walk Check	K-27, Cross Crawl
2. Triple Warmer in Overwhelm	Palm-around-Ear Check	Smoothing behind the Ears, Wayne Cook Posture, Triple Warmer/Spleen Hug
3. Polarity Reversal	Hand-over-Head Check	Crown Pull, Navel/Third-Eye Hook-Up
4. Ocular Lock	Left/Right Eye Rotation	Palming Eyes, Navel/K-27 Massage
5. Homolateral Patterning	X & 11 Check	Homolateral Crossover
Stabilizing		Eights, Polarity Unswitching
Homework		5-Min Routine, Collarbone Breathing, Lymphs

Table 3.1 provides an overview of what you will be learning in the remainder of this chapter. While at first glance this list might seem a bit daunting, as if your whole practice could be taken up with correcting for neurological disorganization, be assured that you can energy check for all five types of neurological disorganization, combined, within a minute. You can then move to the corrections for any type that is present, and these treatments generally require only a minute or two. The chart can also easily be copied, kept nearby, and referred to during treatment sessions. For each of the five types of neurological disorganization, presented below in the order listed on the chart, its description is followed by instructions on how to energy check for its presence, followed by a specific treatment sequence for correcting it.

1. Meridians Running Backward 📼

The energies along each meridian normally flow in a specific direction. At times of exhaustion, upset, or confusion, the meridian system may literally reverse its flow and run backward. This causes activities that typically vitalize the meridian system, such as walking or running (which are in alignment with the normal flow of the energies), to further drain it. Reversing its energies is the body's way of saying, "Slow down, take a rest" while enforcing the suggestion by placing a high energy tax on normal activities.

Energy Checking for Meridians Running Backward (the Reverse Walk Check)

To determine if the meridians are running backward, first use an energy check to find a firm indicator muscle. You can strengthen indicator muscles that do not stay firm by selecting techniques from the 90-second and three-minute sequences you have already learned (such as the Three Thumps). Establishing a firm indicator muscle is the first step in any procedure that utilizes energy checking. Once a firm indicator muscle has been identified, have the client take several steps forward. If the indicator muscle loses strength, the meridian energy is probably moving in a reversed direction. Then have the client take several steps backward. If the same indicator muscle regains its strength, this confirms that the meridian energy is running backward.

Correction Sequence for Meridians Running Backward

1. **Stimulating K-27.** First have the client tap or massage the K-27 points (see Fig. 1.1, p. 19). These, the 27th points on the kidney meridian, are critical juncture points for the entire meridian system. Stimulating them can be thought of as flipping a switch that overrides the body's defensive mechanism of reversing its vital energies when tired or stressed.

Work with the K-27 points while breathing in deeply through the nose and out through the mouth. Continue for about 20 seconds, stimulating both sides simultaneously. To find the exact location of these points, press your index fingers in at the bottom of your neck, beneath your Adam's apple and you will notice that you are at the top of bones (your sternum) that form a U-shaped notch (about where a man would knot his tie). From the top of the U, move your fingers down toward your navel, about an inch and then go to the left about an inch and the right about an inch. Most people have slight indents there. Some people find it more effective to cross their hands, tapping or massaging the left side with the right hand and right side with the left.

2. **The Cross Crawl.** To stabilize the forward direction of the meridian flow after stimulating the K-27 points, have the client walk in place with

the *right* arm and the *left* leg raising simultaneously, and then the *left* arm and *right* leg, for 30 to 90 seconds. Check again for reversed energies. If still present, proceed to the homolateral crossover.

3. **The Homolateral Crossover.** If stimulating the K-27 points, followed by a cross crawl, did not correct for meridians that were running backward:

HOMOLATERAL CROSSOVER

a. Have the client begin by again tapping or massaging the K-27 points, followed by a full-body "reaching for the stars" stretch.

b. The client then marches in place, lifting right arm with right leg and then left arm with left leg.

c. The client is reminded to breathe deeply throughout the entire routine.

d. After about 12 lifts of the arms and legs in this homolateral pattern, stop and change the pattern to a normal cross crawl (lifting opposite arms and legs) for about 12 lifts.

e. Repeat the pattern twice.

f. Anchor it with an additional dozen cross crawls and stimulation of the K-27 points.

2. Triple Warmer in Overwhelm

Triple warmer is the energy system that governs 1) the fight-or-flight response, 2) the immune system, and 3) the maintenance of survival-oriented habits. When a person faces threat or substantial stress, a series of psychological, biological, and chemical events—the fight-or-flight response—is initiated by triple warmer. This emergency response can dominate all other activities and often results in impaired judgment, emotional volatility, and finally exhaustion. When physical or emotional stress is persistent, triple warmer becomes perpetually activated ("goes into overwhelm"), exacting long-term physical and emotional costs.

Energy Checking for Triple Warmer in Overwhelm
(The Palm-around-Ear Check)

Have the client cup either hand, spread the fingers, and place the palm of the hand around either ear with the fingers touching the head a couple of inches from the ear. Energy check. If the muscle loses firmness, triple warmer overwhelm is indicated.

Correction Sequence for Triple Warmer in Overwhelm

Standard corrections for *triple warmer in overwhelm* include Smoothing behind the Ears, the Wayne Cook Posture, and the Triple Warmer/Spleen Hug. The directions are written as you would say them to the client.

1. Smoothing behind the Ears.

Rest your face in your hands, palms at your chin, fingers at your temples. Hold this for two breaths. Breathe in deeply and push your fingers upward two or three inches with some pressure, smoothing the skin from the temples to above the ears. On the exhalation, circle your fingers around your ears, press down the sides of your neck, and hang both hands on the backs of your shoulders, pressing your fingers into your shoulders. Stay in this position through at least two deep breaths. Then drag your fingers slowly over your shoulders with pressure. Once your fingers reach your clavicle, let go.

2. The Wayne Cook Posture. This procedure is described on page 62.

3. **The Triple Warmer/Spleen Hug.** This simple technique provides comfort and reduces emotional overwhelm by balancing the energies between the triple warmer and spleen meridians. Have the client:

a. Wrap the left hand around the right arm with the middle finger pressing the indent just above the right elbow.

b. Wrap the right hand around the left side of the body, with the fingers underneath the underarm, and the hand resting just above the waist.

c. Be still or gently rock. Stay in this position for at least three deep breaths or up to two minutes.

d. Repeat on the other side.

3. Polarity Reversal 📹

Electrical currents move throughout the body and, as occurs wherever electricity flows, a magnetic charge is built. Like a compass, every magnetic charge has a north and a south polarity. The body becomes accustomed to its own magnetic charge and to the magnetic charges in the environment. When the poles of the body's magnetic charge become reversed, which is called a *polarity reversal*, neurological disorganization often follows.

Energy Checking for a Polarity Reversal (Hand-over-Head Check)

The palm side of the hand has an opposite charge from the back of the hand, and this is used in checking for a polarity reversal. The client or therapist places the palm of either hand an inch above the apex of the head. Energy check. The hand is turned, palm up. Energy check. Each of the three possible combinations has a different meaning.

1. If palm down checks strong and palm up checks weak, the polarities are as they should be.
2. If palm down checks weak and palm up checks strong, a polarity reversal is probable.

68

3. If there is no differential between the two palm positions, a polarity reversal is also probable.

Correction Sequence for Polarity Reversals

If you suspect a polarity reversal, the correction sequence will do no harm even if the condition is not present, and it is, in fact, still likely to have a positive effect. The correction is simply a combination of two techniques you have already learned. First do a Crown Pull (p. 60), then the Navel/Third-Eye Hook-Up (p. 21).

4. Ocular Lock

Disturbed coordination of the eyes is called *ocular lock* and can reflect neurological disorganization. The underlying cause is often a cranial fault and might require the services of a cranial-sacral or other specialist. However, the treatment sequence that follows will often correct the condition enough so that the energy psychology treatment can proceed.

Energy Checking for Ocular Lock (the Left/Right Eye Rotation)

The client rotates his or her eyes 360° to the right and 360° to the left. Saccadic (jerky) eye movements when the eyes pass through a particular position indicate the presence of ocular lock and related neurological disorganization. Ocular lock is also indicated if a firm indicator muscle checks weak immediately following the eye rotation.

69

Correction Sequence for Ocular Lock

To provide at least some relief from ocular lock, begin by having the client massage the orbits around the eyes. Press into the bone with the thumb and continue around the circle above and below each eye. Then palm the eyes by rubbing the hands together to generate heat and energy and placing the palms of each hand over the eyes. Have the client breathe deeply, holding for 30 seconds or longer. Finish with the Navel/K-27 Massage. Gently massage the navel with the middle finger of one hand for 10 to 15 seconds while vigorously stimulating the K-27 points with the other hand.

5. Homolateral Patterning

The body's energies are meant to cross over from one side to the other. This pattern is found in microcosm with the double helix of DNA, and it extends to the way the left side of the brain controls the right side of the body and the right side of the brain the left side of the body. When the body's energies are not crossing over from one side to the other, neurological disorganization results, as well as compromised immune functioning. The condition is known as *homolateral patterning.*

Energy Checking for Homolateral Patterning (the X & Parallel Line Test)

To check for homolateral patterning, energy check a firm indicator muscle as the client looks at a large X drawn on a sheet of paper or made with the

practitioner's hands. Then energy check as, or just after, the client looks at two parallel lines. If the X checks strong and the parallel lines check weak, the energies between the left and right sides of the brain are crossing properly. Otherwise, the energies are running in a homolateral pattern.

Correction Sequence for Homolateral Patterning

The homolateral crossover you learned earlier (p. 66) is a standard correction for homolateral patterning.

Stabilizing the Corrections

The Neurological Disorganization: Triggers, Checks, and Corrections Chart (p. 62) summarizes how to recognize, energy check for, and treat five basic forms of neurological disorganization. At the bottom of the chart are five additional correction sequences that are not associated with a specific type of neurological disorganization. These have generic benefits (as, it should be noted, do many of the specific techniques).

Two are used for stabilizing the gains after other corrections for neurological disorganization have been successfully applied. The other three can be done in the treatment setting, but they are also recommended as back-home assignments when neurological disorganization is persistent. After successfully correcting for neurological disorganization, Dancing to the Eights and Polarity Unswitching are brief procedures that serve to stabilize the correction.

FIGURE 3.2
DANCING TO THE EIGHTS 📹

The figure-eight is one of nature's most basic energy patterns. Weaving your energies in figure-eight curves supports the corrections, connects the hemispheres of your brain, activates numerous energy systems (notably the *radiant energies*—see the "Radiant Energies" module on the CD), and brings the body into greater health and vitality.

Put on music if you wish and move your hips to a figure-eight, then your arms. Flow freely, moving your entire body while creating as many small and large figure-eights as occur to you. Allow the dance to evolve into any pattern that feels good.

From *Energy Medicine*.
Drawing by Brooks Garten.

71

Polarity Unswitching 📹

Polarity Unswitching, a generic correction technique for neurological disorganization, involves four steps:

1. Begin with a Crown Pull (see p. 60).
2. Place thumb and first two fingers of one hand over the third eye and the thumb and first two fingers of the other hand at the notch where the neck meets the back of the head. Hold for at least three deep breaths.
3. Briskly tap or rub the K-27 points (the areas under each side of the collarbone next to the sternum).
4. Massage the Wellspring of Life points at the bottom of each foot, below the ball of the foot and between the first and second toes (the K-1 points). Massage deeply for several seconds.

Back-Home Routines

Particularly in cases where neurological disorganization is recurring or resistant to the above corrections, homework can be assigned for establishing and maintaining positive neurological and electromagnetic patterns. In general, the procedures that help most in the office will be the most effective at home. You may print any of them out from the CD or copy them from this book to use as client hand-outs.

Two additional, more complex sequences are also included on the CD. The 5-Minute Daily Energy Routine (see video demonstration 📹 or access text instructions through the Embedded Topics Index) combines some of the most universally beneficial techniques from energy medicine with a daily practice for optimal health and functioning. The "Collarbone Breathing" exercise, developed by Roger Callahan, has long been a standard within energy psychology (see the "Neurological Disorganization" module of the CD). A third, very valuable back-home technique that can be applied for a few seconds several times per day is described here. It is called *neurolymphatic massage*, and it is also a part of the 5-Minute Daily Energy Routine.

Massaging the neurolymphatic points dislodges accumulations of toxins so they can be eliminated from the body. This creates physical space and better conditions for the body's energies to flow more naturally and freely. The most frequently used neurolymphatic point in energy psychology is called the *chest sore spot*, which is near the left shoulder, but any spot that is sore may indicate a blockage of lymph that can be freed by working with the neurolymphatic point at that spot.

Have the client locate any sore spots on the chest and firmly massage each for a few seconds while breathing deeply. The soreness typically indicates lymphatic congestion. When you rub the area, you are dispersing that congestion. The more frequently you massage a point, the congestion becomes dispersed and the soreness diminishes. Working on a daily basis with the spots that tend to be chronically sore is an excellent practice.

Massaging the sore area should not cause more than a little discomfort. If it does, lighten your pressure a bit. Also, if the client has had an operation in that area of the chest or if there is any medical reason not to probe in a specific area, use appropriate caution.

Neurological Disorganization Requiring
Specialized Interventions

While energetic imbalances are always involved when neurological disorganization is present, if the energetic imbalance is caused by any of the following conditions, interventions by an appropriate health care specialist might be required.

- digestive problems (irritable bowel syndrome, diarrhea, constipation)
- chemical toxins or allergic reactions (Radomski, 2001)
- nutritional deficiencies or chronic dehydration
- hormonal imbalances such as hypothyroidism
- severe structural imbalance (particularly at the feet, the sacrum, and the cranium)
- cranial movement dysfunction (this might require cranial-sacral therapy from a specially trained osteopath or chiropractic physician)

Other causes of neurological disorganization that tend to spontaneously correct when the circumstances that caused them change are severe psychosocial stress and sleep deprivation.

73

Practice Session: Neurological Disorganization

1. Check a colleague for each of the sources of neurological disorganization described in the chart on page 64. With a little practice, you will be able to do all five checks in less than a minute. Apply the appropriate treatment sequence to each type of neurological disorganization you identify.
2. Trade roles. You become the "client" and guide the person in energy checking you and applying the treatments.
3. With the other person neurologically balanced, shift into a role-play in which the energy check "reveals" one of the types of neurological disorganization not already worked with. Apply the treatment for that type. Proceed until you have had practice with each type of neurological disorganization. Even if not needed, these procedures will do no harm and will reinforce the healthy flow of energies.

—4—

Psychological Reversals[1]

REMEMBER THE TOY PUZZLE where you stick a finger into each end of a straw tube and the harder you try to pull your fingers out, the more firmly they become embedded? That is how a psychological reversal feels—your efforts to change a situation produce the opposite of the result you intend. This dynamic is familiar to most people who make plans for personal improvement, which they affirm and reaffirm but never quite achieve (the flaw in the "New Year's resolution" approach to personal development). It is as if the conscious mind has one agenda but an opposing agenda, outside its awareness, wins. Because we wind up doing the reverse of what we intended, the dynamic is called a *psychological reversal*. You were introduced to psychological reversals in Chapter 1. They are examined here in some depth.

Psychological Reversals within Energy Psychology

When a client formulates a goal that activates a psychological reversal, the treatment's effectiveness will be compromised until the psychological reversal has been resolved. All effective therapies address psychological reversals in one way or another. Energy psychology focuses on their energetic as well as psychological roots, yielding an intervention strategy that neutralizes most psychological reversals quite rapidly.

---

[1] The concept of the psychological reversal, and the basic treatment strategy, were intoduced by Roger Callahan, Ph.D.

Are Psychological Reversals a Form of Cognitive Dissonance?

At the core of both cognitive dissonance and of a psychological reversal is an *internal contradiction*.

- In *cognitive dissonance* (in which a current experience challenges an existing belief), new information does not conform to a consciously held *idea*.
- In a *psychological reversal*, one's behavior does not conform to a consciously held *intention*.

> *Cognitive Dissonance*: What you believe ≠ what you experience.
> *Psychological Reversal*: What you intend ≠ what you do.

The presence of a psychological reversal *does not mean the client is unmotivated*, simply that other factors are interfering with the conscious intention. Once a psychological reversal has been identified, some clients may need additional explanation and reassurance that it does not mean they do not really want to get over their problem or that deep down they want to fail. Since the term *psychological reversal* can itself be intimidating or seem pathologizing, some clinicians avoid the phrase, referring simply to inner conflicts about the treatment goals.

Self-Sabotage or an Adaptive Mechanism?

Psychological reversals have been described as a form of self-sabotage, but they actually reflect a much broader, and potentially adaptive, process. They can be adaptive because the psyche contains a greater intelligence than only the elements with which a person identifies. As generally thought of, a person wants to change in a healthy direction and the psychological reversal gets in the way. But what if a person wants to change in an unhealthy direction, as seen, for instance, with excessive ambition? Then the psychological reversal may counter the self-destructive impulse. Many well-intentioned aspirations cost a person dearly, and a psychological reversal is a natural mechanism for restoring balance.

If excessive ambition is countered by a psychological reversal, neglected aspects of the personality can flourish, as when a highly driven corporate executive, for reasons he cannot explain and perhaps amidst inner echoes of self-recrimination, allows himself to engage in a truly relaxing, time-consuming, creative but "unproductive" hobby. On the other hand, psychological reversals can keep a person addictively trapped in behavior patterns that are costly and destructive, as when another highly driven executive consciously resolves to bring more balance and relaxation into her life but her behavior is to repeatedly push herself to the edge of physical breakdown.

Psychological Structures in Conflict

Speculation about the physiological dynamics of psychological reversals has focused on the differences between the way the left and right cerebral hemispheres organize information as well as differences between cerebral cortex and back brain activity. The psychological dynamic is clear: a conscious intention is in conflict with motivation that is outside of the person's awareness.

While this can be problematic, it is also part of normal development; it is not in itself a sign of psychopathology. In a comprehensive research program at Northwestern University, psychologist Dan P. McAdams (1996) showed that optimal psychological maturation requires the progressive reconciliation of *opposing qualities* within one's inner nature and within one's life structure. A primary mechanism by which this occurs is in the resolution of conflicts between psychological structures (relatively autonomous constellations of information and emotion) with which a person identifies and those that are outside of consciousness. McAdams's research suggests that it is through this process wherein opposing qualities are reconciled that the psychological structures that organize experience become more comprehensive and better integrated as a person matures.

Psychological structures are both *frameworks* for understanding and *designs* for action. One cognitive scheme may be primarily concerned with insuring safety, while another is oriented toward cultivating fulfilling inter-personal relationships. A person may be fully identified with some of these explanatory and motivational maps, while others operate preconsciously (the maps are known at some level but are not available for articulation). Such independent, yet interrelated, psychological structures can either be in harmony with one another or in conflict. Their conflict is at the root of a psychological reversal.

> A psychological reversal occurs when we *consciously identify* with one psychological schema while another that is in conflict with it is operating *outside of our awareness*.

Psychological Reversals and the Energy System

Psychological reversals exist not only at the cognitive level; they also operate within the person's energy system. Pursuing a conscious intention that is in conflict with an underlying psychological structure can cause, or reflect, a disruption in the meridian system. The person's thinking and effectiveness are correspondingly compromised.

On the other hand, when an action you take is in line with a map that is energetically more deeply embedded than your conscious intention, your energies might return to a more optimal flow, making you feel better and operate more effectively. This is, of course, baffling to the conscious mind, and it is part of the reason that certain addictive or compulsive habits that make little sense in terms of obvious rewards and punishment are still so difficult to break.

Based on an understanding of both the cognitive and energy dimensions of psychological reversals, energy-oriented clinicians have developed some surprisingly simple yet apparently effective interventions for working with them. While talk, introspection, and analysis can address the dynamics that are at play, they do not easily counter the energetic structures that maintain the pattern. Energy methods intervene at precisely that level. Clinical reports from a spectrum of energy-oriented practitioners strongly suggest that when psychological reversals undermine well-formulated treatment goals, they can be corrected relatively easily and quickly using a straightforward combination of cognitive and energetic techniques.

You have already been introduced to a simple procedure for working with psychological reversals, the EFT set-up affirmation ⛭ (p. 32). The two parts to the set-up affirmation are the *affirmation* and an *energy intervention* that involves stimulating specific points on the body. In this chapter, you will learn to distinguish among four types of psychological reversal that tend to interfere with treatment, and you will learn how to resolve each using relatively simple methods that combine cognitive and energetic techniques.

You are, however, again at a choice point about whether to go into greater depth within this chapter or jump to the next. This is the last such choice point. The subsequent chapters should be studied in their entirety in the order they are presented. Developing skills in *energy checking, correcting neurological disorganization,* and *resolving psychological reversals,* however, can be more meaningful once you see how they fit into the overall treatment approach.

If you jump ahead to the next chapter at this point, you will already have a good idea of what is meant by the term *psychological reversal,* and you will already know a simple generic correction procedure. The program will make it evident when you need a more advanced understanding. Either way will work.

Psychological Reversals: Four Variations

Psychological reversals (PRs) interfere with a person's capacity to achieve a desired goal. There are two basic types:

1. **Global PRs** are linked to the desire to be happy or fulfilled. All other treatment goals can be undermined if they are operating.

   "I *want* to be happy" (conscious desire) vs. "I *don't want* to be happy" (agenda that is outside of awareness and often enmeshed with one's self-concept and early programming).

2. **Specific-Context PRs** are linked to the desire to solve a *specific* problem or reach a specific goal. When that problem or goal is the focus of the therapy, treatment will be compromised.

   "I *want* to quit smoking" (desire with which the person identi-fies) vs. "I *don't want* to quit smoking" (desire with which the person does not identify).

Global PRs are involved with large thematic issues, such as esteem, self-concept, core attitudes, and basic lifestyle choices that globally impact many aspects of the person's life. Specific-context PRs are specific to a more concrete problem or goal that might be the immediate focus in psycho-therapy. Both global and specific-context PRs appear in two variations.

Variation 1: Criteria-related psychological reversals emerge when secondary issues conflict with the desired goal (Gallo, 2000). Rather than involving ambivalence about the desire to achieve the goal ("I want to . . ."), they focus on a *conflict* around an *underlying issue*: "It is not *safe* to be happy" (safety vs. happiness); "I am not *capable* of quit-ting smoking" (ability vs. inability). The conflict hinges on a criterion that is more delimited (e.g., safety, ability, deservedness, permission, identity) than simply the desire to maintain well-being or achieve a specific goal. A criteria-related PR will always be a variation of a global PR or of a specific-context PR. That is, it will either involve general well-being (criteria-related *global* PRs) or specific problems or goals (criteria-related *specific-context* PRs).

Variation 2: Intervening psychological reversals appear after any PRs detected at the outset of treatment have been resolved and progress toward treatment goals has been observed. They usually involve a specific tangible treatment goal (intervening *specific-context* PRs), but may also involve the person's general well-being (intervening *global* PRs).

Psychological Reversals to Check Early in Treatment

Global, specific-context, and criteria-related PRs should be checked for during the diagnostic phase of treatment, before introducing energy interventions that target the presenting problem. You will learn techniques for quickly assessing, usually in less than a minute, the presence of PRs that might affect the treatment.

The presence of a **global PR** can be confirmed, or ruled out, by energy checking specific statements (i.e., does saying the statement weaken the meridian system?):

- For statements such as "I want to be happy," "I want to be fulfilled," or "I want my life to be gratifying," if the indicator muscle loses firmness, the reversal exists; if it stays firm, the reversal is not operating.
- For statements such as "I don't want to be happy" or "I want to have a miserable life," a global PR is indicated if the muscle stays firm.

Specific-context PRs appear within a given type of situation. They are of particular concern when the situation is related to a treatment goal because they involve a conflict regarding the desire to reach the goal or solve the designated problem. Once the treatment goal or target problem has been specified, the presence of a specific-context PR can be confirmed, or ruled out, by energy checking:

- "I want to get over this problem," or "I want to get over my anxiety around powerful men" (specifically describing the problem), or "I want to create more time for spiritual development" (specifically describing a goal). If the indicator muscle loses firmness, a reversal exists; if it stays firm, a reversal is not operating.

- "I want to keep this problem," "I want to keep my anxiety around powerful men," "I don't want to get over this problem," or "I don't want to get over my anxiety around powerful men." If the muscle stays firm, a specific-context PR is indicated.

A criteria-related psychological reversal is like a *rider* on the client's good intentions. The client might *want* to be happy or *want* to get over the problem, but might feel or deeply believe that he or she does not *deserve* to get over the problem, or that it is not *safe* to get over the problem. The reversal is organized around specific criteria, such as *deservedness* or *safety*, thus the term *criteria-related*. Criteria-related PRs might operate only in a narrow area of the person's life (criteria-related *specific-context* PR) or might have a more widespread impact (criteria-related *global* PR). Statements that will, based on an energy check, show whether criteria-related psychological reversals are operating include:

> "I deserve to . . . [get over this problem, attain this goal, be happy, etc.]."
> "It is safe for me to. . . ."
> "It is safe for others if I. . . ."
> "It is possible for me to. . . ."
> "I will feel deprived if I get over this problem [PR indicated if muscle stays strong]."
> "Getting over this problem will be good for me."
> "My getting over this problem will be good for others."
> "I will get over this problem."[1]
> "It is my duty/role/job to have this problem . . . [family of origin issue, PR indicated if muscle stays strong]."
> "I will allow myself to get over . . . [the issue is permission]."
> "I will still be me if I get over . . . [the issue is identity]."

The statements can also all be worded in the negative (e.g., "I do not deserve to . . ."). A PR is indicated if a positive statement loses strength or a negative statement keeps the muscle strong.

---

[1] Some practitioners consider this basic expectation in relationship to the issue to be a separate type of PR, and call it a *deep level psychological reversal*.

Some practitioners make the statements in both their positive and negative forms to distinguish between psychological reversals and neurological disorganization. If the results of the two checks are inconsistent (e.g., yes to "I want to be over this problem," and yes to "I don't want to be over this problem"), neurological disorganization is probably present.

Practice Session 1: Checking for Psychological Reversals

1. Qualify an indicator muscle on a colleague with whom you can delve into psychological issues. Energy check the global statement, "*I want to be happy.*" Then proceed through the various possible qualifying criteria: "*It is safe for me to be happy,*" "*I deserve to be happy,*" etc. 📹 If you find any global or criteria-related global PRs (based on an energy check of an indicator muscle done immediately after completing the statement), remember them or write them down to be used in the practice session on correcting psychological reversals.

2. Ask the person to describe a habit, an emotional response, a behavioral pattern, or a way of thinking he or she would like to change. Energy check a statement in the form of "*I want to [change this pattern].*" Proceed through the various possible qualifying criteria: "*It is safe for me to . . .,*" "*I deserve to . . .,*" etc. If you find a specific-context or a criteria-related specific-context PR (based on an energy check), remember it for the practice session on correcting for psychological reversals.

3. Reverse roles. You become the "client" and guide your partner in checking for psychological reversals.

82

Intervening Psychological Reversals

Intervening psychological reversals, by definition, appear only after treatment is underway. This type of PR is distinguished by when it emerges. Where a PR about the presenting problem or treatment goal detected at the outset of treatment is called a *specific-context* PR, an *intervening* PR appears *after* gains have been made in the treatment. The energy techniques that had been working no longer result in subjective improvement or in positive energy shifts as revealed by energy tests. It is as if an invisible barrier has been hit. Progress may cease or there may be a resurgence of the problem, as if the treatment is "bouncing off" the barrier.[2]

An intervening psychological reversal is operating if an indicator muscle loses strength during statements that emphasize the idea of *completely* overcoming the problem:

> "I want to get *completely* over this problem" [or specify problem, e.g., "my obsession for cars I can't afford"].
> "I want to *completely* reach my goal" [or specify goal, e.g., "master this program"].

The statement can also be worded in the opposite way. If an intervening PR is present, the muscle will stay firm during statements such as:

> "I want to keep *some* of this problem" [or, "some of my obsession for cars I can't afford"].
> "I do not want to *completely* reach my goal" [or, "completely master this program"].

The appearance of an intervening PR can be discouraging to both the client and the practitioner, and it might be caused by a variety of factors. A problem that was improving might stop improving or completely return because:

- new stresses or other changes in the client's life are undermining the treatment
- environmental substances (particularly found in food, medications, shampoo, chemicals in synthetic clothing or rugs or from dry cleaning, electromagnetic fields) are disrupting the client's energies (Radomski, 2001)

83

---

[2] The term *recurrent psychological reversal* has sometimes been used for when distress that was decreasing not only stops decreasing—i.e., an *intervening PR*—but then spikes upward. Since the treatment is identical for either situation, the term *intervening PR* is used here for both.

- another *aspect* of the problem has emerged (addressed in Chapters 1 and 9)
- an intervening psychological reversal has emerged

Addressing the Cognitive Dimension of a Psychological Reversal

A psychological reversal has occurred when a psychological schema outside of the person's conscious awareness engages thoughts, emotions, or behaviors that do not conform to the person's intentions. Interventions for resolving a psychological reversal have both cognitive and energy components. While the cognitive dimension of the intervention strategy has many varieties, these variations tend to share a common format.

In working with a psychological reversal, an affirmation or self-suggestion along the lines of "I deeply love and accept myself" is paired with an acknowledgment of the problem that has been targeted for change. Affirmations for addressing a pattern in which a person collapses around certain authority figures might be:

84

> *"Even though I become anxious around powerful men, I deeply love and accept myself"* (*specific-context* PR).
> *"Even though I **still** become **somewhat** anxious around powerful men, I deeply love and accept myself"* (the words "still" and "somewhat" are added so that the statement addresses an *intervening* PR).

We can speculate on how this statement, made with focus and intention, signals to the part of the psyche that manages inner conflict that the person is:

- attuned to the conflict
- speaking directly to aspects of the psyche that were not being consciously addressed (also the mechanism of paradoxical intention)
- accepting and prioritizing the needs of the "deeper self" rather than focusing narrowly on the conscious agenda

This reframes the issue from a polarized conflict, where only one side can win, into a negotiation where the issues of concern to both sides can be considered. The reasons for the conflict may or may not come to light.

Perhaps the fear of authority traces to a specific incident of humiliation, a pattern of abuse, or an unresolved issue with a parent. Whatever the etiology of the conflict about the stated goal, the side with which the person is not consciously identified can move out of a defensive posture when it is acknowledged and accepted.

The reframe addresses another key issue involving psychological interventions for emotional, cognitive, or behavioral change. Every human culture shapes the thoughts, feelings, attitudes, and behavior of its young through a system of reinforcements and punishments. Parental and social injunctions then become internalized. Many of these reinforcements and punishments target the child's self-esteem. When these injunctions are violated, self-negating internalized statements follow, from the toddler's "Bad Robbie, spilled the milk. Bad. Bad!!!" to all variations of adult guilt and self-recrimination.

When, as an adult, you target something about yourself for change, this mechanism of self-judgment and self-negation tends to become engaged. You have the idea "I want to exercise more regularly," and your self-esteem is held ransom when you do not carry out the desired behavior (or bring about a desired internal change).

The correction for such a psychological reversal, as we've seen, includes a statement in the form of *"Even if I"* or *"Even though I"* (followed by a description of a mental state or behavior targeted for change—for example, *"Even if I never exercise regularly"* or *"Even if I'll always be afraid of people in authority"*), *"I deeply love and accept myself."* A statement of this nature, made with focus and intent, tends to circumvent the entire self-negating sequence. Various alternative approaches for formulating affirmations or intentions are also possible and are sometimes required, as when low esteem makes a statement about self-love too incongruent.

While the self-suggestion in itself can shift the energy system, the effectiveness of this cognitive technique is substantially enhanced when it is paired with an intervention that energetically supports the affirmation (i.e., pairing the self-affirming cognitive statement with an energy intervention that simultaneously optimizes the flow of the meridian energies).

85

Addressing the Energy Dimension of a Psychological Reversal

The basic *energy principle* to understand when faced with a psychological reversal is that when a conflict between a consciously held intention for change and an unconsciously held intention to resist change is activated, there will be a corresponding conflict in the meridian energies.

The psychological issues involved in a PR may involve any of the rich and varied dimensions of the psyche. Within the energy system, however, the issue is simple: mobilize the body's energies to *resist* a consciously initiated change or to *support* that change. In a psychological reversal, the conscious intention is to initiate change while the body's energies, driven by inner conflict, are mobilizing to resist it.

Such internal conflict is not unusual. Initiating change, even constructive change, is fundamentally disruptive to the homeostasis of the body's energy system. There are good reasons for this counter-intuitive dynamic. Established codes of behavior, patterns of emotion, and habits of thought are hard-won compromises among many competing agendas and possibilities. The body's energies constellate themselves to support and maintain these established solutions. When the conscious mind says, "I want to make a change," the energy system charged with maintaining established patterns is immediately engaged. That system is governed by the triple warmer meridian.

Triple warmer controls the activation of the *immune* response, the *fight-or-flight* response, and the body's *habitual* responses to stress or threat. Its primary concern is *survival*. When triple warmer goes on alert, its "authority" supercedes most other energy systems in the body (for a more thorough discussion of these dynamics, see Chapter 8 of Eden's *Energy Medicine*).

The implications of triple warmer's role in maintaining survival habits are enormous when the topic is psychological or behavioral change. When you decide to initiate change, triple warmer is instantly activated and poised to resist whatever changes you intend to initiate. After all, the status quo has worked until now. *You have survived!*

Triple warmer is not concerned with your happiness, sense of meaning, or fulfillment—only your survival. It is oriented to fight change, and it can mobilize the meridians and other energy systems to maintain established patterns of thought and behavior. It may sound as if triple warmer is being personified here, but few reading these words have not been impressed by the "intelligence" of the immune system or elegance of the fight-or-flight response, both governed by triple warmer. When threatened, triple warmer can also take control of your mood, combat your will, even extinguish your memory about what you were resolved to do. It is a powerful though largely unrecognized force within the body's energy system.

Resolving Psychological Reversals

The basic approach to working with a psychological reversal involves an affirmation or self-suggestion paired with the stimulation of an energy point. The wording for the self-suggestion uses a three-part format:

1. Begin with *"Even if"* or *"Even though."*
2. Describe or acknowledge the target problem or the goal that is to be achieved.
3. End with words similar to *"I deeply and completely accept myself," "I fully love and accept myself,"* etc.

The self-suggestion also uses qualifiers and syntax that mirror the format of the statement used to energy check for the psychological reversal being addressed.

For example, a self-suggestion worded for a global PR might be:

> *"Even if I don't want to be happy, I deeply love and accept myself."*

A self-suggestion worded for a specific-context PR:

> *"Even if I am the one at work who keeps getting confused, I deeply love and accept myself."* (This differs from a global PR in its focus on a specific issue.)

For intervening PRs, the self-suggestion will include the words "still," "some," or "somewhat":

> *"Even if I am **still** the one in the group who keeps getting confused, I deeply love and accept myself."*

For criteria-related PRs, the self-suggestion includes a description of the criteria:

> *"Even if **it is my role to be** the one in the group who gets confused,* [or *"Even if it is **not safe** not to be confused,"* or *"Even if I **deserve** to be confused,"* etc.], *I deeply love and accept myself."*

Self-suggestions designed to address criteria-related PRs might focus on a global issue or a specific context. They might include:

- **Criteria-related global PR**: "*Even if **I deserve to be** unhappy, I deeply love and accept myself.*" (For an intervening global PR, insert "still" and/or "somewhat": "*Even if I **still** deserve to be **somewhat** unhappy. . . .*")
- **Criteria-related specific-context PR**: "*Even if **I deserve to be** intimidated around powerful men, I deeply love and accept myself.*" (For an intervening specific-context PR, insert "still" and/or "somewhat": "*Even if I **still** deserve to be intimidated around powerful men, I deeply love and accept myself.*")

For other criteria, substitute "*I deserve to be*" with:

"it's still not safe if I were no longer . . ."
"it's still not safe for others if I were no longer . . ."
"it's still not possible for me to no longer be . . ."
"I still won't allow myself to no longer be . . ."
"I still won't do what's necessary to no longer be . . ."
"it still won't be good for me to no longer be . . ."
"it still won't be good for others for me to no longer be . . ."
"I still would be deprived if I were no longer . . ."
"I still would lose an essential aspect of who I am if I were no longer . . ."

88

This of course appears formulistic when you are first learning it. The "formulas" are simply devices to keep your intuition alert to the presence of psychological reversals, which can be decisive obstacles to a successful treatment outcome.

In practice, it is not necessary to track whether you are testing, for instance, for a specific-context or an intervening psychological reversal. If the check is performed prior to other energy interventions, you are not checking for an intervening PR. If the check is performed after treatment that had been progressing becomes stalled, you are. Being able to label the distinctions is most important in coming to understand the nature of PRs in their various forms. Once you have this understanding, your focus while working with PRs will be on the intricate dance between you, your client's conscious intention, and your client's unconscious dynamics in relationship to that intention. Rely on your intuition while keeping the formulas in your back pocket.

For example, an 85-year-old man, whose mind has remained very sharp, is nonetheless increasingly unable to think of common words. This experience, which happens several times each week, has become the cause of considerable anxiety and concern about declining mental abilities. Assurances from others that he is "just fine" make him feel worse and his own attempts at self-assurance also make him more anxious and deeply convinced that senility is setting in. The affirmation "*Even though I sometimes cannot remember the correct word, I know my mind is still strong and clear,*" combined with the stimulation of an energy point, rapidly shifts the constellation so that he is able to keep the occasional mental lapses in perspective and appreciate the preponderance of ways in which his mind is still robust. The second phrase could be "*I deeply love and accept myself,*" but the phrase "*I know my mind is still strong and clear*" speaks more directly to the issue. You do not have to be limited by the formulas.

Still, having the wording for energy checks of the most common PRs in your back pocket can be quite handy. Prior to the energy interventions you will learn in subsequent chapters, you might routinely energy check for a number of likely psychological reversals, using statements such as:

- Before focusing on the problem or goal: "*I want to be happy.*" "*It is safe to be happy.*" "*It is safe for others if I am happy.*" "*It is my role to be unhappy.*" "*I deserve to be happy.*" "*I will be happy.*"
- After the problem or goal has been specified: "*I want to get over this problem.*" "*It is safe to get over this problem.*" "*It is safe for others if I get over this problem.*" "*It is my role to have this problem.*" "*I deserve to get over this problem.*" "*I will get over this problem.*"

Your intuition might suggest other criteria, such as: "*I will lose my identity if I get over this problem,*" "*I will allow myself to get over this problem,*" "*Others do not deserve to have me get over this problem,*" etc.

If treatment stalls, you can check for a variety of intervening or recurrent psychological reversals by simply inserting the word "completely": "*I want to be* completely *over this problem.*"

Of course it is not just a matter of mechanically applying the formulas. The client's history and the relationship of the client's life context to the treatment goals remain in your mind as you stay alert for psychological reversals. Once you have internalized the principles, you will be able to easily devise protocols individualized for the situation. Nonetheless, practitioners who are new to energy psychology frequently express surprise at how easily and how often the simple formulas alone result in the detection and demonstrable resolution of psychological reversals.

89

The Basic "Formula"

With the limitations of over-reliance on formulas duly emphasized (it should also be noted that not all energy-based psychotherapists address psychological reversals in the explicit manner outlined in this chapter), the basic approach to working with a psychological reversal is:

1. Identify the presence and type of psychological reversal via an energy check.
2. Formulate an *"Even if* [. . .], *I deeply love and accept myself"* self-suggestion worded for the type of PR that has been identified.
3. Use an energy intervention that can help overcome a PR while stating the self-suggestion, with focus and intention, several times.

Energy Interventions for Resolving Psychological Reversals 📠

In Chapter 1, you learned to massage the chest sore spots in the treatment of psychological reversals. Energy interventions that have been found to be effective with psychological reversals (performed while stating the affirmation) include:

• Vigorously massaging the chest "sore spots" (two to three inches below the clavicle and two to three inches in from where the arm attaches to the chest).
• Tapping the "gamut spot" (on the back of the hand, between ring and little finger, below the knuckle, and toward wrist).
• "Hooking up" the third eye and navel with the middle fingers, gently pushing in and pulling up.
• Tapping the "spleen points" (about four inches below each armpit).
• Tapping the "karate chop" points.

Any of these techniques is likely to be effective. Many of their actions are identical—they all pair a self-suggestion that embraces both sides of the reversal with an energetic boost—but each also has special strengths. For instance, the procedure might stimulate the electrical connections

90

among all of the meridians and between the front and back portions of the brain (the hook-up), metabolize contradictory information (the spleen tap), work with the fight-or-flight response (the gamut point), resolve psychological reversals related to stress, grief, or pride (the sore spot), or support choices about what information to incorporate (small intestine meridian, one of the karate chop points).

The simplest approach is to apply one of the methods and then do another energy check of the statement that identified the psychological reversal. If it has not been corrected, try another energy treatment while repeating the same affirmation (also, consider that the affirmation may need to be adjusted). Whether a particular energy technique is going to be effective in a specific instance varies from one case to the next, but any of these five techniques will work most of the time.

Practice Session 2: Resolving Psychological Reversals

Begin with the psychological reversals you and your partner identified during Practice Session 1. Formulate the affirmations and experiment with the above energy interventions for resolving each of your partner's PRs. Then instruct your partner on how to carry out the procedure for you. Enlist several other people to check for psychological reversals and correct any you identify.

With the completion of this chapter, you have been introduced to several of the basic elements of energy psychology. In the following chapter, you will see how skills in 1) energy checking, 2) detecting and correcting for neurological disorganization, and 3) identifying and resolving psychological reversals come together in the opening phases of treatment.

—5—

The Opening Phases of Treatment

BEYOND THE TYPICAL CLINICAL TASKS in the early phases of treatment, energy-oriented psychotherapy generally opens with six additional elements (Gallo, 2000):

1. Establishing an energy checking procedure.
2. Checking for and correcting neurological disorganization.
3. Checking for and resolving psychological reversals.
4. Identifying a target problem appropriate for energy interventions.
5. Assessing the person's "subjective units of distress" (SUD) and confirming this with an energy check.
6. Energetically locking the problem into the body (for the purposes of the treatment session).

This chapter addresses each of these tasks and shows how they may be integrated with more generic clinical tasks in the opening phases of treatment.

Attitudes That Support Rapport

Maintaining rapport is an ongoing task and a necessary condition if psychotherapy, regardless of its orientation, is likely to be successful. Five attitudes that support rapport include:

1. Maintaining an appreciation of the client's individuality.
2. Staying open to your own moment-to-moment experience as you interact with this unique person.
3. Being willing to engage the client in terms of this flow of experience.
4. Using any negative responses within yourself as information about the client's problem (while remaining open to the possibility that these reactions might also provide information about you).
5. Practicing "high positive regard" of the other as your default position.

In addition, and consistent with an energy approach, exploring the presenting problem in terms of its "physical address" helps align the client and the therapist. Questions such as, "Notice where in your body you hold an emotional charge about this issue," by attuning both client and therapist to the client's "felt sense" of the problem, can lead the way into an energy-based approach.

Client Expectations to Explore in the Initial Interviews

Expectations the client brings to the treatment that should be explored and clarified include:

1. Where does the client place responsibility for overcoming the presenting problem (self, therapist, family members, a change in external circumstances)?
2. What does the client believe will be the curative elements of the treatment (advice, advocacy, emotional support, "talking out" the problem, analysis, affect release, behavioral interventions, energy work, etc.)?
3. Are extraneous factors influencing the client's hopes and expectations (involvement with the legal system, strategy for establishing a disability claim, desire to please a spouse)?

Psychosocial History

Another task shared by virtually all forms of psychotherapy is attaining relevant biographical and clinical information. Some practitioners new to energy work may, however, wonder if it is still necessary to take a detailed psychosocial history when the interventions are targeted largely toward the client's energy system. Regardless of the therapeutic approach, a psychosocial history gathers essential information, including:

- a background for understanding the origins and context of the presenting problem
- a framework for meeting the client within his or her model of the world
- a survey of potential treatment hazards emerging from a personal or family history of depression, mental illness, traumas, suicide attempts, etc.
- other diagnostic indicators

In addition to providing vital treatment information, taking a psychosocial history establishes a more favorable therapeutic atmosphere by helping to:

- increase rapport
- explore the client's expectations about the therapy
- formulate appropriate therapeutic goals
- engender hope that a good therapeutic outcome is possible
- lead the way into an appropriate treatment strategy

Taking a psychosocial history involves, of course, more than just gathering objective information, and the greater the client's pathology, the more critical and delicate this process may become. Even though energy methods have been reported to be effective for a wide range of diagnostic categories, including serious psychiatric disorders (Gallo, 2002), special skills beyond energy methods are required in the competent treatment of personality and emotional disorders. It is far easier to learn the mechanics of energy psychology than to be an effective clinician, and there is no substitute for clinical training, particularly with clients who have a history of psychological difficulties. Practitioners working with a generally non-psychiatric clientele, such as "life coaches" who bring energy psychology methods into business, educational and other settings should, at a minimum, know how to gather pertinent information about a client's past and know when it is appropriate, based on this psychosocial history and other basic indicators, to make a referral.

Limitations of an Energy-Based Approach

Because energy-based interventions can be so rapid and effective, it is not unusual for therapists who are new to energy psychology to over-apply the methods. Tentative indications and contraindications for the use of energy psychology, based on early clinical data, have been delineated (p. 204) and can serve as provisional guidelines. Particular caution must be applied with people who have suffered severe or multiple trauma, who have borderline or other personality disorders, who have had episodes of psychosis or dissociative identity, who have been hospitalized for other psychological problems, who have severe depression or bipolar disorder, who have not been able to form a productive working relationship with the therapist or who have a history of severe relationship disturbances, or who cannot understand their role in their problems and in the potential solution of those problems.

Another dilemma in having a method that can rapidly and effectively impact emotional problems is that psychological equilibrium may be disrupted. Symptoms have a purpose. An 11-year-old girl, a model child who causes few problems and gets little attention in a home where two other siblings are highly disturbed, develops a phobia of balloons after one she is inflating bursts. The phobia grows so intense that she resists leaving her home for fear of seeing a balloon. The therapist is quite certain that tapping treatments could rapidly ameliorate the phobia, but also suspects that if her symptoms were resolved, the therapy would end before the more pervasive family issues were addressed. Should the phobia be treated by defusing its energetic basis using primarily physical interventions? To "tap away" unwanted emotional responses or intrusive thoughts can upset a delicate psychic or interpersonal ecology.

In addition, a person's "life lessons" or developmental steps are sometimes achieved by psychologically working through difficult feelings or thoughts. In some instances, even if the symptom can be removed through relatively mechanical procedures, the therapist must consider how and if their surgical-like removal will ultimately serve the client's well-being and psychological growth. Energy interventions can also lead to the opposite of what was intended. Such paradoxical responses are seen when procedures that begin to reduce fearful feelings or thoughts have the unintended effect of activating other phychological defenses. While all of these dilemmas can be addressed and worked with and do not necessarily contraindicate the use of energy methods, clinical sensitivity and sophistication are obviously required.

Ethical Considerations

As with any new field, ethical standards for practitioners of energy psychology are evolving. The "Code of Ethics" that has been developed by the Association for Comprehensive Energy Psychology is posted at

www.energypsych.org/coe.html

and their "Standards of Practice" statement can be found at

www.energypsych.org/standards.html.

The "Code of Ethics" established by the American Psychological Association remains a model set of standards for all psychotherapists and can be found at

www.apa.org/ethics/code.html.

Numerous ethical concerns are thoughtfully addressed in the American Professional Agency's Newsletter on Risk Management for Psychologists. Current as well as back issues can be downloaded free from

www.americanprofessional.com/insight.htm.

An ethical consideration that is of direct relevance to the potential applications of this program, and one with which the fledgling field of energy psychology has been wrestling, involves the level of professional training that is required before someone is considered qualified to use the techniques it employs. Controversy about whether energy-based treatment approaches should be offered by nonprofessionals is inevitable.

The at-home treatment routines assigned to a growing number of people by their psychotherapists, along with a spate of self-help books and classes, are simple enough to use and yield results that are impressive enough that people are tempted to try them with family and friends. Nonlicensed counselors and "coaches" are tempted to offer them to the public. But the wisdom of a century of clinical practice holds that psychological interventions that might unearth latent psychopathology require sophisticated and responsible application and are best left in the hands of professionals.

The counter-argument is that an energy-based approach to psychological problems represents a new paradigm in which people can readily influence the energies that affect their physical and mental health, and that these techniques should be widely distributed. Both positions have merit, and their inevitable dialectic will result in guidelines for both the professional and self-help–oriented uses of the developing methods.

Introducing a New Client to an Energy-Based Approach

Areas that should be addressed when introducing a client to an energy-based treatment approach to psychological problems include:

1. The hypothesized underlying role of electromagnetic and more subtle energies in psychological problems (see transcripts for orienting a new client, p. 220).
2. The nature of energy checking and its role in assessing the energetic dimension of psychological problems.
3. Unfamiliar procedures that might be used during the treatment, such as:
    a. tapping or holding specific points on the body
    b. moving the eyes in certain directions
    c. assuming various physical postures
    d. mentally focusing on certain thoughts, feelings, or situations
    e. repeating specific statements or affirmations
4. Reaching an agreement about proceeding with an energy approach (see considerations regarding informed consent, p. 223).

Incorporating the Procedures You Have Already Learned

Energy checking, neurological disorganization, and psychological reversals are all addressed during the opening phases of treatment. Energy checking (Chapter 2) is often introduced as part of the explanation of an energy-based clinical approach. The first step is to "qualify" an indicator muscle. This means identifying a muscle that can be safely and reliably used in checks of the body's overall energy system. Once the muscle has been identified, qualifying it also involves:

- establishing the muscle *firmness* that indicates an affirmative response
- establishing the *decrease in that firmness* that indicates a negative response

Neurological disorganization (Chapter 3) may be a chronic state or it may occur in response to specific situations, including those that arise during the treatment session. Because it can interfere with subsequent work, the practitioner should remain alert for neurological disorganization not only in the diagnostic phases but throughout the treatment. An expedient way to introduce the concept of neurological disorganization while further establishing the validity of energy checking is to assess each of the five types of neurological disorganization, perform the related corrections for any that are present, and energy check again to demonstrate the effects of the correction technique.

The concept of the psychological reversal (Chapter 4) is also introduced relatively early within an energy psychology approach, although wording along the lines of "inner conflict about the treatment goal" might be preferred. Typically, this would come after introducing energy checking, after addressing neurological disorganization, and after the target problem has been articulated but prior to working with it. Initially, the clinician would use energy checking to identify global (and criteria-related global) psychological reversals. Among the statements that might be energy checked, as the clinician's intuition dictates, include:

99

"I want to be happy."
"It is safe to be happy."
"It is safe for others if I am happy" (PR indicated if muscle stays firm).
"I deserve to be happy."
"I will be happy."
"I will lose my identity if I am happy."
"I will allow myself to be happy."
"It is possible for me to be happy."
"I will feel deprived if I am happy" (PR indicated if muscle stays firm).
"My being happy will be good for me."
"It is my role to be unhappy" (PR indicated if muscle stays firm).
"My being happy will be good for others."
"Others do not deserve to have me be happy"(PR indicated if muscle stays firm).

Identifying the Target Problem

The treatment can focus on fear, phobias, panic, anxiety, anger, lack of confidence, grief, worry, jealousy, guilt, shame, obsessiveness, or any other undesired emotional response to a specific situation, thought, image, or memory. Other treatment goals are also possible, from overcoming addictions and allergies to improving athletic or professional performance, but for the purposes of this training program, the focus at this point will be limited to undesired *emotional* responses.

In identifying the first problem area to address using an energy-based psychological approach, the problem should be consistent with both the client's intention and the practitioner's sense of the next step based on:

1. The *psychosocial history*.
2. An exploration of the *meaning*, within the client's worldview, of the identified problem.
3. An analysis of the *aspects* of the problem and a selection of the first aspect that must be resolved before the entire problem can be resolved (see p. 34).

100

The selection and wording of the designated problem is a significant choice, and it may be approached in various ways. A guideline for finding the "top priority issue" is called the *principle of highest leverage*: Which issue will yield the greatest result from the simplest intervention; which issue is going to help the client move forward most effectively? (This is discussed in greater depth in the paper, "Five Keys to Successful Energy Psychology Treatment" by David Grudermeyer and Rebecca Grudermeyer, accessed through the Embedded Topics Index on the CD).

Some practitioners begin with the presenting problem and wait to see if other aspects tied into the person's past will surface. Others identify analogous situations from the client's history that might have been instrumental in the formation of the current pattern. They might focus, for instance, on earlier traumas and the core beliefs that emerged from those traumas. By treating these first, and then turning to the presenting problem, the therapy is believed to be more thorough and lasting. While this is a matter of therapist preference that also varies from client to client, for the purposes of this training program, the initial focus will be placed on the presenting problem.

Checking for Specific-Context Psychological Reversals

After the problem has been formulated, many practitioners use energy checking to identify any specific-context psychological reversal that might be operating in relationship to the designated problem. While you will be guided by the client's history, presentation, and your own intuition, a sample list of possible specific-context PRs includes:

"I want to get over this problem [or specify problem]."
"It is safe to get over this problem."
"It is safe for others if I get over this problem."
"I deserve to get over this problem."
"I will get over this problem."
"I will lose my identity if I get over this problem" (PR indicated if muscle stays firm).
"I will allow myself to get over this problem."
"It is possible for me to get over this problem."
"I will feel deprived if I get over this problem" (PR indicated if muscle stays firm).
"My getting over this problem will be good for me."
"It is my role to have this problem" (PR indicated if muscle stays firm).
"My getting over the problem will be good for others."
"Others do not deserve to have me get over this problem" (PR indicated if muscle stays firm).

Subsequently, if treatment stalls, you can check for a variety of intervening psychological reversals by simply inserting the word "completely," such as "I want to be *completely* over this problem" or "It is safe to be *completely* over this problem."

Accessing the Problem State

Accessing the problem state is a fundamental procedure in energy-based psychotherapy. For the treatment interventions to be effective, they must be administered while the problem state is energetically "active." Once a target problem has been identified, accessing the problem state can be as simple as bringing the problem to mind. Thinking about or imagining a situation activates the *thought field* (discussed in the following chapter) associated with that situation, including a complex of feelings, beliefs, and responses in the meridians and other energy systems. A firm indicator muscle will lose its firmness when this constellation is activated.

The issue of inadvertently retraumatizing a client is a concern in any treatment approach that works with severe trauma. When guiding a client to mentally access a problem state, clinical sensitivity is required to find a balance between psychologically entering the problem and not inducing further trauma.

If there is special concern about retraumatization with a particular client, a variety of techniques can be used to keep the memory or feeling at a distance, such as viewing it through a long tunnel or thinking about "what it would be like" to think about the issue. In his Tearless Trauma technique, when asking for a rating on the amount of distress caused by a traumatic memory, Gary Craig sometimes asks the client to simply "*guess at what the emotional intensity would be* [on a scale of 0 to 10] *if* you were to vividly imagine the incident."

The practitioner can also focus the initial round of treatment on the fears the client is having about accessing the problem, which can also be a powerful affirmation of an energy-based approach. Neutralizing these fears at the outset can be comforting and reassure the client that subsequent fears that emerge will be manageable and that lifelong fears can be treated. Like all good therapeutic pacing, matching the target of the intervention with what is occurring during the treatment aligns the treatment to the client.

If, on the other hand, the client is emotionally blocked around the problem or otherwise having difficulty accessing the problem state or feelings about it (i.e., an indicator muscle stays firm while the problem is brought to mind), he or she can be encouraged to:

1. Take more time to focus inward while relaxing and breathing deeply.
2. Vividly visualize circumstances that activate the problem.
3. Bring to mind other sensory dimensions of those circumstances (kinesthetic, olfactory, auditory, gustatory).
4. Slowly and deliberately replay in the imagination a situation in which the problem was felt or imagine one in which it would be felt.
5. Schedule an in vivo session in a setting where the problem actually arises.

Assessing the Distress Associated with the Problem State

The level of distress associated with the problem state is given a number from 1 to 10 (the "subjective units of distress," or SUD rating), which is veri-fied with an energy check 🎥. With the problem state mentally activated, the client is asked to rate the level of discomfort "at this moment," with 10 being an extreme level of discomfort and 0 being no discomfort at all.

While SUD ratings are *subjective* verbal estimates, they correlate strongly with *heart rate variability*, an objective measurement that reflects activity in the autonomic nervous system. When the SUD level goes down, heart rate variability shifts in a desirable direction (Callahan, 2001). The purpose of translating the feeling into a number is that the rating provides a simple gauge for tracking progress through the treatment. If the client is unable to translate the feeling into a number, less precise language—such as "slight," "moderate," and "extreme" distress or improvement—might be used.

SUD ratings can also be confirmed using energy checks. Like the SUD rating, energy checks for this purpose are also named by their acronym. The energy check to corroborate a SUD rating is called a MUD (muscular units of distress) rating. The client states the SUD level (e.g., "It's a 5") while an indicator muscle is checked. If the muscle loses firmness, other ratings are checked (e.g., "It's more than a 5," "It's less than a 5," "It's a 3"). Often the SUD and the MUD will match.

Sometimes they do not match. The difference between a *subjective rating* and an *energy check* can be puzzling yet ultimately informative. The client is obviously the authority on how he or she feels, but the energy check can provide information about the problem that the client cannot access consciously. When the SUD and MUD do not match, this difference simply provides new information. Often it results in the client delving more deeply into his or her experience in order to explore the discrepancy. Also keep in mind that energy checks should always be interpreted within the context of other indicators; they are not to be relied upon as the sole source of information about a given question.

"Locking In" the Problem State

The problem state needs not only to be accessed; it must also remain active during the energy interventions designed to treat it. It is not necessary, however, to continually hold the problem in mind. You have already learned one technique for keeping the energy of the problem state active, the use of a *reminder phrase* (p. 32).

Although continually thinking about the problem, or repeating the reminder phrase, are effective ways to keep the problem state active, they require the client's ongoing attention. It is also possible to temporarily "lock" the problem state into the client's energy field for the purposes of the treatment. The problem state will remain energetically active, even as the client's attention is focused on other matters.

The Third Eye Up and the Leg Lock are two techniques for keeping the thought field that is associated with a problem energetically locked in (called *resonance locking*) for the purposes of the treatment. Based on anomalies that were discovered and are used within the field of applied kinesiology, these are tremendously valuable tools for energy psychology practitioners.

The Third Eye Up Technique ▣: Prior to the Third Eye Up, the client attunes to the psychological issue. A weak indicator muscle on an energy check verifies that the client has attuned to the problem state, and a SUD rating is usually requested. The client then places the middle finger of either hand onto the bridge of the nose and pushes the skin up until the finger comes off the forehead, about halfway up to the hairline. A thought field will usually remain active through the treatment sequence and can quickly be re-established by repeating the procedure.

The Leg Lock ▣ : Prior to the leg lock, the client sits or stands comfortably and attunes to the psychological issue. Again, a weak indicator muscle on an energy check verifies that the client has attuned to the problem state, and a SUD rating is usually requested. At this point, the legs are turned outward, about 45 degrees (in a Charlie Chaplin stance, or the first position in ballet). The thought field will usually remain active as long as this position is maintained.

With either method, the thought field will stay engaged for a period that will vary depending on several factors. Continued resonance with the problem state can be verified from time to time with an energy check, and the problem state can be re-accessed and locked in again as needed.

A Summary of the Opening Phases of Treatment

Within the first minute of the first session, rapport is being established. The client's expectations about the treatment and the client's goals for seeking treatment are typically addressed early in the treatment. As with most forms of psychotherapy, a psychosocial history is usually taken early in the treatment. In addition to gathering information, the interview helps establish a therapeutic climate.

Because a focus on the subtle energy dimension of psychological problems differs from traditional treatment models and the basic concepts are unfamiliar to many people, substantial explanation of the model might also be necessary early in the treatment. A way to introduce some of the features of an energy-based approach to treating psychological problems is to qualify an indicator muscle for the energy checking procedure and to use it to demonstrate the relationship of mental states and the body's energies (e.g., a firm indicator muscle instantly loses strength when a stressful memory is brought to mind). Once an energy checking procedure has been established, neurological disorganization and global psychological reversals are often assessed and corrected if present.

If the problem has not yet been formulated in a manner appropriate for an energy-based approach, this would be the next step, and then specific-context psychological reversals that might affect the problem would be checked for and corrected. With the problem state accessed, a measure is taken of the degree of distress caused by the problem (using SUD and MUD ratings). Another step before introducing energy-based interventions that focus directly on the target problem is to "lock in" the problem state. Finally, specific energy-based interventions focusing on the problem can be applied effectively.

105

Flow Chart of Tasks in the Opening Phases of Treatment

It is worth repeating that the emphasis on steps and procedures is to help you internalize a basic structure that allows you to operate more freely within a treatment setting rather than that you be confined to a set of rules and formulas. To further internalize the structure, however, we suggest that you memorize the following sequence of tasks from the opening phases of treatment:

Begin building rapport.

↓

Gather information about client's background and treatment goals.

↓

Explain an energy-based approach and obtain informed consent.

↓

Establish a familiarity and some success with energy checking.

↓

Check for and correct neurological disorganization.

↓

Check for and resolve global psychological reversals.

↓

Formulate an appropriate target problem.

↓

Check for and resolve specific-context psychological reversals involved with the problem.

↓

Access the problem state, rate it, and "lock it" in.

↓

Specific energy interventions can now be focused directly on the target problem.

106

Applying specific energy interventions that are focused directly on the target problem is the topic of the following three chapters.

Practice Session: Opening Phases of Treatment

With a colleague role-playing a client coming in with a specific problem or using an actual problem, go through each of the phases of the early part of treatment. The target problem could be a fear, phobia, anxiety, anger, lack of confidence, grief, worry, jealousy, guilt, shame, obsession, or any other undesired emotional response to a specific situation, thought, image, or memory. Use the flow chart to remind you of the sequence of treatment tasks to address. Then solicit feedback. Reverse roles.

Please take care that the problems you target are appropriate given the context of your practice sessions. Discuss possible areas of conflict or negative consequences in advance. If the program is being used in the context of a university or other formal training program, please be certain that its use is in compliance with Standard 7.04 of the American Psychological Association's 2002 *Ethics Code*, "Student Disclosure of Personal Information." The critical word is "require"; no one should be coerced, even subtly, into working with personal issues for training purposes.

—6—

Meridian Treatment Basics

OUR FOCUS CHANGES NOW from the *opening phases* of treatment (including neurological disorganization, psychological reversals, and the various ways of creating a context for energy-based treatments as covered in the previous chapter) to the *energy intervention phase*. The purpose of the energy intervention phase can be described in various ways, but operationally it is to bring the subjective units of distress (SUD) of a well-formulated target problem and each of its aspects down, ideally, to 0. This chapter presents basic theory for understanding how interventions in the meridian energies can resolve psychological problems. The subsequent two chapters present a systematic set of procedures.

The Meridians as the Initial Focus of Treatment

The anatomy of the body's energy system is believed to encompass 1) *centers*, where energies concentrate, 2) *pathways*, along which energy travels, 3) energies that *surround and protect* the body, 4) energies that *connect and harmonize* other energy systems, and 5) energies that control biological and psychological *cycles*. Numerous cultures and healing approaches emphasize one or more of these energy systems. For instance, in the yogic tradition the energy centers are known as *chakras*; in acupuncture the pathways along which energy travels are called *meridians*; and the energies surrounding the body are often referred to as the *aura*. Eight major energy systems have been identified (each is described in Part 2 of Donna Eden's *Energy Medicine*), and energy interventions can concentrate upon any of them. They include the meridians, the chakras, the radiant circuits, the aura (or biofield), the triple warmer, the five elements, the Celtic weave, and the basic grid.

The initial focus of this program is on the meridians. Some energy-oriented therapists routinely begin with one of the other systems or assess the client's energies to determine which system is most strongly indicated for the initial intervention. Most psychological problems, however, can be addressed by attending to the meridian system alone, partially because bringing the body's energy pathways into balance simultaneously impacts all of the other energy systems. Additional psychological benefits of working with specific systems, particularly the chakras and the radiant circuits, are covered in later modules of the CD.

110

The Nature of the Meridians

In the way an artery carries blood, a meridian carries energy. The flow of the meridian system is no less critical than the flow of blood. *No meridian energy, no life!*

The meridians affect every organ and every physiological system, including the immune, nervous, endocrine, circulatory, respiratory, digestive, skeletal, muscular, and lymphatic systems. As the body's "energy bloodstream," the meridians bring vitality and balance, remove blockages, and adjust metabolism. They also influence the speed and form of cellular change.

Each bodily and energetic system is fed by at least one meridian. If a meridian's energy is obstructed or unregulated, the system it feeds is compromised.

The primary function of the meridian system is to carry vital energy—called *chi* or *ki* in the traditional Oriental healing arts—to every organ and every other physiological and energetic structure. The meridian system is a complex energy pathway that runs deep into the body and also surfaces to run along the skin in 12 places, appearing as 12 segments. Each segment is called a meridian, and each of the meridians is named for the primary organ or system it services.

There are actually 14 major meridians carrying energy into, through, and out of the body: the 12 *segments* of the primary meridian pathway just mentioned, and two additional energy pathways, the *central* and *governing* meridians. Eleven of the 12 meridian segments are named after an organ they energetically feed. These include:

Bladder	Large Intestine	Small Intestine
Gall Bladder	Liver	Spleen/Pancreas
Heart	Lungs	Stomach
Kidney	Pericardium	

The twelfth meridian segment, *triple warmer*, is not named after an organ, but rather after the *energy system* that stimulates 1) the fight-or-flight response, 2) the immune response, and 3) the formation of the body's habitual responses to stress and threat. Triple warmer functions both as a meridian and as a radiant circuit. Its complex role in the body's defenses requires that it also be thought of as a unique and independent energy system (see Chapter 8 of *Energy Medicine* for a detailed discussion).

The remaining two meridians, central and governing (also called *extra meridians* or *collector vessels*), are special meridians. Rather than serving as links in the chain of the 12 major meridian segments, central goes up the center of the front of the body and governing goes up the spine, through the brain, and connects with the central meridian at the back of the throat.

Like the other meridians, central and governing are energy pathways. But, like triple warmer, they also exhibit the properties of the radiant circuits (the topic of one of the CD modules). So central, governing, and triple warmer are meridians, and they are also radiant circuits. A fourth energy pathway, spleen meridian, also functions as a radiant circuit as well as a meridian.

Empirical Investigations into the Meridians

The meridians emit electromagnetic radiation that can be recorded by infrared photography, and they have been detected by other instrumentation as well. The pathways revealed by infrared photography corroborate the accuracy of the maps found in the ancient texts (Wang, Hu, & Wu,

1993). MRI measurements reveal that an acupuncture treatment in a toe, for instance, affects blood activity in the brain, though no nerve, vascular, or other physical connections are known to exist (Cho, 1998). The flow of meridian energies can also be detected by a sensitive individual's hands (Eden, 1999) and verified by measures of electrical patterns in the skin (Motoyama, 1998).

While the ancient Chinese maps of the meridian system were at first discounted in the West because they had no known anatomical correlates, a number of studies dating back to the 1960s identified correspondences between physical structures and the energy pathways described in the early texts. In an experiment conducted in Korea, for instance, a liquid containing radioactive phosphorus isotopes, injected into the acupuncture points of rabbits and other animals, demonstrated the existence of a fine duct-like tubule system of approximately .5–1.5 microns in diameter (a human hair is approximately 1.5 microns). The liquid flowed along the tubules, paralleling the ancient descriptions of the meridian pathways (the correct translation of the word for these pathways is actually "vessel" or "channel," not "line," as the word "meridian" implies). Concentrations of the isotope in tissue that was adjacent to the meridian or near the acupoint that was injected were negligible. The tubular system included a superficial system and a deep system with a complex of subsystems. All were connected and ultimately traveled to the nuclei in all of the body's cells (Rose-Neil, 1967).

French researchers in the 1980s used a similar strategy with human subjects, injecting several acupoints with radioactive technetium, and obtained similar results (de Vernejoul, 1985). Fluid extracted from the meridian tubules is high in concentrations of DNA, RNA, and various hormones, and it contains an electrolytic fluid that some believe conducts various forms of subtle energy (Gerber, 2001, pp. 122–127).

Joaquín Andrade, M.D. (an *Energy Psychology Interactive* Advisory Board member who spent many years as a young man learning acupuncture in China and who frequently returns for further study and investigation) estimates that 60 to 65 percent of the acupuncture mechanisms described in the ancient system have been validated through vigorous scientific research. For instance, decreased electrical resistance on the skin corresponds with many of the acupoint locations described 5,000 years ago. But some concepts, such as the flow of meridian energy, continue to elude decisive empirical demonstration. The studies in France and Korea

112

mentioned above, for instance, have not been precisely replicated and there is debate about some of their methods and conclusions. Dr. Andrade explains that scientists in China respectfully consider the ancient concepts as provisional assumptions based on the cultural context of the historical periods in which they originated. But they also attempt to verify these concepts with modern research techniques.

Investigating the time-honored system scientifically sometimes leads to clinical innovations and sometimes corroborates earlier methods. For instance, electrical acupuncture machines, a logical modern extension of the ancient concepts, have been tested as a way of diagnosing meridian energies based on the skin resistance at selected acupoints. But they are not favored in China because so many variables affect electrical conductivity, such as the temperature and humidity of the room, the thickness of the skin, basal metabolic conditions, the presence of hair over the point, etc. According to Dr. Andrade, "They prefer the poor man's Dermatron [an electrical acupuncture machine, whose newer versions are priced from $3,000 to $50,000], the sensitive finger pads of a trained clinician."

The Meridians and the Emotions

Each meridian regulates a particular set of emotions and behavioral themes. While these vary from person to person, some generalizations hold. For instance:

1. The functions of the *heart meridian* tend to correspond with poetic associations to the heart: loving feelings flourish when it is in a healthy balance; heartache and heartbreak correspond with a disturbance in the energies of the heart meridian.
2. The *stomach meridian*, when in balance, supports a sense of basic trust; but when its flow is impeded, the reactive emotion is obsessive worry. This is a plausible energetic link between worry and indigestion or stomach ulcers.
3. The *governing meridian* (which runs along the backbone) seems related to confidence ("standing tall") when its energy flow is unimpeded and a lack of courage ("no backbone") when it is out of balance.

The emotions associated with each meridian when it is in balance and when it is not in balance (the "reactive emotion") have been mapped (see page 234). Through simple physical interventions that balance the energies of a meridian involved in an emotional problem, the reactive emotion can be deactivated.

The Meridian Energies in Fight-or-Flight

The manner by which a triggering event or image can disrupt the meridian energies has a biological analog in the body's instinctual forms of self-protection: the immune response and the fight-or-flight response. In the way a pathogen (a disease-producing microorganism or substance, such as a virus, bacterium, or environmental pollutant) causes a progression of chemical events within the bloodstream (immune response) and a perceived physical threat mobilizes an emergency response in the auto-nomic nervous system (fight-or-flight), an experience that is psychologi-cally stressful or threatening results in a sequence of programmed responses within the meridian energies. This series of events in the energy system, in fact, *precedes* and *regulates* the physiological responses. The entire mechanism is governed by triple warmer.

Just as autoimmune illnesses are caused when the immune system is chronically activated though no actual pathogens are threatening the system, and stress-related illnesses are caused by the fight-or-flight response being chronically activated though no actual physical danger is present, many emotional problems are caused when triple warmer goes into a reactive mode that impacts the emotions though no actual inter-personal or other emotional threat is present. In all three instances, an overgeneralization is made; a "false positive" initiates a maladaptive and costly response.

One of the unique functions of triple warmer is its ability to conscript energy for the purposes of defense from any of the other meridians (except heart meridian, whose energies are protected at all costs). These conscripted energies are utilized in both the immune response to microor-ganisms and its behavioral analog, the fight-or-flight response to threat or stress. The emotional consequences of this process correspond with the emotions associated with the meridians that are depleted by these threat-related responses. If triple warmer conscripts energy from large intestine meridian, for instance, which governs issues involving holding on and releasing, emotional problems concerning the issue of control might emerge. The continuum from tolerance to judgmentalness is governed by gall bladder meridian; disturbances often lead to feelings of rage. Bladder meridian governs hope; when its energies are disrupted in service of the fight-or-flight response the result might be a sense of futility.

The fight-or-flight mechanism is activated when the autonomic nervous system's ability to operate optimally is overwhelmed (see Porges, 1997, and related papers available at www.trauma-pages.com/articles.htm). At that point, triple warmer mobilizes the body's energies for the fight-or-flight response. When understood at the level of the body's energy systems, the fight-or-flight response is an even more intricate and pervasive mechanism than when understood only in terms of biochemistry. It is, in fact, believed to be the underlying mechanism involved in many psychological problems:

1. Whenever *psychological stress* or *perceived threat* reaches a critical threshold, an analog of the fight-or-flight response occurs within the energy system (this, again, *precedes and regulates* the biochemical reaction).
2. This response can be activated by:
   - *direct experiences* of stress or perceived threat
   - *experiences associated* with *previous* stress or threat
   - *internal events* (thoughts, images, memories) that *evoke* stress or a sense of threat
3. The *psychological impact* generally includes: quickened impulses and reactivity, increased acuity, and diminished perception of pain, *but also* a significant *decrease in perspective* and other cerebral functioning and a tendency to rely on *habitual* stress-induced behavioral patterns rather than to form a creative response to the situation. In addition:
   - *Anger* or *rage* tends to accompany and support the fight response.
   - *Fear* or *panic* tends to accompany and support the flight response.
   - *Hysteria, overwhelm,* or *numbness* tend to result when the fight-or-flight response is activated but then inhibited or otherwise not acted upon.
4. The *specific* psychological impact also depends on *which meridians* have been activated in the service of the fight-or-flight response (recall that the triple warmer system may, using its own unique calculus, conscript the energy from any of the meridians for the fight-or-flight response, *and* each meridian governs specific emotional and behavioral themes).

Examples of this sequence are commonplace. John's wife raises her voice slightly while asking John once more not to leave his clothes on the floor. This evokes a habitual pattern within John's energy system that traces back to his mother's criticism when he was a boy. Triple warmer treats the increased volume and trace of irritation in the voice of an intimate female as a threat to John's well-being. It conscripts energy from the liver and gall bladder meridians, as it has been doing for decades in similar circumstances, and uses these energies to activate the stress response into a "fight" reaction.

John's anger is instant and intense (in addition to anger being characteristic of the fight response, rage is the reactive emotion when the gall bladder meridian is disturbed). He simultaneously is angry with himself, first for again having left his clothing on the floor and then for his angry response to his wife (anger toward the self is the reactive emotion when the liver meridian is out of balance). Neither response is tempered by his usual good humor or good judgment, as is often the case when stress reactions trigger behavior. His wife, having witnessed this sequence too many times, stomps out of the room with derogatory observations about how he refuses to grow up and, with her own fight-and-flight mechanisms now activated, she withdraws and will not speak with him.

116

Interventions into the Meridian System

An energy-based treatment approach to intervening in this long-standing pattern might (after correcting for neurological disorganization and psychological reversals) involve having John bring to mind his wife's raised voice, assessing the meridians that become disturbed (the liver, gall bladder, and triple warmer meridians; possibly others) and balancing them until the image can be held with no disturbance in the meridian system. The mechanics of balancing meridians involved in a psychological problem are straightforward.

Along each of the 14 meridians are points that, when stimulated, affect the flow of energy within that meridian. Called *acupuncture, acupressure,* or simply *acupoints,* these spots have significantly lower electrical resistance (Voll & Sarkisyanz, 1983) than other areas of the skin (12,000 to 14,000 Ohms compared with 300,000 to 400,000 Ohms). At least 360 such points are distributed throughout the surface of the body along the meridian lines.

Perhaps because of this lower resistance, acupoints have been called windows into the body's energy system (Pulos, 2002). Stimulating an acupoint will affect the energy flow of the meridian on which it is located. Some acupoints are dedicated to bringing energy into the body, some to releasing energy from the body, some to increasing the movement of energy through the body, some to slowing it, and some serve several of these functions. Acupoints can be stimulated not only with needles, but also by non-invasive means (e.g., tapping, massaging, twisting, or holding, even through the use of imagination or focused intention) to switch the energies that flow along the meridian pathway "on" or "off."

The Mechanics of Acupoint Stimulation

The acupoints appear to serve as resistors and amplifiers that regulate the flow of energy through the meridians. Situated along each meridian are between 9 acupoints (heart and pericardium meridians) and 67 acupoints (bladder meridian). Because any current will grow weaker with distance, due to resistance along the transmission cable, theorists wondered what boosted the meridian energies to allow them to maintain a balanced circulation.

The orthopedic surgeon and Nobel Prize nominee Robert O. Becker likened some acupoints to the amplifiers found along a telephone cable, boosting the signal so that it can continue to the next amplifier. His research yielded preliminary evidence that "the acupuncture points were just such booster amplifiers, spaced along the course of the meridian trans-mission lines" (Becker, 1990, p. 47).

117

Stimulating an acupoint whose function is to increase the movement of energy in a blocked meridian will tend to restore the meridian's optimal flow. Stimulating an acupoint whose function is to slow the movement of energy in a meridian that is overcharged will similarly restore an optimal flow. Some acupoints will increase *or* inhibit the movement of energy as needed for balance in the meridian system, and these are the points that are generally used within energy psychology.

Using Acupoints to Alter a "Thought Field"

Many approaches have been developed within energy psychology for iden-tifying the acupoints that when stimulated will have the greatest impact for alleviating a particular emotional or psychological difficulty. In Roger

Callahan's pioneering Thought Field Therapy (www.tftrx.com), 14 acupoints are emphasized, one for each of the 14 major meridians. Treatment involves identifying the meridians enmeshed in the problem and tapping the associated acupoints while the problematic "thought field" is accessed mentally. Subsets of the 14 points have also been delineated as "algorithms," or protocols for working with specific emotional conditions or thought field disturbances.

Systematic investigation of how clairvoyants "see" thought forms dates back to a fascinating series of studies in the early 1900s (Bessant & Leadbeater, 1905/1969). Scientific evidence has been accumulating that thought fields, though invisible, impact the physical world, including the firing of neurons. In this sense they are as "real" and verifiable as are magnetic and gravitational fields. Growing numbers of established scientific publications have introduced concepts analogous to the thought field to explain observed phenomena. Based on findings from within their respective disciplines, informational *fields* (a field is a "region of influence") that are involved with consciousness and behavior have been postulated by neurologists, biologists, anesthesiologists, physiologists, psychologists, physicists, and engineers (Feinstein, 1998). In addition to the known chemical, neurological, linguistic, and subjective components of thought, the hypothesis that another component of thought consists of a *field of information* which directly impacts and is impacted by psychological functioning and physical health is rapidly gaining credibility.

You have already seen photographs comparing a microscope's enlargement of a frozen crystal derived from the same source of water before a prayer was offered and after a prayer was offered (p. 7). The following images contrast water that was in the presence of an appreciative thought and water that was in the presence of a hateful thought:

118

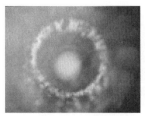

Crystal from distilled water after it has been frozen and magnified.

Crystal from distilled water after the words "Thank you" were typed on a piece of paper and pasted to the bottle.

Crystal from distilled water after the words "You make me sick. I will kill you" were typed on a piece of paper and pasted to the bottle.

This vivid illustration[1] of the presumed impact of thoughts on the physical world, combined with the fact that the human body is 70 percent water, lends credibility to efforts to examine the impact of *thought fields* on psychological processes.

If we operationally define a thought field as a field of information that influences emotions, perceptions, cognition, and behavior, then:

> A thought field that might be a *focus for treatment* is a physical field *that influences mental activity and behavior* that has become disturbed.

This disturbance in the thought field is believed to be the *energetic structure* that maintains many emotional and behavioral problems. Callahan emphasizes the way a disturbance in a thought field triggers a disturbed meridian response. While no physical measure has yet been devised to directly determine if there is a disturbance in a thought field, energy checking (Chapter 2) affords a way of identifying disturbances in the meridian energies that appear to be associated with disturbed thought fields. Many factors might disturb either a meridian or a thought field, and the cause-effect influence between them seems to run in both directions. Whether the disturbance that is at the energetic root of a psychological problem originates in the thought field or the meridian flow:

> Thought fields that cause psychological problems
>
> ↓   result in   ↑
>
> disturbances in the meridian energies

The interventions in the meridian-based psychotherapies alter the thought field by targeting the disturbed energy response in the meridian system. This is accomplished by:

1. Mentally accessing a disturbed thought field.
2. Identifying the meridians that reflexively become disturbed when this thought field is activated.

---

[1] From *Messages from Water* by Masaru Emoto, 1999, pp. 74, 91, and 94, respectively. Reprinted with permission. For further information, visit www.hado.net.

3. Eliminating the disturbed meridian response by stimulating selected acupoints while the thought field is engaged; this in turn eliminates the disturbance in the thought field.

The *trigger* (an event, image, memory, or idea) that activated the psychological problem becomes associated with a *balanced energetic state*, the thought field is correspondingly altered, and the psychological problem is no longer activated by the original trigger.

Selecting the Acupoints to Treat

The detail to which the energy dynamics underlying a psychological problem must be analyzed before effective energy treatments can be formulated is being debated within energy psychology. Clinical reports vary on this matter, and decisive research that establishes the "active ingredients" or the "necessary and sufficient conditions" for mediating the disturbed energy response within a thought field is not yet available.

In Chapter 1 you were introduced to Gary Craig's Emotional Freedom Techniques (EFT), one of the most popular self-help variations on Callahan's Thought Field Therapy (TFT). Rather than attempting to assess which meridians are disturbed by the problematic thought or situation, EFT uses a subset, usually at least 7 of the 14 TFT points, and taps each in every instance in order to activate the energies in the entire meridian system.

Other practitioners believe that even if the successes reported using uniform protocols such as EFT are verified by controlled investigations, an assessment-based approach is required to insure reliable outcomes when working with a wide range of problems and clients.

For instance, the choice of which points to treat may have distinct clinical consequences. In a double-blind study conducted by Joyce Carbonell, Ph.D., at Florida State University with 49 individuals who had a fear of heights, a protocol based on TFT was given to one randomly selected group and a "placebo" tapping treatment to the other. The placebo protocol involved tapping various parts of the body that are not used in TFT. The TFT group showed significantly greater improvement on a post-test than the placebo group. A summary of this study can be found at www.tftrx.com/ref_articles/6heights.html.

A reasonable clinical strategy is to begin with a relatively simple protocol, using the most effective points known, and to introduce more elaborate procedures when the simpler ones do not produce the desired results. Among the postulated advantages of the more elaborate protocols are that they allow for greater diagnostic[2] precision and they allow for treatments that are more precisely tailored to the client's unique energies and problems. In the remainder of this book and CD program you will learn:

- how to identify the specific meridians affected within a problematic thought field
- additional treatment points for each meridian (and how and when you might need to use them)
- additional energy systems beyond the meridians (and how and when you might use them)
- protocols for specific problems

The abbreviated EFT protocol you learned in Chapter 1 used eight acupoints and applied them to all problems. In the remainder of this chapter you will learn a somewhat more complex 14-point protocol in which one point is treated for each of the 14 meridians. In the following chapter, Formulating Energy Interventions, you will learn how to apply this meridian balancing sequence within a treatment session. In Chapter 8, Advanced Meridian Treatments, you will learn how to assess which specific meridians are involved in a psychological problem, as well as additional treatment points for each of the 14 meridians. When a meridian associated with the problem state has been identified but the first intervention does not balance that meridian, the advanced techniques provide additional strategies for achieving that balance.

Most of the points you learned in the abbreviated EFT protocol will also be used in the longer protocol presented here. You can, alternatively, continue to use only the set of points you learned earlier. They are simple, widely known, now familiar to you, and good results are often reported. A more complex protocol, however, is introduced in this chapter for a number of reasons. Among them is that you will later find it is valuable to have memorized at least one treatment point for each of the 14 meridians.

Since for this protocol you will be learning only one point per meridian (of the 9 to 67 acupoints on each meridian), great care has been taken to

---

[2] In energy psychology, diagnosis is used for assessing energetic patterns within a problem state as well as for *DSM-IV* diagnoses. Treatment has a similar dual usage, specific energy interventions and the overall therapy.

identify the points that are most likely to be effective in the greatest number of situations. If however, you already know a different set of points, such as the complete set of TFT or EFT points, they will do for the purposes of this and the next chapter.

The issue in selecting treatment points is not about some of a meridian's points being "right" and others being "wrong." Rather, since none of the points will be effective in all cases, it is a judgment call, a best guess, about which points are likely to be effective with the greatest frequency when a simplified treatment protocol is used. In the more sophisticated approach that is presented in Chapter 9, these considerations are not at issue since single pre-selected points for each meridian are not relied upon. Instead, assessments about which of several possible treatment points are continually being made.

By assessing the meridians that are involved in the target problem, the treatment can be tailored to focus on those meridians. Another reason for meridian and acupoint assessment is that, of the 9 to 67 acupoints that fall along each meridian, some will correct disturbances in the meridian's energies more reliably than others.

The clinician who knows several points on each meridian, and who is able to assess whether stimulating the standard treatment point was effective, will have ready access to viable options when the "best-guess" point was not the best guess. In these cases, another treatment point can be used.

How to Tap an Acupoint

The method for stimulating acupoints that is used most frequently in energy psychology is to tap the points. Tapping should be done at a comfortable rhythm, perhaps two to four taps per second, and hard enough that there would be a sound if you were tapping on a desk but not hard enough to risk bruising even a very sensitive person. An instruction sheet on how to tap acupoints can be found in Appendix I, page 227. One alternative to tapping is called the Touch and Breathe method (see page 229).

Regarding how long to continue tapping, you will usually get the desired effect by tapping anywhere between 5 to 10 times. However, you will increase your percentage of attaining the desired effect if you tap 10 times, pause, take a deep breath, and tap 5 to 10 more times. The energies in the meridian system move according to a rapid pulse as well as a slower pulse that penetrates more deeply. The pause, followed by the second set of taps, is more likely to activate this second, deeper energy flow. One way to pace your tapping is to tap during a deep inhalation and exhalation, pause during a deep inhalation and exhalation, and again tap the same point on a third inhalation and exhalation. Still, tapping just a few times and with no pause is often enough to significantly improve the meridian flow.

The One-Point-per-Meridian Protocol

Of the 14 acupoints used in the one-point-per-meridian protocol, the points for each of the 12 major meridian segments are tapped, while those for the central and governing meridians are held. The 12 tapping points can be stimulated in any order (face to torso to arm to hand might be the easiest to remember), followed by a "hook-up" of central and governing. Most of the tapping points are *bilateral*. Though only one side is usually shown on the chart, either side can be tapped, and there are some benefits to tapping both sides simultaneously or in sequence.

FIGURE 6.1
ONE-POINT-PER-MERIDIAN TREATMENT CHART

123

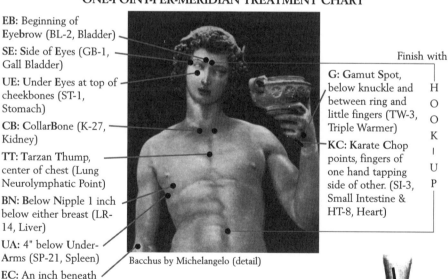

EB: Beginning of Eyebrow (BL-2, Bladder)

SE: Side of Eyes (GB-1, Gall Bladder)

UE: Under Eyes at top of cheekbones (ST-1, Stomach)

CB: CollarBone (K-27, Kidney)

TT: Tarzan Thump, center of chest (Lung Neurolymphatic Point)

BN: Below Nipple 1 inch below either breast (LR-14, Liver)

UA: 4" below Under-Arms (SP-21, Spleen)

EC: An inch beneath inside Elbow Crease in line with pointer finger (LI-10, Large Intestine)

Bacchus by Michelangelo (detail)

Finish with

G: Gamut Spot, below knuckle and between ring and little fingers (TW-3, Triple Warmer)

KC: Karate Chop points, fingers of one hand tapping side of other. (SI-3, Small Intestine & HT-8, Heart)

H O O K I U P

MW: Middle of Wrist, tap with three fingers (PC-5, 6, & 7, Pericardium)

Jeno Barcsay, 1958

The acupoints, and the associated meridians, are listed in parentheses.

Follow the 12 taps with a hook-up of central (CV-8) and governing (GV-24.5):

1. Middle finger of one hand in belly button.
2. Middle finger of other hand at third eye.
3. Press in and pull the skin gently upward.
4. Hold about 30 seconds or until there is a spontaneous deep breath.

These points are easy to learn and the entire treatment sequence requires only one to three minutes (depending upon how long each point is tapped). The points can be tapped in this order:

1. EB: Beginning of Eyebrow (BL-2, Bladder)
2. SE: Side of Eyes (GB-1, Gall Bladder)
3. UE: Under Eyes at top of cheekbones (ST-1, Stomach)
4. CB: CollarBone (K-27, Kidney)
5. TT: Tarzan Thump, center of chest (Lung Neurolymphatic Point)
6. BN: Below Nipple 1 inch below either breast (LR-14, Liver)
7. UA: 4" below UnderArms (SP-21, Spleen)
8. EC: An inch beneath inside Elbow Crease in line with pointer finger (LI-10, Large Intestine)
9. G: Gamut Spot, below knuckle and between ring and little fingers (TW-3, Triple Warmer)
10. MW: Middle of Wrist, tap with three fingers (PC-5, 6, & 7, Pericardium)
11. & 12. KC: Karate Chop points, fingers of one hand tapping side of other (SI-3, Small Intestine & HT-8, Heart)
13. & 14. Use the hook-up for the last two meridians, central and governing (middle finger of one hand in belly button, middle finger of other hand at third eye, press in, and pull the skin gently upward—about 30 seconds or until there is a spontaneous deep breath).

Practice Session: Balancing the Meridians

Balance your own meridians by tapping the 12 points on the One-Point-per-Meridian Chart (for each point, tap during an inhalation and exhalation, pause during an inhalation and exhalation, tap again) and then hooking up the central and governing meridians. Instruct a partner in balancing his or her meridians.

124

Must all 14 Meridians Be Balanced with Every Treatment?

One approach to working with psychological problems is to access the problem state and then treat all 14 meridians using the points to which you were just introduced, or a standard subset, as in chapter 1. Another approach is to access the problem state, determine which of the 14 meridians have become disturbed, and treat *only* those meridians.

We will use the first approach in the following chapter. While it may be redundant to keep treating meridians that are already balanced, it is simpler to tap without assessing the meridian system, it does no harm, and this procedure alone seems effective a reasonable portion of the time. It also allows you to move forward before learning the more complex meridian assessment techniques.

—7—

Formulating Energy Interventions

THIS CHAPTER BUILDS UPON CHAPTER 1, The *Basic* Basics, expanding from the initial self-help focus into a full clinical treatment approach that incorporates what you have learned in each of the subsequent chapters. The chapter is oriented around a series of practice sessions. For this reason, it would be particularly valuable to work through this chapter with a partner. If you cannot do it with a partner, you can still get a good overview of the procedures by reading through the instructions, choosing a problem area to experiment with, and applying the treatment procedures to yourself. Still, nothing can adequately substitute for hands-on, interactive experiences in a real or at least simulated clinical situation.

The instructions for the practice session in Chapter 5 are repeated in the first practice session below. If you have already completed this with a partner, *and* your partner is still available to continue working with you, *and* the work you did is still fresh, skip this practice session and jump to the following section, the Basic Single-Point-per-Meridian Treatment Protocol. You and your partner will, within this chapter, each do an entire session as therapist and an entire session as client.

Practice Session 1: The Opening Phases of Treatment

With a colleague role-playing a client coming in with a specific problem or using an actual problem, go through each of the phases of the early part of treatment. The target problem could be a fear, phobia, anxiety, anger, lack of confidence, grief, worry, jealousy, guilt, shame, obsessiveness, or any other undesired emotional response to a specific situation, thought, image, or memory. As emphasized on p. 107, please take care that the problems you target are appropriate given the context of your practice sessions. The treatment tasks to cover in this practice session are to:

- build rapport
- gather information about the client's background and treatment goals
- explain and obtain informed consent about using an energy-based approach
- establish a familiarity and some success with energy checking
- check for and correct neurological disorganization
- check for and resolve any global psychological reversals
- formulate an appropriate target problem
- check for and resolve any specific-context PRs that are involved with the problem
- access the problem state, rate it, and "lock it" in (alternately, use a "reminder phrase" as described on p. 28).

128

After this sequence, solicit feedback. Switch roles.

The Basic Single-Point-per-Meridian Treatment Protocol

With the problem state selected, rated, and locked in and initial neurological disorganization and psychological reversals resolved, the remaining steps in a basic single-point-per-meridian treatment protocol are:

1. The Basic Treatment Sandwich:
    a. Treatment point sequence (Practice Session 2)
    b. Bridging technique (Practice Session 3)
    c. Treatment point sequence again (Practice Session 4)
2. Subsequent Rounds of the Sandwich (Practice Session 5)
3. Anchoring the Gains (Chapter 9)

Practice Session 2: Treatment Point Sequence

The First Part of the Sandwich

You have some choices here. Beginning with the simplest:

1. Tap each of the 8 treatment points from Chapter 1 ⛚ (see p. 27) between five and nine times. *Or*
2. Use a treatment point sequence you have learned elsewhere (TFT, TEST, BSFF, a different subset of EFT points). *Or*
3. Stimulate each of the 14 points from Chapter 6 ⛚ (p. 123) by tapping the first 12 points between five and nine times each and then hooking up central and governing. *Or*
4. Same as numbers 1, 2, or 3, but tap each of the points for the length of an inhalation and exhalation, stop for the length of an inhalation and exhalation, and tap again.

Research is not available about which sequence is likely to be most effective. It might seem that using all 14 points would be more potent for balancing the associated meridians and that the longer tapping sequence would be more effective in more situations. This might, however, be more intervention than is necessary, and a tremendous amount of anecdotal evidence suggests that simpler sequences are effective a good deal of the time. The 14-point protocol was, in fact, introduced primarily so you would know at least one point for each meridian by the time you are learning the more advanced approaches in the following chapter, not because it is necessarily used that frequently in clinical practice. Stimulating a subset of the meridians will usually suffice.

In one sense, it does not matter which set of points you use: If the sequence is not effective in bringing down the client's distress level (SUD) while the problem state is activated, you would then move to the procedures taught in Chapter 8. It is truly dealer's choice.

Select a treatment sequence that you will use for the remainder of this chapter and, with the problem state locked in, show your "client" how to stimulate the points. As soon as the SUD decreases, even slightly, it is often reassuring for clients to realize that they are responsive to this method. Even if the SUD moves down slowly, the fact that it is moving at all means the indications are good for obtaining the desired results by applying the technique persistently while remaining alert for any neurological disorganization, psychological reversals, or unresolved aspects of the problem. A small proportion of people, however, apparently do not respond to meridian tapping, and in these cases, other techniques may be employed, such as the Touch and Breathe method of meridian stimulation (see page 229) or working with other energy systems, such as the chakras or the radiant circuits (CD modules are devoted to each).

It is better now to go through the remainder of the treatment sequence with one of you in the therapist role and the other in the client role. Switch roles at the end of the treatment session.

Practice Session 3: Bridging Techniques

The Middle of the Sandwich

The Nine Gamut Procedure, which you learned in Chapter 1, has become a standard within energy psychology. Other techniques, loosely called *bridging techniques* because they are performed between procedures that specifically focus on the designated problem, can also be used as the *middle* of the "treatment sandwich." These techniques enhance the effects of the interventions they bridge. Four bridging techniques are described below. You can use any one of them between rounds of tapping. Most practitioners find a favorite and use it most of the time, introducing others as intuition dictates. On subsequent rounds through the practice treatment, experiment with any of these—they are easy to do and require only a minute or two each. The techniques include the Nine Gamut Procedure, the Blow-Out/Zip-Up/Hook-In, the Elaborated Cross Crawl, and Separating Heaven and Earth. Experiment with each of them.

The Nine Gamut Procedure 📺 . While steadily tapping the gamut spot (the point on the back of the hand that is just below the knuckles and between the ring finger and the little finger), have the client do each of the following:

1. Close eyes.
2. Open eyes.
3. Move eyes to lower left.
4. Move eyes to lower right.
5. Rotate eyes clockwise 360 degrees.

6. Rotate eyes counter-clockwise 360 degrees.
7. Hum a tune for a few seconds ("Happy Birthday," "Row, Row Your Boat," "Zipadee Doo Dah").
8. Count to five.
9. Hum again.

Variations on the Nine Gamut Procedure:

1. Instead of the fifth and sixth steps, move the eyes in a horizontal figure-eight (the therapist might draw an infinity sign in the air), first in one direction, then the other.
2. End by bringing the eyes down to the floor and then slowly bringing them up to the ceiling, projecting sight out into the distance as the eyes move up the arc.

Blow-Out/Zip-Up/Hook-In 📇.

1. **Blow Out:** Make fists and put arms in front of you with your fists facing up. Take a deep inhalation and swing your arms above your head. With the fists facing toward you, bring your arms down swiftly to the sides, opening your hands, exhaling and releasing the energy charge. Repeat several times.
2. **Zip Up:** Place hands at groin and drag them, slowly and deliberately, straight up the front of the body on an inhalation, leaving the body at the lower lip and continuing up and over the head. Repeat three times.
3. **Hook In:** Place middle finger of one hand at third eye and of the other hand at navel. Gently press in and pull up. Hold for 15 to 20 seconds.

Elaborated Cross Crawl 📇. A good preliminary before the Elaborated Cross Crawl is to briskly tap the shoulders and neck while breathing deeply. Alternate the tapping between the left and right sides. Then:

1. March in place, touching the right hand to the left knee and the left hand to the right knee.
2. Continuing the Cross Crawl, hum-count-hum, for about five seconds each.
3. When completed, circle the eyes in each direction or make figure-eight patterns with the eyes.

131

Connecting Heaven and Earth 🔖. You learned this technique as part of the Three-Part/Three-Minute generic correction for neurological disorganization (p. 61). It is also an excellent bridging technique. To review:

1. Rub hands together and shake them out.
2. Stand with hands on your thighs and fingers spread apart.
3. With a deep inhalation, circle your arms out.
4. On the exhalation, bring your hands together in a prayer position.
5. Again with a deep inhalation, separate your arms from one another, stretching one high above your head and flattening your hand back, as if pushing something up above you.
6. Stretch the other arm down, again flattening your hand as if pushing something toward the earth. Stay in this position for as long as is comfortable.
7. Release your breath through your mouth, returning your hands to the prayerful position.
8. Repeat, switching the arm that raises and the arm that lowers. Do one or more additional lifts on each side.
9. Coming out of this pose the final time, bring your arms down and allow your body to fold over at the waist. Hang there with your knees slightly bent and take two deep breaths. Slowly return to a standing position with a backward roll of the shoulders.

132

Practice Session 4: The Treatment Point Sequence (again)

The Last Part of the Sandwich

Repeat the treatment point sequence exactly as you did in the first part of the sandwich. When you have completed the sandwich (treatment point sequence, bridging technique, treatment point sequence), again assess the intensity of the problem. Clients may be able to focus more easily on the problem if they close their eyes. Have them tune into the problem, bring the original problem or memory to mind, and give it a rating from 0 to 10 on the amount of distress it causes them now, as they think about it.

If no trace of the previous emotional intensity remains, then you are done with the sandwich and ready to move on to *anchor* the gains. If, on the other hand, the SUD goes down, lets say, to a 4, perform subsequent rounds until 0 is reached or until you can reduce the number no further.

Practice Session 5: Subsequent Rounds of the Sandwich

Sometimes a problem will be resolved after a single round of treatment. More often, only partial relief is obtained and additional rounds are necessary. Between rounds, discuss anything about the treatment that concerns the client or does not seem to be going as planned. Three areas to consider checking for between rounds are:

1. Neurological disorganization
2. Psychological reversals
3. Another SUD rating

Before returning to the next round of treatment, also be sure the problem is still locked in (the indicator muscle still goes weak during an in-the-clear energy check), particularly following periods of dialogue or intense emotion. For this practice session, go through the following guidelines and apply them with your partner as appropriate.

Considerations about neurological disorganization *between* rounds of acupoint stimulation. Simply accessing the problem may introduce subtle disruptions within the client's neurological system. The bridging techniques done within each round tend to counteract this tendency, but they are not always enough. While it is not necessary to frequently test for neurological disorganization, stay alert for signs of confusion, jumbled words, or loss of mental acuity. If these appear, consider introducing the three-part/three-minute sequence (p. 59) for neurological disorganization (Crown Pull, Separating Heaven and Earth, Wayne Cook Posture). This will usually correct the problem for the purposes of treatment. If it does not, do the five tests for neurological disorganization described in Chapter 3 (all five require only one minute) and use the correction techniques shown there as appropriate.

Any of the procedures in the Five-Minute Energy Routine (access instructions from the CD's Embedded Topics Index) can also be introduced between rounds of treatment, as well as other exercises for keeping the energy system clear and flowing.

Considerations about psychological reversals *between* rounds of acupoint stimulation. Psychological reversals may emerge at any point during the treatment, and when they do, they can inhibit further progress. Psychological reversals that emerge *during* treatment are called *intervening psychological reversals.*

The check for an intervening psychological reversal might be worded something like, "I want to be *completely* over this problem [or describe problem]." "Completely" is the element that distinguishes an intervening psychological reversal. Like other PRs, intervening PRs might also be organized around specific criteria. The wording to check for a criteria-related intervening PR might be "I deserve to be *completely* over this problem" [or: "It is safe to . . ."; "It is safe for others if I . . ."; "It is possible for me to . . ."; etc.]. Review Chapter 4 for more details on working with psychological reversals.

Considerations about SUD ratings *between* rounds of acupoint stimulation. The SUD rating is a subjective verbal estimate, on a scale from 0 to 10. It can be corroborated with an energy check (e.g., client says "It's a 3," followed by checking an indicator muscle). The energy check to corroborate a SUD rating is called a MUD (muscular units of distress) rating.

Periodic assessments of the distress still experienced in association with the problem (SUD and MUD) may be taken regularly. They provide a gauge on the effects of the acupoint treatments. Each assessment also leads to a choice point. The five basic possibilities are that the SUD will have:

134

- decreased but is still above 2
- stopped decreasing and is still above 2
- as above, but no psychological reversals or neurological disorganization are present
- gone down to 2 or less
- reached 0

Since you are in the middle of a practice session, simply scan down to the "next step" instructions for the situation you are working with. You can return later to study the options for each of the five possible conditions.

1. **The next step** if the SUD has decreased but is still above 2:
   - Do another round of the acupoint stimulation sandwich.
2. **The next step** if the SUD has stopped decreasing and is still above 2:
   - Check for any intervening psychological reversals (e.g., "I want to be *completely* over this problem") and their variants based on specific criteria (e.g., "It is safe to be *completely* . . .", etc.).
   - Resolve any that are found and return to the next round of the sandwich.

- If there were no PRs, check for neurological disorganization, correct if detected, and return to the next round of the sandwich.

3. **The next step** if the SUD has stopped decreasing, or is still above 2 and no psychological reversals or neurological disorganization are present:

- Do another round of the sandwich, concentrating particularly on the bridging techniques, perhaps using more than one of them.
- Explore whether another *aspect* of the problem (see p. 33) requires attention before further progress can be made.
- If the SUD still will not go down, the techniques in the following chapter, Advanced Meridian Treatments, can be applied. You may jump there now, if necessary, to continue this session.

4. **The next step** if the SUD has gone down to 2 or less: Once this threshold has been reached, another bridging technique or the eye roll will often bring it all the way down.

The Eye Roll Technique 🖅 : While steadily tapping the gamut spot (the point between and just below the knuckles of the little finger and the ring finger on the back of either hand), slowly and steadily roll the eyes upward from the floor to the ceiling. During this "sweep," send the energy from the eyes outward. Hold the eyes in the raised position for a few seconds. Reevaluate the SUD level.

If the SUD is still above zero after doing one or more of these techniques, and you are quite certain that PRs, neurological disorganization, and other *aspects* of the problem are not interfering, do another round of the sandwich. Sometimes, however, the SUD will go down to 2 or 1 but will not reduce any further. This is not necessarily a bad outcome. Some clients cannot conceive of the SUD going down to 0, so a 1 or a 2 is essentially a 0 in their subjective world. In some circumstances, such as in taking a test, a small measure of anxiety increases a person's ability to function. So while 0 might be thought of as a kind of ideal, it is not always realistic or necessary. In addition, it is often still possible to get the "positive belief" rating (see Chapter 9) up to the desired 8 or above even with the SUD at 1 or 2.

5. **The next step** if the SUD has reached 0 or near 0, the additional steps presented in Chapter 9 will:

- anchor in the new response
- project the positive state into the future
- fix the gains into the person's life

After the SUD has reached 0, you will complete the treatment in the first practice session of Chapter 9. If you are already at a 0, you may wish to go directly to that chapter now and return later to the following chapter, Advanced Meridian Treatments.

If you are unable to significantly lower the level of distress, you may next want to consider either of two approaches (also, see the "self-help" handout "Taking Energy Psychology Another Step," on p. 245, discussing what to do when the interventions do not produce the desired result). Suppose the issue that is not responding to treatment involves feelings of intense shame that are readily evoked in a variety of situations. Two basic next options are:

1. **Micro-Focus on the Aspects of the Problem.** Gary Craig uses the metaphor of a table to describe the way he approaches a problem such as generalized anxiety or incessant feelings of shame. If the presenting problem is the top of the table, the legs are the aspects of the problem, particularly specific events in the client's life that produced similar feelings. By chipping away at the legs, the table top often falls away spontaneously or with minimal further intervention. So rather than beginning with the "table top" or global problem, such as "I feel shame," Craig works with the "legs," addressing the problem's history—specific event by specific event— until every memory involving shame is cleared (after addressing several specific events—Craig estimates the typical range as being between 5 and 20—there is a "generalization effect" so the remainder become emotionally resolved). Sometimes, to clear a memory, it is necessary to separate it into smaller aspects still ("the feeling of ice in my heart," "the look in her eye when she discovered me," "the sound of his voice," etc.) and treat them one at a time. Craig reports not only an extremely high success rate when focusing on these micro-aspects of a problem, but also that the gains are far more durable than when only using a global (table top) formulation of the problem. Craig's website, www.emofree.com, has a powerful search engine where you can find discussions of EFT with hundreds of specific issues.

2. **Isolate and Treat the Meridians that Are Involved with the Problem.** Other therapists will next identify the specific meridians that are involved with the problem and focus the energy interventions on those meridians (frequently doing muscle-based energy checks as sometimes after one meridian becomes balanced another that had been balanced goes into a disturbed state). You continue until the problem can be mentally accessed with no disturbances in any of the 14 meridians. The specifics of this method are taught in the following chapter.

—8—

Advanced Meridian Treatments

THIS CHAPTER (patterned after Gallo, 2000) adds three skills to your repertoire of clinical interventions. These additional capabilities will—according
to an influential contingent of practitioners—help you become more sensitive and more attuned to a client's energies and help you to formulate
more potent interventions. The skills include:

1. The ability to assess the *specific* meridians that are affected by a
   psychological problem.
2. The ability to formulate *self-suggestions* that are attuned to the
   emotional themes of the specific meridians that are affected.
3. The ability to select from several treatment points for each of those
   meridians.

A Multipoint Approach

The *single-point approach* you have learned up until now (one treatment
point for each meridian) is based on a best guess, a point for each meridian
that is likely to be effective with the greatest proportion of clients and
issues. The *multipoint approach* is based on the fact that each meridian has
between 9 and 67 acupoints and, in any given circumstance, some of these

points are more able to balance the flow of energies in the meridian than others. In a multipoint approach, several potential treatment points are considered for each meridian.

A single-point approach will often get the desired results. You may wish to rely on it and only use the more complex approach taught in this chapter when it does not. However, the multipoint approach is more flexible, perhaps more reliable, and is easy enough to learn and apply so that many practitioners favor it. Once you are comfortable with the single-point approach, as presented in the previous chapter, the multipoint method will be quite straightforward to learn.

Is a Multipoint Approach More Effective?

While some practitioners use only a single-point approach and believe it is as effective as the more complex methods, others believe that a multipoint strategy is often more effective, particularly with more challenging issues and with clients whose energies are more disturbed. Research that referees this debate is not yet available, but numerous practitioners are persuaded by their own clinical experience that, in many instances, knowing only a single point for each meridian is not enough.

A fundamental question that might occur to you as you are being introduced to a procedure that considers several acupoints for each meridian is this: *If two acupoints are both on the same meridian, why would one acupoint correct a disturbance in the meridian's energies while another would not?* Several factors may be involved.

The proximity of the acupoint to a blockage in the meridian could be involved, although the most effective point is not necessarily the closest to the energy irregularity. In acupuncture, for instance, the "law of opposites" dictates that the left side of the body is sometimes treated for a problem on the right side, and vice-versa. Another factor involves whether the disturbance in the meridian has to do with over-energy or under-energy. Either can be involved in psychological and behavioral problems. Some acupoints increase the flow within the meridian and others decrease it, so stimulating the wrong kind of acupoint will not lead to an improvement and could potentially exacerbate a client's symptoms.

Another advantage of a multipoint approach and the assessment it entails of the specific meridians that are involved in the problem is that often, after one disturbed meridian has been corrected, another meridian that did not initially show a disturbance now does show one. The rabbit disappears from one hole and pops up in another. Each time a meridian is balanced, the entire gestalt shifts. Sometimes, for instance, deeper energy imbalances are revealed only after those that are more easily accessed are resolved. It is a bit like the way that, in talk therapy, deeper layers of a problem often emerge only as surface issues are resolved.

A point is finally reached, however, where no additional meridians need correction. That is the objective. Meridian diagnosis[1] allows you to stay in close touch with and work with the entire meridian system until all of the meridians stay in balance while the target problem is mentally activated.

In this chapter, you will be checking the *alarm points*, an acupuncture diagnostic technique, to more reliably determine which meridians are disturbed when a problematic thought field is active and which acupoints are most likely to correct the disturbance.

The Alarm Points

The *alarm points* are used in traditional Chinese medicine to determine whether the flow of energy in a meridian is disturbed. They are aptly named. Like a smoke detector, an alarm point is activated when there is a problem in the energies of the meridian to which it is associated. Rather than a ringer or siren, the "alarm" is indicated by tenderness at the point:

139

- If tenderness is experienced when an alarm point is palpated lightly, the corresponding meridian is deficient in its energies.
- If tenderness is experienced when an alarm point is palpated firmly, the corresponding meridian has excess energy.

The technique you will be learning here combines the traditional alarm points with energy checking to determine which meridians are involved in a psychological problem. The technique:

- is based on whether an indicator muscle stays firm or loses firmness rather than relying on a subjective sense of the degree of tenderness when the point is palpated;

---

[1] Again, the terms *diagnosis* and *treatment*, as used in energy psychology, refer to the assessment and correction of specific disturbances in the body's energies *as well as* the more customary uses involving assessing and treating psychological problems.

- identifies whether a meridian's energies are disturbed or not disturbed[2] while a psychological problem is engaged.

In addition to alarm point assessment, the nature of the psychological problem may in itself provide clues about which meridians are involved with it. Specific meridians are associated with specific emotions (see the Meridian Emotions list, p. 234). The practitioner might, based on the client's history and current issues, already have an idea of which meridians are involved in the problem. Energy checking the alarm points (also called "the meridian diagnostic points"), however, provides a more objective way to determine which meridians are disturbed when the problem state has been accessed.

Checking the Alarm Points 📺

For each meridian, while the problem state is locked in:

1. Find its alarm point on the Meridian Assessment Chart (p. 257).
2. Have the client touch this point with the pad of one or more fingers of one hand while the opposite arm is used for an energy check.

This way of checking whether a meridian is involved in the problem state by touching an alarm point is called *energy localizing*. Energy localizing is based on the principle that when you touch an electrical point you create a circuit and the energy check is localized to that circuit.

Alarm points and acupoints are precisely located on the skin, but because everyone's anatomy differs, they can be difficult to pinpoint from a chart. To be sure the correct point is being localized, the pads of several fingers can be placed upon the skin in the general vicinity shown on the chart.

The Information Derived from Checking an Alarm Point

When checking an alarm point, while the problem state is locked in, a firm indicator muscle means:

1. The meridian associated with that alarm point is involved in the problem.
2. Any of several acupoints on that meridian might correct the disturbance.

---

[2] This method does not focus on whether the disturbance is based in excess energy or an energy deficiency. Rather, the acupoints selected as treatment points tend to adjust for either kind of imbalance.

Later in this chapter, you will learn how to identify which acupoint to treat. For now, the principles to remember are that:

1. Each alarm point is associated with a specific meridian.
2. Each alarm point is a diagnostic point but not necessarily a treatment point.
3. The alarm points are shown on the Meridian Assessment Chart (p. 257), and this chart is the reference you will be using as you move from one meridian check to the next.

Why a Firm Rather Than a Weak Indicator Muscle Signals a Problem

If you were to test "in the clear," that is, without having locked in the problem or without having the client think about the problem, the indicator muscle would stay *firm* when you check meridians that are in *balance* and would *lose firmness* when you check meridians that are *disturbed*. Alarm points show where there is a problem by switching off the energy to the indicator muscle.

But after you have locked in the problem, the situation is reversed. If the meridian is *disturbed*, the indicator muscle stays *firm*. This may seem backwards, but when the problem state is locked in, it is like a double negative. The problem state itself (the first negative) switched off the flow of energy to the indicator muscle. Touching the alarm point of a meridian that is involved in the problem again switches the flow of energy (the second negative), this time turning it on.

This can seem paradoxical because meridians that are in a *balanced* state (i.e., not involved in the problem) will energy check as weak while meridians that are in a *disturbed* state (i.e., involved in the problem) will energy check as *firm*.

Practice Session 1: The Alarm Points

Have your partner access and lock in a new problem state or the problem state used in the previous chapter if that problem has not been resolved. "Lock it in" using the Third Eye Up or the Leg Lock (p. 104).

Using the Meridian Assessment Chart (p. 257), energy check each alarm point 🔋. When testing while a problem state is locked in, a strong indicator muscle means that the energy in the related meridian is disturbed. Make a note of which meridians need treatment while the problem state is locked in. Switch roles.

141

From Assessment to Treatment 📱

When the indicator muscle stays firm while energy localizing a particular alarm point, the next step is to stimulate a treatment point on the meridian associated with that alarm point. There are meridian treatment charts for each of the 14 meridians (Appendix II). They follow immediately after the Meridian Assessment Chart. Once you have identified, through the alarm points on the Meridian Assessment Chart, a meridian that is involved with the problem, turn to its treatment chart. These charts show various points that can be tapped, held, or massaged, and they indicate which form of stimulation to use for each point.

Several treatment options are given for each meridian because, as already emphasized, there is probably no one-size-fits-all formula; different points are more effective for different individuals and for the same individual in different circumstances. The points on the meridian charts are selected from the many points on each meridian because clinical experience has shown them to be most effective for the largest number of people the largest proportion of the time.

Of these "most effective points," you can determine which one to use in two ways. The first is to choose any one of the recommended points, stimulate it, and re-check. The points you worked with in the previous chapter (listed on the One-Point-per-Meridian Treatment Chart) provides, for each meridian, a point that is a good first bet.

To determine if stimulating the point was effective, re-check by touching the original alarm point to see if the indicator muscle that had checked firm loses its firmness (this would mean the treatment was effective). If stimulating the first point did not result in a correction, locate other possible points by accessing the treatment chart for that meridian (which will show the point on the One-Point-per-Meridian Treatment Chart as well as viable alternatives). Stimulate another point, do an energy check, and if the disturbance has still not been corrected, proceed to yet another point. If a series of treatments does not correct the imbalance, neurological disorganization or psychological reversals might have reemerged and should be checked for and corrected, or the formulation of the problem may need to be reconsidered.

The second method for determining which point to use is to energy localize (touch the point and energy check) each of the points on the Meridian Treatment Chart for the meridian being corrected *before* stimulating any of the acupoints. If the indicator muscle stays *firm* while the point is being touched, this is a point to stimulate. Because it takes almost as long to do the energy check as to do the treatment, however, the first method—simply treating one of the points on the chart and then checking to see if the treatment was effective—is more commonly used.

You are not required to memorize the numerous treatment points for each of the 14 meridians in order to utilize energy-based interventions. Many practitioners, in fact, openly refer to the meridian treatment charts during treatment sessions. You can also keep a laptop computer nearby, opened to the Meridian Assessment Chart on the CD, which not only shows the alarm points, it gives instant hyperlink access to the treatment points for each meridian. If it is not convenient to have a computer nearby, the charts are included in Appendix II of this book and can also be easily printed from the CD in color and indexed in a binder. The Meridian Treatment Checklist (p. 242) also lists the recommended treatment points for each meridian, and since it is used for back-home assignments, you will probably keep it conveniently located.

After you have worked with the points a bit in practice sessions, you will also find that they are becoming familiar. If it is important to you, you can with a few memorization drills quite readily memorize the points on the Meridian Assessment Chart and the One-Point-per-Meridian Treatment Chart.

The client or the practitioner can stimulate a treatment point by tapping it. Tap with the tips of the fingers during an inhalation and exhalation, stop tapping during an inhalation and exhalation, and then tap again (see Tapping Instruction Sheet, p. 227). Alternatively, fewer taps (five to ten) without a pause will still be effective a large proportion of the time. Another alternative to tapping is the Touch and Breathe method (instructions accessed from the CD's Embedded Topics Index). Other ways of stimulating a point, such as pressing it, massaging it, twisting it, or holding it, are suggested, where relevant, on the meridian treatment charts.

Practice Session 2: Stimulating Treatment Points

If you are not working with the same partner, or if some time has passed, repeat Practice Session 1. Then check to be sure the problem state is still locked in, or lock it in again. Next, identify the meridians that you noted

143

as needing correction when you checked the alarm points in Practice Session 1, and locate the meridian treatment chart for each.

Treat each meridian using one of the points listed on the chart and re-check the alarm point 🔳. If the indicator muscle is *weak* (meaning that the treatment was effective), go on to check the next meridian. If the indicator muscle remains *strong* during the alarm point check (meaning this meridian still *requires treatment*), stimulate another point from the chart for that meridian.

Self-Suggestions Attuned to a Meridian's Emotional Themes

If the problematic thought field has been locked in using a technique such as the Third Eye Up or the Leg Lock (p. 104), it is not necessary for the client to concentrate on the problem state for the acupoint treatment to be effective with that problem. This makes it possible to focus the client's attention in other therapeutically beneficial ways. A potent method used within energy psychology is to have the client:

- state a positive affirmation that is attuned to the emotional theme governed by a meridian that is involved with the problem *while*
- stimulating a treatment point for that meridian.

Rather than being *generic* positive affirmations, such as, "Every day and in every way I am getting better and better," the self-suggestions are formulated based on the properties of the meridian being treated. Each meridian *tends to be* associated with a specific emotion. The affirmation is tailored so it is *meaningfully connected* with this emotion and with the target problem. While sample affirmations can be found on each meridian treatment chart (and are also compiled as a Meridian Emotions and Affirmations list, p. 234), the affirmations that are actually used should be adjusted to the clinical situation and its psychological meaning for the client. This can be a highly creative aspect of the treatment.

For instance, a sample affirmation for the stomach meridian is "I trust the larger picture" (see chart, p. 270). For some people this might be so difficult to conceive that wording that is paced for the client might simply involve an acknowledgment of the "reactive emotion," such as "I am consumed with worry." For others, a positive affirmation might fit but need to be reduced in its scope (such as "I am *learning* to trust the larger picture"). The affirmation may lead the person a bit, but it should be essentially believable to him or her.

144

Wherever the sample affirmations have brackets in the charts, such as "*I am decisive in* [overcoming this problem]," the brackets should be replaced with as specific a statement as possible. When instructing a client to state an affirmation while stimulating a treatment point, the client should be reminded to breathe fully.

It is not necessary to introduce such a "verbal treatment" with every acupoint that is tapped. If and when to use these self-suggestions is a judgment call. Many clients, however, find the affirmations to be a meaningful and memorable part of the treatment because of the way the verbalization constructively engages the conscious mind in the process. For instance, a client does not instinctively know what it means to tap a bladder point. But combining the tapping with an understanding that fear is the reactive emotion of the bladder meridian, along with a self-suggestion about "moving forward with courage and trust," facilitates the client's conscious involvement with the tapping treatment.

So, in addition to the involuntary mechanisms that may be invoked, such as the hypnotic effects of autosuggestion and the reconditioning of the emotional response to the stimulus that had been the catalyst for the problem state, the affirmations also serve as a bridge to understanding. New insight may emerge regarding:

- the psychological issues involved with the problem state *as well as*
- the meaning of the disruptions in specific meridians.

Tapping the meridian while stating an affirmation is sometimes referred to as "tapping in" the positive idea, as if the tapping opens the energy system to the suggestion.

Practice Session 3: Verbal Treatments

Review the Meridian Emotions and Affirmations list (p. 234). Focusing on the same problem used in the previous practice session, or a new problem, experiment with the verbal treatments:

1. Using the alarm points as before, find a meridian that needs treatment when the problem state is locked in.
2. Formulate an affirmation or self-suggestion based on the information provided on that meridian's treatment chart.
3. Have the "client" state this affirmation while stimulating one of the treatment points.

4. Re-check the meridian using the alarm points.

Experiment with different meridians. Change roles.

After the First Correction

After correcting the first meridian indicated by an alarm point (i.e., the indicator muscle stays weak when touching its alarm point while the problem state is locked in), use the Meridian Assessment Chart to identify the next meridian needing correction, find its treatment chart, and make the necessary corrections, adding affirmations or self-suggestions as feels appropriate. You will ultimately continue until no further meridians need correction, but on the way, several additional methods might be employed.

In the single-point approach you learned in the previous chapter, the tapping was routinely followed by a bridging technique and then another round of tapping (the sandwich). The multipoint approach does not routinely use a sandwich, but rather makes a choice after each tapping sequence (tapping sequence = *each* meridian that showed a disturbance based on its alarm point is treated until the alarm point checks show that the meridians are no longer disturbed). Then another SUD rating is taken, and usually verified with a MUD rating. Each of the assessments leads to another choice point.

Choice Points

After a problem state has been locked in, the core of the treatment in the multipoint approach is to energy check the alarm points and correct each disturbed meridian. Along the way are various choice points based on the periodic SUD and MUD assessments (p. 230).

If the SUD has:

1. Decreased but is still above 2:
    • Introduce a bridging technique (Nine Gamut, Blow-Out/Zip-Up/ Hook-In, Elaborated Cross Crawl, Separating Heaven and Earth, pp. 130–132).
    • Return to the alarm points and meridian treatments (be sure the problem state is still locked in).

2. Stopped decreasing and is still above 2:
   - Check for any intervening psychological reversals (e.g., "I want to be *completely* over this problem") and their variants based on specific criteria (e.g., "It is safe to be *completely* . . .", etc.).
   - Resolve any that are found and return to the alarm points and meridian treatments.
   - If there were no PRs, check for neurological disorganization (see Neurological Disorganization Summary, p. 231), correct if found, and return to the alarm points and meridian treatments.
3. Stopped decreasing, is still above 2, and no psychological reversals or neurological disorganization are present:
   - Use one or more of the bridging techniques until the SUD decreases and then return to the alarm points and meridian treatments.
   - If there is still no further decrease in the SUD rating, explore whether another *aspect* of the problem (see p. 34) requires attention before further progress can be made.
4. Decreased to 2 or less:
   - Consider another bridging technique or the Eye Roll procedure (p. 135).
   - Continue with the alarm points and meridian treatments. Note: Sometimes the SUD will go down to 2 or 1 but will not reduce any further, and this is not necessarily a bad outcome. See discussion on p. 135.
5. Reaches 0 or near 0. The additional steps presented in Chapter 9 will:
   - anchor in the new response
   - project the positive state into the future
   - fix the gains in the person's life

Practice Session 4: Choice Points

With your partner, review and discuss each treatment choice point that depends upon one of the periodic SUD ratings.

Supporting Success in the Client's Back-Home Setting

When the SUD gets down to 0 or near 0, additional steps are taken to anchor the new response to the problem, to project the positive state into the future, and to fix the gains into the person's life. Methods for accomplishing these goals are the topic of the following chapter.

One of these methods, however, is initiated at this point in the treatment, which is to provide the client, often in writing, the energy corrections to use if the problem state is experienced in the back-home setting (based on those that were the most effective during the treatment session). A practical way to provide the client such a handout is to:

1. Keep notes during the session of the meridians needing correction, the correction points that proved effective, and the affirmations that were used. The Meridian Treatment Checklist (p. 242) is designed to assist you with this.
2. At the end of the session, decide which points you wish to suggest be worked with if/when the problem state returns or as a regular routine for a week or two. This may be done through:

   - selecting points on meridians that needed correction more than once
   - emphasizing meridians whose associated emotion and affirmation are most involved with the problem state
   - assigning the last five points that were used to bring balance to the meridians
   - having the client imagine being in a back-home setting that could be challenging, intensifying the imagery until an indicator muscle loses its firmness on an energy check, touching the treatment points used in the session, and selecting those points where the muscle becomes firm during the energy checks

3. On the Meridian Treatment Checklist, circle the corrections and note or write in the affirmations you are recommending.
4. Provide instructions for stimulating the indicated points and using the related affirmations on either a regular basis or when/if the problem state returns. The amount of back-home work to provide, and its nature, are clinical judgment calls.

Practice Session 5: A Complete Session

With your partner, go through a complete session, from 1) the opening phases, to 2) assessing the acupoints needing treatment, to 3) moving through the various choice points based on the periodic SUD ratings for getting the SUD rating down to 0, or near 0, to 4) providing the client with

148

a copy of the Meridian Treatment Checklist. You might also want to keep the Opening Phases (p. 226) and the Advanced Meridian Intervention flow charts (p. 241) nearby.

When the SUD reaches 0 or near 0, you will complete the treatment in the Closing Phases chapter. Considerations if the SUD cannot be brought down to 0 or near 0 are addressed in the following discussion.

Then, with your partner, switch between the client and therapist roles.

When Stimulating the Meridian Points Is Not Enough

If stimulation of the meridian points—interspersed with bridging techniques and the ongoing resolution of psychological reversals—does not get the SUD down to 0 or near 0, it is possible that:

1. Straightforward discussion will reveal that the target problem needs to be adjusted or the client's relationship to the practitioner and the treatment need to be addressed.
2. Different *aspects* of the problem are confounding the treatment. Aspects are further addressed in the following chapter.
3. Neurological disorganization has emerged and needs correction.
4. Environmental substances are disrupting the client's energies, estimated to require attention in up to 10 percent of cases, before other energy treatments can have their full effect (Radomski, 2001).
5. Another energy system is involved.
6. If the SUD could not be brought down at all, the client may be one of a relatively small proportion of people who seem not to respond to meridian tapping methods and an alternative method, such as Touch and Breathe or an alternative energy system, might be considered.

If Another Energy System Is Involved

Even if another energy system was initially involved with the presenting problem, it does not necessarily need to be addressed. Working with the meridian system often simultaneously corrects disturbances in other energy systems. The procedures for correcting neurological disorganization, for instance, may also correct for many possible energy disruptions, such as gaps in the auric field or disruption in a chakra.

While other systems (chakras, aura, basic grid, five elements, radiant circuits) may need special attention, if the meridians stay strong and in good balance when the problem state is accessed, improvement will be seen in the vast majority of cases. If the problem persists, the chakras or the radiant circuits are the next systems to consider working with. They lend themselves to the same basic approach used with the meridians and are each addressed in modules on the CD.

Final Notes on Working with the Meridians

It may take many rounds of treatment before corrections hold with each of the 14 meridians. Gallo (2000) has developed a variation on the approach taught in this chapter, the Advanced Multipoint Protocol, which he feels is somewhat more effective, particularly in cases where many meridians are disturbed by the problematic thought field. Instructions for using this protocol can be found in the Advanced Meridian Treatments module on the CD.

First, however, master the skills presented in this chapter. They will usually get the meridians into balance, and the Advanced Multipoint Protocol builds on them. To review this chapter, study the Meridian Intervention Flow Chart (p. 241) and consider repeating Practice Session 5 several more times with other partners or other problems. You might also at this point wish to read some of the cases in the Clinical Illustrations module on the CD to see how the techniques you are studying have been applied in clinical settings.

—9—

Closing Phases[1]

I AM TEACHING a six-day residential workshop in South Africa. Many of the participants are leaders in their communities who have come to learn about the unconscious beliefs and motivations that shape a person's life. The first evening, one of the participants tells the group that she is terrified of snakes and is afraid to walk through a grassy area from the meeting room to her cabin, about 100 feet away. Several participants offer to escort her. Sensing that she could rapidly be helped with this phobia, I arrange— with her tense but trusting permission—for a guide at the game reserve where the workshop is being held to bring a snake into the class at 10 a.m. the next morning.

I set up the chairs so the snake and the handler are 20 feet away from her, but within her range of vision. I ask her what it is like to have a snake in the room. She lets us know she has been dissociating: "I am okay as long as I don't look at it, but I have to tell you, I left my body two minutes ago." Within less than half an hour, using methods presented in this program, she is able to imagine being close to a snake without feeling fear. I ask her

---

[1] "Closing phases" in this chapter refers to work with a particular treatment goal, not necessarily the closing phases of the therapy process, in which all the basic considerations for achieving a positive termination of the clinical relationship are relevant.

if she is ready to walk over to the snake that is across the room. As she approaches the snake, she appears confident. The confidence has soon grown into enthusiasm as she begins to comment on the snake's beauty. She asks the handler if she can touch it. Haltingly but triumphantly, she does. She reports that she is fully present in her body. This proves to be a most satisfactory way of introducing the participants to the "energy" component of the workshop. Three days later, the group is driven out into the bush and returns on foot, about a 60-minute nature walk. When they are back, another class member asks the woman if her fear of snakes made the walk difficult. A surprised look comes over her face. She realizes, "I never even thought about it." Her lifelong fear had evaporated, and on follow-up, has not returned.

In this case, with a highly specific symptom that readily responded to tapping within a half-hour session, there was no need for elaborate measures to complete the treatment. More often, a number of steps are advisable to help insure that a positive clinical response will be main-tained. When the SUD drops to 0 or close to 0 while a problem state is locked in, additional steps for completing the treatment include:

152

- anchoring the new response into the person's energy system
- projecting the positive state into the future
- installing the gains into the person's life structure

This chapter addresses each of these steps.

How Long Do Energy Corrections Typically Hold?

Two opposing principles[2] influence whether an energy correction will be effective, and if it is, how long it will hold. They are:

1. *The Principle of Rapid Adaptability.* It is because of this principle that the "instant cures" which have brought energy psychology so much attention in the popular press are possible.
2. *The Principle of Deep-Seated Survival Strategies.* It is because of this principle that even behavioral habits and patterns that are obviously dysfunctional and self-destructive can be so difficult to change.

---

[2] These principles are derived from the stress response literature, Chinese medi-cine, and clinical observation.

Both principles are reflected in the activities of the triple warmer energy system.

Rapid Adaptability

The principle of rapid adaptability is seen in the immune response to an unrecognized substance in the bloodstream and the fight-or-flight response to physical danger in the environment. A rapid assessment is made about whether the situation being encountered poses a threat. If it is determined to be dangerous, a pre-programmed response is instantly set into motion.

Triple warmer is continually scanning for danger. Whenever a threat or potential threat is identified, it mobilizes the body's energies to respond to the threat, building upon inherited defense strategies such as the immune response or the fight-or-flight mechanism.

Triple warmer's basic "decision" involves only two possibilities: mobilize for threat or don't mobilize. The decision is made instantly based on whether previous decisions in similar circumstances were or were not reinforced. After each new experience, the underlying strategy can be updated in either direction (mobilize, don't mobilize). If the mobilization for danger is provoked by a stimulus but no danger follows, and this cycle is repeated, the mobilization eventually ceases even in the presence of the original stimulus, a process known as "extinction." Brief electrical stimulation of the prefrontal cortex in rats in the presence of a stimulus that mobilizes a fear response also extinguishes the fear response (Milad & Quirk, 2002). This mechanism may be highly significant for energy psychology. It is possible that the stimulation of certain acupoints while a stress-evoking stimulus is mentally accessed sends signals to the prefrontal cortex that extinguish the conditioned emergency response to that stimulus.

In many psychological problems, the emergency response is set into motion by a single event involving danger or perceived danger, and from then on is reflexively evoked in all similar situations. The emergency response—costly in terms of the diversion of attention, the generation of intense affect, the distortion of perception, and the expenditure of biological resources—is regularly triggered by circumstances that do not constitute actual physical or psychological danger. When a conditioned emergency response of this nature is interrupted by an energy intervention, and the perceived threat proves to have been innocuous (nothing bad happens), triple warmer can quickly update its emergency strategy. This is how the principle of rapid adaptability helps explain the unexpectedly rapid treat-

153

ment responses, such as instant phobia cures, that are so frequently reported within energy psychology.

Deep-Seated Survival Strategies

There is economy in habit. A survival strategy can be implemented for a new threat more readily if it is patterned after strategies that have worked in the past. This economy, however, carries two risks:

1. The survival strategy may not be sufficiently attuned to the present danger.
2. The survival strategy may become deeply embedded and then triggered in circumstances where it is not needed, the "false alarm" factor that is at the root of many psychological problems.

As with rapid adaptability, *deep-seated survival strategies* are also maintained by triple warmer. A stimulus (such as an internal image or external situation) is perceived to be a threat, triple warmer mobilizes the meridians for physical or emotional danger, and it maintains this pattern whenever a similar image or situation is encountered. These survival-oriented habits are conditioned (learned) elaborations upon the genetically programmed fight-or-flight mechanism. The meridian system often sacrifices its own energetic balance and coherence in service of the triple warmer–mediated emergency response.

Whether or not the situation that triggers that survival response is an actual threat, the disruption to the meridian system, the rush of chemicals, and the accompanying threat-related emotions are still just as physiologically and psychologically costly, and restabilizng after the crisis has passed requires just as many resources. More to the heart of psychological problems, because the threat response overpowers reason, the resulting perceptions, thoughts, and actions are often blindly reactive, non-adaptive, and sometimes self-destructive.

Working with the acupoints while accessing the problematic thought field can reliably interrupt the emergency response and recondition the body so the triggering stimulus no longer initiates the pattern. The principles of rapid adaptability and deep-seated survival strategies are both involved.

In cases such as an uncomplicated phobia, the principle of rapid adaptability usually prevails. The threat response is interrupted, nothing bad happens, the strategy is updated. In cases where a problem has many

154

aspects, where the threat response is connected to a complex of experiences and issues, the deep-seated survival strategy can be enormously resistant to change. The same basic energy interventions are still used, but numerous aspects of the problem need to be identified and energetically neutralized. Once this has occurred, the steps presented in this chapter can support the positive internal changes within the client's back-home setting.

Anchoring Techniques

After the problematic situation no longer evokes a disturbed response in the energy system, any of several techniques that help to immediately stabilize this new response can be introduced. Among them:

1. The Eye Roll 📠
2. The Third Eye Tap 📠
3. The Auric Weave 📠

The Eye Roll not only serves to *lower* the SUD when it is at 2 or less (p. 135), it also helps to *anchor* the distress-free state into the body's energies while the original problematic stimulus is present. Two additional anchoring techniques are the Third Eye Tap and the Auric Weave.

155

The Third Eye Tap 📠 . The Third Eye Tap is used when a person is already feeling good. It takes the vibration of a joyous feeling and patterns the nervous system to more easily support that vibration. The first acupuncture point on the meridian that governs the nervous system (bladder) is also the spot that yogis refer to as the "third eye," between the eyebrows, above the bridge of the nose. When you are feeling happy, deeply satisfied, spiritually connected, in love, or any other joyful feeling, you can, by tapping at your third eye, direct this energy to leave an imprint on your entire nervous system.

At a moment a client is feeling joy or hope or enthusiasm about a future that is untainted by the target problem, he or she may "tap" this feeling into the "third eye" point. The tapping is firm yet gentle, for about 10 to 20 seconds. The breathing is deliberate.

The Auric Weave 📠 . The human biofield is an electromagnetic field that is detectable using established measuring instruments (Ochman, 2000). It comes several inches out from the skin and surrounds the entire body. The concept of the *aura* has its basis in the biofield. The aura has been described as an envelope that *contains* a person's own energies, protects against harmful energies in the environment, and at the same time connects the person with harmonious energies, including those of other people. Energy healers report that the "health" of the biofield or aura reflects the health of the body along with its vulnerability to taking on diseases and other outside intrusions.

Because your hands carry an electromagnetic charge, you can use them to smooth and trace and strengthen your aura or biofield. This is almost like giving it a massage. The aura seems to have the best response when "massaged" in figure-eight patterns. When your energies are in a positive state, you can use your hands to "weave your aura" so it constitutes itself around this positive state. Hold the image that initially triggered the problem, with the distress level now at 0 or close enough to 0 that you would like to lock it in, and you can energetically reinforce this internal state by weaving your aura as follows:

1. With your feet firmly planted, rub your hands together. Then bring your hands a few inches apart and notice if you feel an energy charge between them. Whether or not you can detect it, it is there, and you will be using it to magnetically weave the energies on the surface of your body in figure-eight patterns.
2. Take a deep breath as you hold your hands about six inches from your ears. Tune into the image or thought that no longer evokes a stress reaction.
3. Make small figure-eights at your ears and begin to increase the movement until your hands are making small and large figure-eight patterns all the way down your body, on the sides, front, and back. Use a free-flow rather than rigid structure, moving the energy to your own inner rhythm.
4. As you do, imagine that you are weaving your energies into a seamless fabric. Some people like to move to a favorite piece of music.

Practice Session 1: Anchoring Techniques

First, access a *positive* internal state and do the Eye Roll, the Third Eye Tap, and the Auric Weave in sequence, keeping the positive state active. Teach your partner the three techniques.

Then, with your partner, review your work in Practice Session 5 of the previous module (a complete treatment sequence that brings the SUD of a target problem down to 0 or near 0). Continue experimenting with the three anchoring techniques in relationship to the problem that has now been neutralized. Switch with your partner between the client and therapist roles.

Projecting a Successful Treatment Outcome into the Future

While cognitive and behavioral techniques for translating therapeutic gains into back-home settings are part of most clinical approaches, the energy-based psychotherapies also use procedures to get specific images of positive outcomes to resonate with the client's energy system. A series of steps called the Outcome Projection Procedure[3] can help anchor the positive internal changes into the client's daily life. You will see that the internal logic is similar to sequences you have already learned. Each step is presented in the language you might use in guiding a client through the technique, followed by an italicized description that elaborates on the dog bite example presented in Chapter 1.

1. Vividly visualize or otherwise imagine a situation that would pull for the old response. *A man who has been neutralizing his fear of dogs imagines coming to a neighbor's house where a friendly but large dog is barking upon his approach.*
2. Visualize or imagine responding to or handling that situation in a manner you consider ideal. *The man imagines himself calmly putting his hand out for the dog to smell and speaking reassuringly to the dog.*
3. Rate, on a scale of 0 to 10, how *believable* this scene is to you. This time, the higher the number the more favorable the score. This measure is called a Positive Belief Scale (PBS), in contrast with the SUD (Subjective Units of Distress). An indicator muscle may be tested for corroboration. If the belief level is already between 8 and 10, the results will probably transfer satisfactorily to the real-life context. *This scene, while desirable, does not feel particularly believable to the man. He rates it at a 3.*
4. State a set-up affirmation around the issue while rubbing your "chest sore spots" (or using one of the other energy interventions described on p. 87). The format for the set-up affirmation at this point focuses on the believability of the scene, such as: *"Even though it is hard for me to believe that [I could calmly put my hand out for the dog to sniff], I deeply love and accept myself."*

157

---

[3] Patterned after the procedure described in Gallo (2000).

5. Do a series of tapping/bridging/tapping sequences until the rating is at least up to 8 (use any standard set of tapping points, such as those found on p. 27). Keep active in your mind the vision or sense of handling the situation in a manner you consider ideal. Also give a name to this scene and use it as a reminder phrase while you are visualizing or sensing the scene. *After four rounds of tapping while sensing into the scene and stating "comfortable with dogs," the believability of the scene where the man puts out his hand for the dog to smell has increased to 9.*

6. Whenever you are in or about to enter a situation that is starting to evoke the old response, use the earlier set-up/tapping/bridging/tapping routine to further neutralize that response, and follow it with the above five steps. *The man arranges to visit a friend who has a large dog and uses the techniques to prepare for the visit and for whenever anxiety begins to arise.*

If the belief level will not move up to 8, the same basic strategy as for lowering a SUD level can be employed: Check and resolve neurological disorganization and psychological reversals, employ general balancing procedures while the client is thinking about the desired state, and stimulate treatment points while the desired state is mentally active.

Checks for psychological reversals focus on the belief that the desired state can be obtained and are worded along the lines of:

"I want to thoroughly believe that I will be able to . . ."
"I will believe that I am able to . . ."
"It is safe for me to believe that I will be able to . . .", etc.

General balancing procedures may be as simple as tapping the gamut point (just below the knuckles of the ring and little fingers, slightly toward the wrist) or the points in the hollows at the side of each eye while thinking about being able to achieve the desired outcome. Any of the other bridging techniques (the Nine Gamut, Blow-Out/Zip-Up/Hook-In, Elaborated Cross Crawl, Separating Heaven and Earth) can also be paired with the thoughts about the desired outcome. These will often elevate the belief level to the desired range.

The alarm points may also be checked while the client thinks about being able to achieve the desired outcome. Since a problem state is not being locked in, corrections in this case should be made when the indicator muscle loses its firmness. If touching the alarm point for liver meridian weakens the indicator muscle, for instance, a liver meridian point is stimulated while the client thinks about the desired outcome.

These procedures are repeated in various combinations until the client is able to create a strong internal representation of the desired outcome (seeing, hearing, feeling) without experiencing any indications of stress or a drop in the belief level. To further affirm the treatment outcome, points that had needed attention in the earlier phases of treatment can be re-checked using the alarm points while the client thinks about the original problem.

Practice Session 2: Outcome Projection Procedure

Working again with the original problem, whose SUD level is now down to 0 or near 0, and having anchored in that SUD level in Practice Session 1, go through the steps of the Outcome Projection Procedure with your partner. Switch roles.

Aspects Revisited

According to Gary Craig, many practitioners would increase their effectiveness if they were more specific in their formulations about the issues they target. Rather than to focus on a global condition, such as "anxiety," he recommends identifying specific experiences, often from childhood, that involve the condition, or current situations that trigger it, and neutralizing the emotional charge to them, one by one, until this eventually generalizes to all related situations.

Complex psychological problems have numerous such "aspects" (introduced on p. 34), and an apparently successful treatment is less likely to prove durable unless its most critical aspects have been addressed. "Peeling the layers of the onion" is one of the most common clichés used within energy psychology. A recent trauma or loss, for example, often unearths a network of earlier traumas or losses:

> A man entered treatment for anxiety attacks following an automobile accident. He understands his psychological symptoms as being a direct result of the trauma sustained in the accident. He feels substantial relief within three sessions, his treatment appears to have been successful, and he is glad the incident is behind him.

But at the end of what might have been the third and final session, he is challenged to think of anything that might make the SUD level rise again. This time, his focus goes to the moment he realized the crash was inevitable. The disturbing thought is about his helplessness in that moment rather than the actual trauma of the crash. Another round of treatment focuses on the feeling of helplessness.

His SUD is lowered to 0 when thinking of the helplessness caused by the car accident, but when asked to see if he can make himself upset about being helpless in the situation, he becomes aware of how helpless he felt when his parents divorced when he was eight. This becomes the focus of the next round of treatment.

While energy psychology interventions can appear relatively mechanical and are often effective without focusing on the history of the problem or insight into its etiology, this case suggests how they can also be used as a powerful adjunct to a psychodynamic therapeutic approach.

160

In debriefing someone immediately following a trauma, the aspects of the incident are usually primary and visceral. Patricia Carrington, Ph.D., a member of the *EPI* Advisory Board, advises focusing on the visual, auditory, and kinesthetic aspects of the event. As she puts it: "It could be a great help if the person didn't have to figure out what to tap on but simply remembered to ask themselves what *visual* aspects of the scene are particularly distressing, and then what *sounds* seem shocking to them to recall, and then what physical *sensations* were distressing." Using this approach immediately following a trauma can, simply put, circumvent a tremendous amount of difficulty at a later point, as is illustrated in the case presented under Trauma Debriefing in the Embedded Topics Index of the CD.

Most long-standing psychological problems have, among other aspects such as intruding sensations or images, correlates in the person's history. These early experiences are often revealed in the course of treatment, but can also be uncovered through standard techniques such as the clinical interview, dream analysis, or examining transference and counter-transference. While this could be the topic of another book, the basic strategy is to: 1) identify critical decision points in the client's past, 2) create conditions, using energy interventions, in which the client is able to recall these circumstances with no subjective distress, 3) in this stress-free context review the deep decisions made as a result of those early circumstances and identify a core life decision that is proving dysfunctional, 4) formulate a new decision, and 5) project this new decision into the future using methods such as the Outcome Projection Procedure (also see the CD module Transforming Core Beliefs).

Challenging Apparently Positive Treatment Results

Challenging the apparently successful outcome of an energy treatment sequence is a standard procedure within energy-based psychotherapy that may reveal aspects of the problem still requiring attention. *The Energy Psychology Desktop Companion* (Grudermeyer & Grudermeyer, 2000) suggests that the treatment is not complete until "the last distress about the last aspect of the issue is cleared away" and the desired effects "have proven durable in relevant real life conditions" (p. 61).

Aspects of the problem that have not been addressed are often identified by challenging an apparently successful outcome, as you saw in the case of the man being treated for the trauma sustained in an automobile accident, and this technique is also a way of confirming and, to a reasonable degree, insuring results. Typically, the client is asked, in one way or another, to "try to get upset" about the presenting problem, e.g., "Try to feel your grief [rage, withdrawal, etc.]." If the disturbed energy pattern has been corrected—that is if the presenting problem is now paired to a stable response in the energy system—the client will not be able to activate the earlier feelings.

A difficult situation will still be recognized for its inherent injuries, dangers, or injustices, but triple warmer's emergency response (with the corresponding perceptual distortions and emotional overwhelm or shutdown) that had been part of the response to that situation will no longer be evoked. If the client is unable to reproduce the initial emotional response, the probability is strong that the issue has been deactivated and the client can expect to meet the original provocative back-home situation without initiating the stress response sequence or being pulled into other dysfunctional habits of thought or behavior that were the focus of the treatment.

If imagining the situation still triggers unwanted emotions, thoughts, or impulses to act in undesired ways, further treatment of the issue is indicated. This may involve another round of the earlier treatment, with careful assessments for psychological reversals, or it may involve focusing on a different aspect of the problem.

It is not always necessary to challenge the apparent results of the treatment, but the interchanges that may result can increase the reliability of the treatment results in the back-home setting. Whether or not you challenge the results, life will, and ample opportunity is always there to revisit related issues if the treatment does not hold.

For the purposes of our practice sessions, we will skip this step because challenging the results can lead to a more complex treatment sequence. However, if you are working within a context that is appropriate for going deeper and addressing multiple aspects of the original problem, this would be a good point to experiment with "challenging the results."

Back-Home Assignments

Once the client believes that the successful outcome will bridge into the back-home setting, and this has been corroborated with PBS ratings and appropriate energy checks, debriefing and back-home assignments that will support a successful outcome include:

1. Explaining that it is neither unusual nor a sign of failure if the problem state is reactivated in the back-home context, but a clue as to what the next step is for completely overcoming the original problem.
2. Providing instructions (usually written; see, for instance, the Meridian Treatment Checklist on p. 242) for repeating the procedures that alleviated the problem during the treatment session, to be used:
   • if the problem state returns
   • routinely for a period of time (e.g., "when you get in the shower; when you are watching TV and a commercial comes on; when you get in the car, before you turn on the ignition")
3. Offering other procedures, such as the Temporal Tap (accessed from the CD's Embedded Topics Index), that will support the gains and provide tools for taking progress in new directions.

Addressing Setbacks

Difficulties the client experiences in translating gains from the treatment setting into problem situations can result in an exploration of:

- *psychological reversals* that have emerged since the last treatment session
- *other aspects* of the problem that need to be addressed before there is a full resolution (e.g., anxiety about asking for a raise may activate anxiety around authority figures, around status, around career concerns, around becoming destitute, etc.)
- *core beliefs* that may be in conflict with the problem's full resolution (the CD's Transforming Core Beliefs module addresses this issue)

As in any other approach to psychotherapy or personal development, "setbacks" such as these become grist in a deepening process of evaluation and evolution.

Practice Session 3: Back-Home Assignments

With a positive outcome projected into the future:

1. Discuss with your partner the possibility of setbacks.
2. Formulate back-home assignments and clearly agree about how they will be implemented.
3. Establish with your partner the ways you will be available to one another to support each other's ongoing progress.

A Final Method Clients Can Keep in Their "Back Pocket"

A technique that can be readily used in situations where a client needs a quick way of calming an emotion or changing a troubling internal reaction combines a self-affirmation with a simple tapping technique.[4] The instructions given to the client are along the lines of:

1. Begin by rating the problem on the amount of distress you feel when you think about it, using the 0 to 10 scale you have already learned.
2. Fold your arms, rest your fingers on your bicep muscles, and pat your right and left biceps alternately with your hands, about a second for each tap (the "butterfly hug").

---

[4] This procedure, suggested by psychiatrist Daniel J. Benor, M.D., blends methods used in EMDR (Eye Movement Desensitization and Reprocessing) and EFT (Emotional Freedom Techniques).

3. Continuing the butterfly hug and tapping, state aloud an affirmation in the form: *"Even though I* [have this problem], *I deeply love and accept myself"* (or end with a different strong, positive, affirming statement).
4. Take a deep breath.
5. Reassess the amount of distress that thinking about the problem causes you on the 0 to 10 scale.
6. Repeat until the rating has gone down as low as you can get it.
7. If you have been able to get the rating down to 2 or less, you can finish by repeating the procedure with a positive affirmation. Use steps 2, 3, and 4 as above, but this time the affirmation describes what you would consider an ideal response in a situation that might have triggered the troubling emotion, such as, "I can speak in front of any audience with confidence and comfort, and the universe supports me in every way" (or "and God loves me," or another closing phrase that evokes a positive, assuring feeling).

Next Steps

With this chapter, you have completed the nine units that correspond with the first major section of the CD, Elements of Treatment. The program could stop here and you would have been introduced to the basic concepts and tools for bringing an energy-based approach to psychological problems into your clinical practice.

The subsequent seven units on the CD, however, will broaden your knowledge and skill base, expand the scope of possible applications of an energy-based approach, and increase the resilience of therapeutic gains by addressing:

- Core Beliefs
- Protocols for Specific Emotional Problems
- The Chakras
- The Radiant Energy System
- Clinical Illustrations
- Other Energy Approaches
- Energy Interventions and Other Forms of Psychotherapy

—10—

The State of the Art

CONSULTING WITH SOME 30 of the field's leaders and innovators while developing *Energy Psychology Interactive* was, among other things, a study of the areas in which energy psychology practitioners agree and disagree. Major differences exist not only in the clinical procedures that are used but also in the explanations of the phenomena that are observed. The great paradox about energy psychology in its current stage of development, in fact, is that never before has a method emerged from psychology that is so widely practiced *and* so poorly understood.

While research will eventually address and resolve many of the areas of confusion and controversy, the best source of information available at this time is probably the collective experience of the methods' practitioners. This chapter is organized as a series of questions to get you thinking about some of the major areas of disagreement and their clinical implications. It introduces each topic by posing one or more questions for you to consider, and it then offers commentary about that topic based upon the interviews conducted in developing the *EPI* program. Introducing each commentary is also a report of the results of an informal survey (show of hands during the opening plenary address) of 265 participants at the Fifth International Energy Psychology Conference held in

May 2003 in Phoenix who identified themselves as energy psychology practitioners with a substantial experience base. The professional affiliations of those who participated included approximately 10 percent psychologists, 10 percent social workers, 40 percent mental health or marriage, family, and child counselors, 3 percent physicians, 6 percent nurses, 5 percent other licensed health care providers, and 26 percent unlicensed counselors. Approximately 65 percent considered energy psychology their primary or one of their primary psychotherapeutic modalities; 35 percent considered it secondary to another modality.

I. Efficacy

The *existing clinical evidence* justifies making the following statement to clients and colleagues:

> "The techniques of energy psychology appear to yield rapid positive results in anxiety-related cases, even those that other treatments have not been able to substantially help, at least 80 percent of the time."

Agree _____ Disagree

Commentary. Eighty percent of the energy-oriented psychotherapists agreed that the existing clinical evidence supports the statement that strong efficacy has been demonstrated; fifteen percent disagreed; and 5 percent were closer to the middle or offered no opinion (the "offered no opinion" category includes those who answered that they did not know as well as those who did not indicate an answer for a given question).

Research in energy psychology is still in its infancy. The South American studies, reported on page 197, had a high n (31,400), used a controlled, randomized design, and yielded statistically impressive results. That study, however, must be considered heuristic rather than conclusive. As is emphasized in the report, the study was always considered to be preliminary in nature, has not been replicated, outcome assessments were based on an interviewer's subjective rating, and record-keeping was relatively informal. The most solid research at this point is to be found in related areas, such as acupuncture and Therapeutic Touch. Numerous small or preliminary studies have also been conducted investigating energy psychology interventions (see www.energypsychresearch.org), and as this book is going to press, the first of these had just been accepted for publication based on a peer-review process (*Journal of Clinical Psychology*, Wells et al., in press).

II. The Core Mechanism

When we have figured out exactly what is going on within energy psychology—when we understand how stimulating certain points helps with anxiety as precisely as we understand how insulin shots help with diabetes—what will the essential, underlying, critical mechanism be:

> **Primarily Mechanical**—tapping and other physical interventions initiate biochemical and electromagnetic processes that interrupt and reprogram the biochemical and electromagnetic sequences that trigger disturbed emotional responses.

> **Primarily beyond the Mechanical**—the physical interventions are secondary—a bridge through which there is an interchange of healing energies, an evocation of spiritual forces, or the initiation of other phenomenon that cannot be fully explained in biochemical and electromagnetic terms but which produce the clinical outcomes.

167

What do you believe:

Primarily _ Beyond
Mechanical   Mechanical

Commentary. In the survey, only 1 percent of the energy therapists believed the primary therapeutic ingredient can be explained in exclusively biochemical/electrical terms; 70 percent believed the essential ingredient is not mechanical at all; 20 percent thought it is a combination of biochemical and electromagnetic mechanisms with processes that cannot be explained in mechanical terms alone; 9 percent did not offer an opinion.

Many neurological correlates of treatment effects have been mapped. Digitized EEG brain scans dramatically illustrate the shifts that occur in anxiety disorders based on tapping acupuncture points (a representative set of scans can be accessed from the CD). Acupuncture points contain high concentrations of receptors that are sensitive to mechanical stimulation on the skin. When certain acupoints are stimulated, electrochemical signals are sent to parts of the brain that are involved in anxiety.

Specific alpha, beta, and theta wave ratios in given parts of the brain are markers of anxiety. In cases where acupoint tapping is followed by a decrease of anxiety, a corresponding normalization of brain wave ratios is found. In samples from the South American studies, the wave normalization tended to persist at one-year follow-up, although the self-application of tapping methods may have helped maintain the improvements. A small minority of practitioners think that this or another related biochemical/electromagnetic explanation provides an adequate accounting of the observed treatment effects. A striking 90 percent felt, based on their experiences, that other explanations are necessary.

Several clinical phenomena that are frequently observed and are not explained according to the neurological sequence described above include:

1. A range of methods (tapping, massaging, or holding the points; varying the points; working with chakras; working with neurovascular points; lateral eye movements) appear to achieve similar clinical outcomes.
2. A range of emotions whose neurochemistry is far different from that of anxiety, and even certain physical conditions, appear to respond positively to similar interventions.
3. Many therapists report their belief that subtle energies, a healing presence, or other forces that cannot be detected by current instrumentation are involved in the treatment effects.
4. Reports and studies of non-local healing, such as prayer and surrogate treatments (a provocative clinical example of surrogate treatment is detailed on the CD), are accumulating and must be accounted for. The role of "thought fields," discussed below, provides a possible complement to the biochemical/electromagnetic explanations.

III. Procedural Issues

1. Within the set of acupoints usually used within the field of energy psychology, assessing and stimulating the points that are *specific* to the problem is critical at least 10 percent of the time for achieving the desired outcome in energy psychology treatments (i.e., there are "effective points" and "ineffective points").

    Agree _ Disagree

168

2. The *order* in which the points are stimulated is critical at least 10 percent of the time for achieving the desired outcome.

Agree _ Disagree

3. The inclusion of "brain balancing procedures," such as the Nine Gamut Procedure, is critical at least 10 percent of the time for achieving the desired outcome.

Agree _ Disagree

Commentary. In the survey, 35 percent agreed that there are "effective" and "ineffective" points, 35 percent felt that virtually any subset of the acupoints typically used within energy psychology could bring about the therapeutic effect, and 30 percent were in the middle or offered no opinion. The identical percentages were found in relationship to the importance of the order in which the points were stimulated, with 35 percent feeling that it mattered and 35 percent feeling it did not matter. Regarding the importance of introducing techniques into the treatment protocol designed to balance the cerebral hemispheres, 45 percent felt such methods were critical in a reasonable proportion of cases, 20 percent felt they were not, and 35 percent were in the middle or offered no opinion.

In the 1980s, procedures for addressing psychological issues drawing upon methods from Applied Kinesiology were independently established by psychologist Roger Callahan and psychiatrist John Diamond. However, so many variations on their early formulations appear to yield favorable clinical outcomes that it is very difficult to know which of the procedures are the "essential ingredients." Informal clinical trials in the South American studies, varying the order of points, the number of points, which points, the inclusion or exclusion of the Nine Gamut Procedure, et cetera, all produced similar results with most but not all anxiety disorders.

Despite the lack of consensus among the field's practitioners and the lack of definitive information about the active ingredients of an energy approach, there is evidence that an energy approach *does have* active ingredients, that it is not just placebo. For instance, many of the practitioners who were interviewed in depth reported that introducing energy psychology methods has substantially improved their treatment success rates in comparison with their earlier use of the most promising *established* treatments for anxiety—such as cognitive behavior therapy. Many combine the approaches. Which of the energy interventions are essential remains a puzzle.

IV. Assessment

1. Energy checking (also called *muscle testing*) is a critical tool in energy psychology.

Agree _ Disagree

2. Energy checking, if properly applied, yields reliable information about the state of a meridian.

Agree _ Disagree

3. Energy checking, if properly applied, yields reliable information (at least 80 percent of the time—other sources of information should also always be used) about questions that go beyond the immediate meridian response, such as "there are no other psychological reversals that need to be dealt with at this time," "Tapping is the treatment of choice for this problem," or "this growth is non-malignant."

Agree _ Disagree

4. In a reasonable proportion of cases, say at least 10 percent, the treatment will be more effective and faster if, using techniques such as checking indicator muscles, you diagnose which meridians are disturbed when the problem is activated and focus the treatment on those meridians.

Agree _ Disagree

Commentary. In the survey, 40 percent felt that energy checking is a critical tool in energy psychology, 30 percent felt it is not, and 30 percent were in the middle or offered no opinion. Sixty percent believed that energy checking could accurately assess the state of a meridian, less than 1 percent disagreed, with the remainder saying they were in the middle or did not know. Fifty percent believed that energy checking could also yield reliable answers to questions that go beyond the immediate meridian response, 10 percent disagreed, and 40 percent were in the middle or offered no opinion. Twenty percent felt it was important in a reasonable proportion of cases to assess and treat the specific meridians involved in the problem, 20 percent did not, 40 percent were in the middle, and 20 percent offered no opinion.

Almost all energy-oriented psychotherapists agree that stimulating at least one of several standard sets of pre-selected treatment points while a psychological problem is mentally accessed will resolve the problem in some proportion of the cases. When it does not, there are strong differences in what the next steps should be. Some refocus on the formulation of the problem; some next look to break it down into its aspects; others recheck for psychological reversals, neurological disorganization, or "energetically toxic" substances that might be interfering. Still others energy check to identify which meridians are involved with the problem, determine which of the many points on those meridians are most likely to correct the problem, and use these points in the subsequent treatment.

Those who diagnose and stimulate specific meridians believe that they are able to focus the treatment in a way that substantially improves clinical success, particularly with complex or entrenched problems. Others believe that stimulating the same carefully selected points in all cases is adequate, arguing that since all the meridians are systemically connected, activating key points within the meridian system activates the entire system.

In theory, energy checking allows for a quick and accurate assessment of the energy flow in a particular meridian or energy pathway. Meridian flow can be affected when a psychological problem is accessed. Some practitioners find it is more effective, at least in some cases, to focus treatment on the specific meridians that are affected while the psychological problem is active. Energy checking is a primary means used for identifying such meridian disturbances.

A number of controlled studies published in peer-reviewed scientific journals support the efficacy of energy checking under specific conditions (see abstracts of 12 studies and citations for 18 more on the CD). There is, for instance, a difference in the amount of pressure that is required to mechanically overpower an indicator muscle following a statement the subject believes to be true as contrasted with a statement believed to be false. But other studies show that different practitioners testing the same subject can get contradictory results. Firm conclusions cannot be drawn from the research, and many of the most respected energy-oriented practitioners emphasize that energy testing is as much an art as it is a science.

171

For instance, if subtle energies are involved, and if the mind influences subtle energies, then the practitioner's and the subject's beliefs, expectations, and hopes must be prevented from skewing the outcome if the test is to be accurate.

This is where the "art" comes in. Experienced practitioners believe such safeguards and precision are possible and that the procedure can be used quite reliably to determine how the energies are flowing through specific meridians. But caution is also advised, and many practitioners who confidently use the procedure still refrain from making clinical decisions based on checking muscles alone. They emphasize that clinical intuition and other indicators should always be given *at least* as much credibility as an energy test.

When the information being sought goes beyond the basic nature of an energy test (determining whether or not the energy flowing within a meridian is disturbed), the test becomes even more theoretically problematic. Questions such as "Are there other psychological reversals that need to be addressed?" or "Is tapping the treatment of choice?" are of this sort. Some practitioners believe this is a naive misuse of the technique. Others believe it is precisely because beliefs and thoughts influence subtle energies that such questions are valid. They believe that the energy test serves as a vehicle through which a deeper knowing or an unconscious wisdom can be revealed within the treatment setting.

172

V. Thought Fields

Roger Callahan postulated that mental activity is influenced by "thought fields" which are comprised of energy and which carry information. In this formulation, psychological problems are caused by disturbances or "perturbations" in the thought field which then impact the neurochemical and cognitive processes that lead to a disturbing emotion. Are you more inclined to believe that:

1. A "thought field" is a *metaphor* which is being used to attempt to explain the essentially neurological, electromagnetic, and cognitive processes involved in emotional problems.
2. A "thought field" is not just a metaphor but *exists in time and space*, much as do magnetic and gravitational fields.

Commentary. Approximately 90 percent of the group felt that thought fields exist in time and space. Less than 1 percent disagreed, with the remainder not expressing an opinion.

The concept of an invisible field carrying information that impacts psychological functioning is not popular among scientists who are hard at work demonstrating that all mental and behavioral processes are neuro-chemically coded. Other scientists, however, representing numerous disciplines, from neurology to anesthesiology, have postulated the existence of *energy fields* or *organizing fields* (see "fields" paper on CD) that influence thought and behavior in order to explain findings produced within their area of specialization. They believe that mental activity is governed by both biochemistry and invisible fields working in tandem. Many phenomena that are difficult to explain via biochemistry alone lend themselves to this two-part formulation. For instance, in energy psychology, the rapid changes that are often witnessed—in which a long-standing emotional response is permanently shifted within a few minutes—have been explained in terms of changes in the field that *organizes* biochemical processes. The therapeutic effects are viewed as being more like changing the radio station than rewiring the radio.

173

VI. The Role of Intention

1. One person's thoughts and intentions can influence other people or the environment from a distance.

Agree _____ Disagree

2. There are healing forces in the universe that can be channeled into the treatment setting through prayer, ritual, or focused intention.

Agree _____ Disagree

3. You cannot go too deep into energy work without getting into spiritual questions.

Agree _____ Disagree

Commentary. In the survey, 95 percent agreed that thoughts and intention could influence other people or the environment from a distance and 90 percent agreed that healing forces could be channeled into the treatment setting. Less than 1 percent disagreed with either statement. Seventy percent felt you cannot go too deep into energy work without getting into spiritual questions, 5 percent disagreed, and 25 percent were in the middle or offered no opinion.

Well-controlled double-blind studies, published in peer-reviewed medical journals, indicating that cardiac patients who were prayed for had a better prognosis than those who were not, disturb the prevailing paradigm. Other studies show that intention as well as prayer impacts physical events, from electronic instruments to the chemistry of the person's DNA on a slide 400 miles away. By sending calming or disturbing thoughts to someone in another room, individuals can influence that person's galvanic skin response as well as other measures of relaxation and agitation. Through mental focus, individuals can impact the growth rate of geraniums as well as enzyme activity in a test tube.

All of these experiments underline the need for a concept that bridges thought and physical events. The energy fields or thought fields postulated within energy psychology provide such a concept and are consistent with formulations from other disciplines. Not only does this suggest that the therapist's caring and intentions physically influence the clinical atmosphere, procedures designed to directly impact the energy field that is involved with the problem might not be as bizarre as they may seem when viewed through traditional paradigms.

This opens up additional areas that have typically been relegated to religion at best, superstition at worst. Are there larger forces in the universe that also impact the thought field? Can those forces be brought to bear upon the healing process through invocation, ritual, or prayer? The neatly tailored biochemical paradigm that has ascended in psychiatry, which increasingly relies on psychotropic medication, is challenged with complications when these doors are opened.

VII. Interpersonal Influences

Subtle or unexpected or difficult-to-explain influences of the client and the therapist upon one another have long been recognized and described using terms such as *transference, counter-transference,* and *projective identification.* A psychiatrist known for her success in helping children who have been traumatized described how she suspects a child has been abused if

174

she herself begins to have fantasies of abusing the child. Which explanation makes the most sense to you:

1. Role expectations and subtle cues are more powerful than most people realize and account for most of the information people subliminally register about one another.
2. An energetic exchange between client and therapist gives each information about the other that cannot be obtained from the other's defined role, behavior, facial expressions, posture, or other physical signs.

Commentary. Less than one percent felt that subtle cues fully account for the psychiatrist's ability to identify child abuse based on her own fantasies. Eighty-five percent believed an energetic exchange that provides information is involved.

Role expectations and subtle cues are far more powerful than most people realize. Both clinical observation and well-controlled social psychology experiments demonstrate this impressively and conclusively. However, other dynamics may also be involved. The magnetic field produced by the heart can be detected anywhere on the surface of the body and also extends a number of feet away from the body, going out in all directions. When two people are within conversational distance, fluctuations in the heart signal of one correspond with fluctuations in the brain waves of the other. An even stronger relationship is found in the way the heart signals and brain waves of healers fluctuate with those of their clients. Information is being exchanged at a physical if often subconscious level. This information might serve as one source of "clinical intuition." Many intriguing experiments of this nature have been reported by the Institute of HeartMath in California and the Human Energy Systems Laboratory at the University of Arizona.

Virginia Larson, a psychologist trained by Rollo May, describes such attunement as "psychotherapeutic resonance." She tells the story that alerted her to this dynamic:

> A new client entered my office for the first appointment. I spontaneously began experiencing very subtle, unusual sensations in my own lower torso. Prior to this appointment I had completed a deep relaxation exercise, so I was quite aware when the subtle, tingly sensations began. I first reflected inwardly trying to discover the source of the mysterious sensa-

175

tions. I asked myself if the new client reminded me of someone I had previously known. I searched myself to ascertain if my own personal memories were related to the tingly sensations. Then I bracketed the experience noting it, watching it, and reflecting further upon it. Finally, my curiosity was overpowering. At a seemingly appropriate point, I described my experience to the young woman client, and asked if my experience had some meaning for her. The young woman immediately replied, "Oh yes, I have cancer of the cervix, and I've been having chemotherapy there."

The *non-specific* factors that are involved in the therapeutic relationship have always been recognized as an important ingredient in the healing process. Possessing the tools to focus on the energetic dimension of the therapeutic relationship is a potential contribution that energy psychology holds for the healing arts.

VIII. Meridians and the Emotions

176

Each meridian tends to be associated with a particular emotion or theme, and you can significantly enhance the therapy if you use a verbal affirmation targeted for this emotion or theme at the same time you apply the energy intervention for that meridian.

Agree _ Disagree

Commentary. Eighty percent agreed that specific meridians are associated with particular emotions or themes and that understanding these relationships is clinically relevant. Less than 1 percent disagreed, with 19 percent in the middle or offering no opinion.

Some practitioners are particularly taken by the elegance of energy treatments. Mentally access the problem that causes a disturbed emotional response, stimulate a set of points on the surface of the skin, and the disturbed emotional response is permanently reprogrammed. No insight required. No messy emotions to process. Just tap them away.

Other practitioners, not as persuaded that this streamlined approach is likely to be reliable in a high enough proportion of cases, add other elements. These often address the emotions that are involved with the target problem. Because of the possible relationships between specific meridians and specific emotions—delineated in the "five element theory" that is at the conceptual heart of traditional Chinese medicine (see p. 234)—an energy-informed approach to the emotions may have special strengths.

Still, many energy-oriented psychotherapists do not utilize these methods. The methods require an assessment of which meridians are involved with the problem, and not all practitioners make meridian assessments. By understanding the constellation of meridians involved in a problem, and its emotional and thematic implications, however, the dynamics of the problem can often be more deeply understood. And as with other energy interventions, relatively straightforward techniques can be used for intervening, thus shifting the energetic underpinnings of the emotional response. Combining these with carefully formulated affirmations adds a cognitive component to the intervention that more meaningfully involves the client's conscious mind in the therapeutic process, while bringing additional advantages that are associated with cognitive therapy.

IX. The Role of Insight in Energy-Based Psychotherapy

When the presenting problem is an unwanted emotional response that easily lends itself to energy interventions, and you know the client to be a stable, psychologically well-integrated individual, and you have established good rapport, one option is to begin the energy treatments, attempting to "tap away" the problem. Another is to examine the role of the problem in the client's life. What is your inclination:

| Tap It | | Examine in |
| Away | | Depth |

Commentary. Ten percent were inclined to treat the problem without examining its meaning. Fifteen percent would tend to first examine the issue in depth. Sixty-five percent were in the middle and 10 percent did not offer an opinion. Parenthetically, among lay people who self-apply energy interventions, a far larger proportion undoubtedly does so before examining the target problem in depth.

Issues concerning the importance of clinical insight emerge not only with energy interventions but also in other physically based psychological interventions, such as in the decision to prescribe psychiatric medication. It is gratifying to be able to provide a "quick fix." Clients like this. Therapists like it. Clinical outcomes are often satisfactory. A large proportion of therapists, however, believe that many of the emotions people want to overcome, such as grief or anger, play a constructive role in the client's psychic ecology and need to be fully processed rather than short-circuited by "cutting them off at the energies."

These clinicians routinely devote substantial time and attention to examining the role of the problem in the person's life prior to any energy interventions. Some, on the other hand, feel there is no concern about robbing a person of needed insight or lessons by "tapping away" unwanted emotional responses. They point out that the requirements for psychological maturation are not so easily cheated: life has a way of enforcing the necessary steps no matter how hard a person may try to circumvent them. Nor is it that easy to tap away emotions that are intricately woven into a larger issue without examining and understanding that larger issue and its various aspects.

While staying alert to the role of emotional problems in the client's life is always advised, the degree of discussion prior to energy interventions is a matter of clinical judgment, and energy interventions are often applied after a minimal amount of analysis. Some practitioners, in fact, see neutralizing emotional turmoil as a way of supporting rather than blocking insight and understanding.

178

X. Energy Psychology Concepts

1. **Neurological Disorganization:** Correcting for neurological disorganization is critical in at least 10 percent of cases before other energy interventions will yield the desired results.

Agree _____ Disagree

2. **Psychological Reversals:** Correcting for psychological reversals is critical in at least 10 percent of cases before other energy interventions will yield the desired results.

Agree _____ Disagree

3. **Energetically Toxic Substances:** Addressing "energy toxins" in the client's environment is critical in at least 10 percent of cases where other energy interventions are not yielding the desired results.

Agree _____ Disagree

Commentary. Forty-five percent felt it is sometimes critical to correct for neurological disorganization, no one disagreed, 35 percent were in the middle, and 20 percent offered no opinion. Eighty-five percent felt that corrections for psychological reversals are sometimes important, 1 percent felt they are not, and 14 percent were in the middle or offered no opinion. Forty percent felt that corrections for energy toxins are sometimes critical, 60 percent were in the middle.

Neurological disorganization, psychological reversals, and energetically toxic substances are terms used primarily within energy psychology. The relative importance placed on each varies considerably from practitioner to practitioner. Other healing modalities often address corresponding dynamics using their own terminology.

Most psychotherapists, for instance, stay attuned for internal conflicts the client might have or develop about the treatment goal (the essential dynamic in a psychological reversal). Such conflict, when it arises, must be addressed in one way or another for treatment to proceed effectively, regardless of the treatment approach. Energy psychology seems to provide a surprisingly simple and straightforward method for resolving the energetic as well as cognitive dimensions of conflict around a treatment goal.

Practitioners of energy psychology tend to stay more closely attuned to the effects of subclinical disturbances in the client's neurochemistry than those of other forms of psychotherapy because energy interventions are less effective when there is "static" in the system, whether caused by internal imbalances (neurological disorganization) or environmental substances ("energy toxins"). As with psychological reversals, relatively straightforward procedures are available for energetically rebalancing the subclinical disturbances to optimize the brain's chemistry and the body's energies for subsequent interventions that directly target the presenting problem.

179

XI. The Role of the Past

1. Some practitioners prefer to focus the initial energy intervention on a current problem rather than childhood events, even with issues that probably trace to formative events in the client's past. They feel that those issues will come up in their own time. Others feel the interventions will be more decisive if they start with formative events. What is your inclination?

Current _____ Formative
Problem   Events

2. In at least the occasional case, the presenting problem will never be fully resolved until a past life issue has been resolved.

Agree _ Disagree

Commentary. Sixty percent in the survey were inclined to begin with the current problem, 10 percent on formative events, and 30 percent reported being in the middle. Thirty percent believed that, for at least some patients, past life issues must be treated before the presenting problem can be resolved; 10 percent disagreed; 45 percent indicated that they were closer to the middle; and 15 percent did not offer an opinion.

Energy psychology, in its most basic format, is psychodynamically atheoretical. It is not rooted in any particular assumptions about the relative roles of childhood experience, genetics, or environment in the origin of psychological problems. Again, as with traditional Chinese medicine, its most venerable ancestor, the theoretical core of energy psychology is: *Whatever the presenting problem, it has a counterpart in the client's energy system and can be treated at that level.*

However, many clinicians and non-clinicians believe that understanding current issues and problems in the context of one's life story is an essential part of the human journey. Using energy interventions like a drug for suppressing problems that will fester and later emerge, often more urgently and destructively, has been identified as a potential hazard of these potent techniques. With serious psychological disturbances, in particular, great caution must be exercised regarding the role of the past. Focusing on a current life difficulty with someone who has been multiply traumatized, for instance, may unearth emotional damage that an inexperienced practitioner is not prepared to address. For these, as well as numerous other reasons, many of the energy therapists who helped in the development of *EPI* conduct a thorough clinical interview before commencing with energy treatments, especially when serious disturbances are suspected. Some of these practitioners favor the strategy of energetically resolving emotional problems from the past, one by one, before current problems are directly confronted.

Instances in which a focus on a purported "past life" issue has helped to resolve a current psychological difficulty are reported so frequently now that they warrant mention, particularly since energy psychology seems to be well suited for addressing such issues. Whether you view the stories told under hypnosis, in "channelings," and through spontaneous memories as

180

metaphors or evidence, the phenomenon appears often enough that you are likely to encounter it in your own practice with clients who otherwise seem to exhibit sound judgment and perceptions. And many reports suggest that treating unresolved trauma that the client understands to have originated in a past life, using energy interventions exactly as they would be used for any other issue from the past, has had a positive impact on a current problem.

XII. Appropriate Issues for Energy Psychology

Successful energy interventions have been most widely reported in the treatment of anxiety-related disorders, such as generalized anxiety disorder, phobias, panic disorder, and PTSD. Many psychotherapists use energy psychology interventions primarily for these diagnoses and use other modalities the remainder of the time. Others find ways to apply energy-based interventions to virtually any conceivable problem, from personality disorders to spiritual alienation. Where do you draw the line?

Anxiety-Related Disorders	Virtually Any Psychological Problem or Goal

Commentary. Less than 1 percent of those in the survey limit treatment to anxiety-related disorders only. About 15 percent indicated that they use the methods with a broader range of issues than anxiety-related disorders but not with every presenting problem. Approximately 85 percent reported that they have found ways to apply the methods to virtually any psychological problem or goal.

In the South American study, initial impressions were that energy interventions are more effective than other therapies for treating anxiety-related disorders and for working with specific emotions, such as excessive anger, guilt, jealousy, fear, grief, or shame. Energy interventions were considered to be approximately as effective as other therapies in treating mild to moderate reactive depression, learning skills and motor skills disorders, substance abuse disorders, and eating disorders. For these diagnoses, the South American team attempts to integrate the strengths of energy methods with the strengths of other selected therapies. Energy interventions were considered less effective than other therapies for major depression, bipolar disorders, personality disorders, dissociative identity disorder, and psychotic disorders. The South American group tends to use energy methods only as an adjunctive therapy for these diagnoses. However, the energy therapy community is continually reporting in its literature and professional meetings new strategies for more effectively applying energy interventions for every conceivable diagnostic category. In addition, the impressions from the South American study are based on very early observations, are continually being refined, and also may not generalize to other contexts.

XIII. Multiple Energy Systems

1. The meridians are generally the most important energy system for energy-based interventions.

    Agree _____ Disagree

2. The chakras are generally the most important energy system for energy-based interventions.

    Agree _____ Disagree

3. It is sometimes important to assess which energy system—meridian, chakras, aura, radiant circuits, basic grid—is most involved with the problem before formulating an intervention.

    Agree _____ Disagree

4. If you thoroughly balance one of the systems, say the meridians or the chakras, the other energy systems will generally become balanced in a chain-like reaction.

    Agree _____ Disagree

Commentary. Fifty-five percent were in the middle regarding the relative importance of the meridians, with only 1 percent stating they were the most important system, 25 percent stating they were not, and 19 percent not offering an opinion. Sixty-five percent were in the middle regarding the importance of the chakras, with no one saying they were the most important system, about 2 percent stating they were not, and 33 percent not offering an opinion. Fifteen percent felt it is important to assess which system to treat first, 15 percent did not, 60 percent were in the middle, and

10 percent did not offer an opinion. Twenty percent believe that bringing one energy system into balance will balance other systems in a chain-like reaction, 55 percent did not, and 25 percent were in the middle or did not offer an opinion.

Reports from societies throughout history, as well as from people who clairvoyantly see or sense the body's energies, suggest that many interrelated energy systems affect health, psychological states, and well-being. At least eight discrete energies have been identified in one society or healing tradition or another (Eden, 1999). Most well known within Western culture are the meridians, the chakras, and the aura or biofield. Others include the basic grid, the five elements or five rhythms, the Celtic weave, the triple warmer system, and the strange flows or radiant circuits.

Sophisticated energy healers suggest that there are times and reasons for concentrating specifically upon one system or another. Most of the early work in energy psychology focused on the meridians, tracing to Callahan's and Diamond's training in Applied Kinesiology, which pioneered an accessible method for diagnosing the flow of meridian energies. The chakras and aura have also received substantial attention. Practitioners trained to work with multiple systems report that thoroughly balancing and optimizing any specific system is likely to have a positive impact on the entire energy system. They also suggest that there are times to carefully select where to focus. The radiant circuits, for instance, are involved with feeling joy, and getting them into an optimal balance and flow may hasten the effects of other treatments for overcoming depression and dysphoria. Trauma that has damaged the basic grid may never be fully healed until the grid energies have been repaired. The triple warmer, which is not only a meridian but also functions as an independent system, governing fight-or-flight, survival habits, and the immune response, may interfere with other interventions until it is brought into harmony with the treatment.

183

XIV. Licensing Energy-Based Psychotherapists

People who provide the public with energy psychology sessions for a fee should be licensed psychotherapists or other health care professionals who have been trained in depth in the diagnosis and treatment of psychological problems.

Agree _____ Disagree

Commentary. Twenty percent of those surveyed felt that practitioners should be licensed, 25 percent did not, and 55 percent were in the middle.

Whether you feel that the techniques of energy psychology should be tightly controlled by the professions or should be taught to every child in elementary school, the fact is that the techniques are becoming widely distributed. One of the major websites for bringing the methods to the lay public, Gary Craig's www.emofree.com, was receiving 1,500 to 2,000 hits per day in January 2002; the number had doubled by January 2003; and 3,000 to 5,000 people per month were downloading his training manual. Meanwhile, growing numbers of professionals are recognizing that an energy-based approach to psychological problems represents a new paradigm where people can readily influence the energies that affect their physical and mental health and they are supporting a wider distribution of the techniques.

While the methods are rapidly entering the public domain, this does not mean that standards, competence, and responsibility become less important. They, in fact, become more important. If you are offering services to the public, inform yourself, at a minimum, about issues such as scope of practice, informed consent, suicide risk assessment, and appropriate record-keeping within your professional context. Scope of practice, for instance, means that you stay within your area of competence. Just because you helped someone overcome an allergy to strawberries does not make you an allergy doctor. Just because you helped your neighbor shrink a growth on his back does not make you a cancer specialist. Just because you helped your mother-in-law overcome her depression after the canary died does not make you a bereavement counselor or qualify you to treat bipolar disorder. Many key professional issues are thoughtfully addressed in the American Professional Agency's newsletter on risk management for psychologists, called *Insight*. You can download current and back issues free, at www.americanprofessional.com/insight.htm.

It seems energy psychology is here to stay and, like it or not, it will not just be in the hands of professionals. So far, this has not thrilled the professions. But the professions are shooting themselves in the credibility foot by being the last to recognize that these methods are both effective and unusually rapid. And even if the lay public is learning the methods on their own, this does not mean that mental health professionals need be bypassed. They can and will play a crucial role as energy methods become more widely distributed. Here are four things you can do as a professional psychotherapist to stay relevant:

1. *Develop a high level of proficiency* for using energy methods effectively within a broad range of conditions. After solid training in classes and home study programs such as this one, establish back-up supervision, attend conferences, stay abreast of the field's emerging literature, and get on at least one e-list (see Links, p. 247) to keep yourself informed about new methods and applications.

2. *Develop an understanding of the issues underlying the various controversies* discussed in this chapter and their implications for practice. There are at least two sides to every controversy. Be ready to learn from each of them.

3. *Develop a familiarity with ongoing research*, particularly as it informs you about what works best and under what conditions. You can expect to see an explosion of studies over the next several years. A good resource for staying on top of significant new findings is the Association for Comprehensive Psychology's research site, www.energypsychresearch.org.

4. *Develop an integration of energy methods within the context of your broader training* in human behavior and psychiatric disturbances. Energy interventions are not a panacea. They are a powerful set of tools, and their application will be far more effective when informed by and integrated into other bases of knowledge and practice. For instance, practitioners who are reporting high success rates in treating recalcitrant obsessive-compulsive disorders are able to apply energy interventions to resolve formative traumatic experiences and then integrate other energy interventions with the patient's existing rituals and avoidance behaviors. Energy methods are also being introduced into educational settings, business, government, and health care. The same principles apply. By systematically integrating the methods into the body of knowledge and practice of each discipline, their impact will be more potent and their application more appropriate.

In brief, if you can deliver a versatile, competent, and well-informed approach to energy psychology, you can freely encourage the democratic distribution of these methods without ever becoming irrelevant. You may not always get the easiest cases, but the base of people who are looking for expert assistance with the methods emerging from energy psychology will only multiply.

Energy psychology is such a new addition to the clinical menagerie that we still do not quite know exactly what we have by the tail. Early findings, however, suggest that it may be a far more powerful, agile, and speedy creature than seems possible at first glance. While it might ultimately follow the path of a hundred therapies before it, which briefly captured the imagination of a large group of practitioners and then faded with a bit of time and empirical investigation, it seems to represent a new paradigm that is gradually becoming viable within scientific thinking as well as the broader culture. If its methods prove as effective and reliable as early reports suggest, we will find that we have, literally in our hands, some very strange-looking tools that may prove powerful allies for reducing psychic pain and empowering people to lead more fulfilling lives within the contexts destiny has provided them. It is a precious trust. Use it with love. Use it with generosity. And know that the preliminary indications suggest that you can also use it with confidence.

Epilogue

Subtle Energy—Psychology's Missing Link

A RECENT MINI-REVOLUTION WITHIN PSYCHOLOGY has involved the emphatic recognition that positive thinking and "learned optimism" can be self-fulfilling. *Positive psychology*, as the trend is called (www.positivepsychology.org), can point to solid evidence showing that people who hold a positive attitude are more effective in the world, attain greater success, make more adaptive choices, stay healthier, and heal more quickly than people who are more negative in their outlook (Seligman, 2002). Therapies that focus primarily on the problems and negative dimensions of a person's life may be emphasizing the wrong part of the story. A positive orientation leads to positive outcomes.

While psychology cannot lay exclusive claim to this eternal principle, it can help people to learn how to acquire attitudes that have positive repercussions in their lives. Insight, will, and intention—the commonsense approaches—are often not enough to change deep attitudes. Energy interventions, combined with methods such as visualization and affirmation, provide one of the most powerful ways of initiating such shifts. Stimulating energy points while mentally activating a problem or a goal appears to 1) create instantaneous neurological changes that, assuming the procedures are carried out properly, deactivate the biochemical underpinnings of the problem and 2) activate an energy field and related biochemical processes that promote the desired goal.

The methods can be used to promote desired psychological states as well as to counter undesired states. If a man visualizes himself attaining a well-considered goal and disturbances instantly occur in his kidney and stomach meridians, his focus and effectiveness will be compromised. If a technique is applied that remedies the energy disturbances, he can move toward the goal without conflict in the energies that influence his thought and behavior. With these obstacles removed, energy methods combined with active imagination can be introduced to surround him with an energy field that organizes his body's energy systems in a manner that corresponds with attaining the goal. Aligning the man's subtle energies with his positive intentions is a powerful intervention.

Subtle energy may long remain an elusive concept, but if you are told that a positive person carries an energy that enriches others, or a negative person carries an energy that is self-defeating, you intuitively know what is meant, even if you cannot precisely define or point to these energies. Energy psychology adds to our repertoire techniques for *identifying* the energies that are involved with psychological problems or goals and for *influencing* them to support desired outcomes. Energy interventions do not take the place of will and insight; they simply enter from a different angle and have strengths that purely psychological interventions do not have.

In that sense, energy psychology provides such a vital and missing link between intervention and outcome that psychological practices which are not attuned to the actions of subtle energy may one day be viewed as archaic. While we may never be able to adequately explain subjective experience in physical terms such as neurochemistry, or even subtle energy, an understanding of the role of subtle energy begins to fill in our understanding about many other mysteries, from the way that stimulating a set of acupuncture points can rapidly neutralize an unwanted emotional response, to the persuasively demonstrated role of focused intention on physical events, to the equally well-established telepathic exchange of information, to the many reported instances where certain personality traits of an organ donor mysteriously appear in the organ recipient, to the way positive images and prayer can facilitate healing from a distance. Psychology does not have ready explanations for such phenomena, and some formulation of an energy field that holds information—perhaps with attributes we can barely imagine, such as a macro-level version of quantum nonlocality or unfamiliar space-time relationships—is the probable missing link.

Epilogue

The nature of subtle energies is still shrouded in mystery, but enough is known to suggest that they influence physical health and can be harnessed to help people overcome mental problems and increase mental capacities. Subtle energies may even prove to be a link between life in a physical body and nature's archetypal or spiritual realms. A whole universe of subtle energies might, in fact, be waiting to be explored, and skillfully working with such energies is already showing great promise for empowering people to influence their own feelings, thoughts, and behavior in desired ways.

A Skeptic's Journey

MY PERSONAL VOYAGE INTO THE PERSPECTIVE expressed in *Energy Psychology Interactive* occurred over many years and with much resistance. I happened to marry a woman (Donna Eden) who was destined as it turned out to become one of the world's most renowned natural healers. For the first nineteen years or so of our relationship, I did not know what to make of her work. I did witness people coming from all over the world with serious illnesses report improvement after a session or two, but I explained it to myself in terms of her charisma, deep empathy, and healing presence. I did not think it was a system that could be taught or replicated, and the "subtle energy" explanations seemed more confusing than clarifying.

Donna was receiving overtures to write a book. She kept passing up these opportunities, for a number of reasons: Her healing work was all-consuming. Conceptualizing was not her forte. And she did not want to hold herself up as being particularly special (she believes that everyone is born with the capacity to see energy as she does, but that the capacity is usually lost very early in a culture that does not validate the experience), plus she is allergic to having people put her in a guru role. One evening, however, after telling me about her four clients that day, each of whom took a somewhat miraculous turn, she said, "You know, David, it would be a shame for my work to die with me." I mark that comment as the point where she became open to describing her approach in a book.

When she had firmly decided to move forward, she asked me, as the conceptualizer in the family, to help her write the book. The next 18 months were an amazing process for me. I interviewed her, day after day after day. I could not pose a question that she could not persuasively answer from within her energy paradigm. Granted, she has one little quirk that is hard to verify, her claim to a lifelong ability to "see" energy as clearly as you are seeing the words on this page. While she has again and again made diagnoses that were later confirmed medically by simply looking at a person's body, the ability to see and read energies is so far outside my own experience that I cannot directly verify it. But given a great deal of indirect evidence, such as her accurate medical diagnoses based on very little other information and impressive cure rate, I finally came to accept that it is so.

Once the ability to read and derive meaningful information from the body's energies is accepted, then Donna's approach turns out to have a strong internal logic. In our interviews, I realized that she operates according to a set of principles that are based on empirical observation and that can be systematized and taught to others. Now with the book widely distributed and many students trained, there is much anecdotal evidence that the procedures work whether self-applied or applied by individuals who do not match Donna's charisma or "healing presence."

192

The book was released in January 1999, and we headed out for a six-month book and workshop tour. I went on sabbatical from my private practice as a clinical psychologist in Ashland, Oregon. As the close of the six months approached, the book was rapidly becoming the classic in its field and the demands on Donna to speak and teach were compelling. I returned to Ashland, and with strong misgivings, closed what had been a deeply satisfying clinical practice in order to support her work, which seemed to be hitting a cultural nerve. I was sad that I might be leaving my own career forever. I was in my fifties and did not know where this would lead me. Where it led was right back into psychology. Many of Donna's students were psychotherapists who were applying energy interventions to psychological issues. Through their influence, I began to study with some of the pioneers in this area. I found it daunting. While I was now open to an energy paradigm, as I educated myself about the new field, which had developed independent of Donna's contributions—they are just both part of the same Zeitgeist—I found that despite this being a relatively new area, it was already rife with warring factions, incompatible explanations, and deep schisms about procedures and appropriate claims.

Something else happened, however, that in my mind overshadowed the field's confusion. The outcomes I was seeing were remarkable. Because I read the field's fractionated literature before I learned how to apply its methods, I was quite skeptical at first. But I began to obtain results for a wide range of complaints that were more rapid and consistent with anxiety-related disorders in particular than anything I'd seen in some 30 years of practice. One of my first sessions outside of a supervised setting was with one of Donna's friends who had recently been spurned by the first man who had opened her heart in years. She was in agony and had been for several weeks. Within an hour of relatively mechanical procedures, the spell was broken. She still felt the loss of a dream. She still missed his love and presence. But she radiated in her relief ("My heart isn't hurting!!!"), and she was no longer incapacitated. After she returned home, her responses to him were no longer pleading and bereft. I'd never before facilitated such a healing of intense heartbreak in a single session. I now have had many cases that were similarly dramatic and have interviewed dozens of practitioners whose claims corroborate my personal experiences. This does not constitute scientific proof, but it is not a one-person medicine show either.

Energy Psychology Interactive began as my way of trying to learn about the field and sort through all of the claims and confusion. Bringing on an Advisory Board with many of energy psychology's leaders and pioneers transformed my computer into a lightening rod for the field's controversies. It turned out that learning how to reach consensus between Donna's and my deeply contrasting intellectual styles was great practice for this task. The Advisory Board, however, was wonderful in positioning themselves behind a project whose purpose was to draw the field together. Many many hours were devoted freely and intelligently. *Energy Psychology Interactive* is the product. It is the most comprehensible statement I am capable of pulling together at this point about the state of the art in this very new and potentially revolutionary area of study.

193

With the book and CD in galley form, I sent the program to one of the most respected clinical psychologists of the past half century. His reply began, "If your claims turn out to be true, it will stand everything I have ever learned and believed about human behavior and physiology on its head." He went on to pose strong doubts about the program's claims. In my response, I shared some of this history and closed by noting, "I am only one witness, but I have been slowly persuaded that the findings from this area of investigation will, as you put it, 'stand' some of our understanding 'about human behavior and physiology on its head.' But I should mention that the claim that perhaps should first turn our understanding about human physiology 'on its head' is anesthesia through acupuncture, which is now used throughout the world and has been widely documented in procedures from appendectomies to brain surgery. Those reports may be challenging for Westerners to assimilate into their worldview. But from there, entertaining the possibility that anxiety can be reduced by stimulating a set of acupuncture points is only a small conceptual step."

194

APPENDIX I

Articles, Lists, and Resources

First Large-Scale Preliminary Study of Energy Psychology   197
Energy Psychology: Theory, Indications, Evidence   199
The Body's Energies   215
Principles of Energy Medicine   218
Orienting a New Client to an Energy-Based Approach   220
Informed Consent   223
Opening Phases Task Sequence   226
Tapping Instruction Sheet   227
A Basic Tapping Sequence   230
Neurological Disorganization Summary   231
Psychological Reversal Summary   232
Bridging and Anchoring Techniques   233
The Meridians and the Emotions   234
Advanced Meridian Intervention Flow Chart   241
Meridian Treatment Checklist   242
Common Elements of Energy Sessions   244
Taking Energy Psychology Another Step   245
Energy Interventions and Other Forms of Psychotherapy   249
Representative Approaches within Energy Psychology   251
The Future of Energy Psychology   252
The CD's Embedded Topics   255

First Large-Scale Preliminary Study of Energy Psychology

IN PRELIMINARY CLINICAL TRIALS involving some 31,400 patients from 11 allied treatment centers in South America during a 14-year period, a variety of randomized, controlled pilot studies were conducted. In one of these, approximately 5,000 patients diagnosed at intake with an anxiety disorder were randomly assigned to an experimental group (imagery and self-statements paired with the manual stimulation of selected acupuncture points) or a control group (Cognitive Behavior Therapy/medication) using standard randomization tables and, later, computerized software. Ratings were given by independent clinicians who interviewed each patient at the close of therapy, at 1 month, at 3 months, at 6 months, and at 12 months. The raters made a determination of complete remission of symptoms, partial remission of symptoms, or no clinical response. The raters did not know if the patient received CBT/medication or energy interventions. They knew only the initial diagnosis, the symptoms, and the severity, as judged by the intake staff. At the close of therapy:

- 63% of the control group were judged as having improved.
- 90% of the experimental group were judged as having improved.

- 51% of the control group were judged as being symptom free.
- 76% of the experimental group were judged as being symptom free.

At one-year follow-up, the patients receiving acupoint treatments were less prone to relapse or partial relapse than those receiving CBT/medication, as indicated by the independent raters' assessments and corroborated by brain imaging and neurotransmitter profiles from a sampling of the patients. In a related pilot study by the same team, the length of treatment was substantially shorter with energy therapy and related methods than with CBT/medication (mean = 3 sessions vs. mean = 15 sessions).

If subsequent research corroborates these early findings, it will be a notable development since CBT/medication is currently the established standard of care for anxiety disorders and the greater effectiveness of the energy approach suggested by this study would be highly significant. The preliminary nature of these findings must, however, be emphasized. The study was initially envisioned as an exploratory in-house assessment of a new method and was not designed with publication in mind. Not all the variables that need to be controlled in robust research were tracked, not all criteria were defined with rigorous precision, the record-keeping was relatively informal, and source data were not always maintained. Nonetheless, the studies all used randomized samples, control groups, and blind assessment. The findings were so striking that the team decided to report them.

198

One other intriguing observation was that, in a sample of patients, the research team found that the superior responses attained with the acupoint treatments compared with the CBT/medication treatments were corroborated by electrical and biochemical measures. Brain mapping revealed that subjects whose acupuncture points were stimulated tended to be distinguished by a general pattern of wave normalization throughout the brain which, interestingly, not only persisted at 12-month follow-up, but became more pronounced. An associated pattern was found in neurotransmitter profiles. With generalized anxiety disorder, for example, acupoint stimulation was followed by norepinephrine levels going down to normal reference values and low serotonin going up. Parallel electrical and biochemical patterns were less pronounced in the CBT/medication group. While these reports are as preliminary as they are provocative, if subsequent research supports them, key mechanisms explaining the surprising effectiveness of acupuncture-based treatment approaches will have been identified. The principal investigator was Joaquín Andrade, M.D. A more complete report follows.

Energy Psychology:
Theory, Indications, Evidence

Joaquín Andrade, M.D.
David Feinstein, Ph.D.

DESPITE ITS ODD-SEEMING PROCEDURES and eye-raising claims, evidence is accumulating that energy-based psychotherapy, which involves stimulating acupuncture points or other energy systems while bringing troubling emotions or situations to mind,[1] is more effective in the treatment of anxiety disorders than the current standard of care, which utilizes a combination of medication and cognitive behavior therapy. This paper:

1. Presents preliminary data supporting this assertion.
2. Discusses indications and contraindications for the use of energy therapy with anxiety as well as other conditions.
3. Speculates on the mechanisms by which
   a) tapping specific areas of the skin while
   b) a stimulus that triggers a disturbed emotional response is mentally accessed apparently alleviates certain psychological disorders.

A Winding Road to Effective Anxiety Treatment

The first author describes his initial encounter with panic disorder, in a crowded urban hospital emergency room, some 30 years ago: The patient was trembling, dizzy, and terrified, pleading, "Help me, Doc, I feel like I'm gonna die!" My medical training had not prepared me for this moment, and I emerged from it determined that I would have a better response the next time I was faced with a patient in acute panic.

This was the first step on a long and winding road. I studied with acknowledged experts on anxiety disorders, attended relevant professional meetings, talked with famous international specialists, read the books they recommended, did my own literature searches, prescribed medications, applied various forms of psychotherapy (from psychodynamic to Gestalt to NLP), learned acupuncture in China, made referrals to alternative practitioners (including those specializing in homeopathy, cranial sacral therapy, chiropractic, flower remedies, applied kinesiology, ozone therapy, and Ayurvedic), sent people on spiritual retreats, used all forms of machines from biofeedback to electric acupuncture, even resorted to sensory deprivation (confining a panic patient in a sensory deprivation tank is a distinguishing sign of a therapist's desperation).

The consistent finding: disappointing results. My colleagues and I were making a difference for perhaps 40 to 50 percent of these people, albeit with multiple relapses, partial cures, and many who never completed treatment. Later, we combined alprazolam and fluoxetine with cognitive behavior therapy, obtaining slightly better outcomes. But never were we able to reach the 70 percent in 20 sessions we had read about. Then came Eye Movement Desensitization and Reprocessing (EMDR), which we learned as an almost secret practice some friends were doing in an East Coast hospital. We began to get more satisfactory responses, yet along with them, disturbing abreactions.

We then learned about tapping selected acupuncture points while having the patient imagine anxiety-producing situations. It was a huge leap forward! We began to obtain unequivocal positive results with the majority of panic patients we treated. At first we used generic tapping sequences. Then tapping sequences tailored for panic. Then tapping sequences based on diagnosing the energy pathways involved in each patient's unique condition. All of these strategies yielded good results, slightly better with diagnosis-based sequences, averaging about a 70 percent success rate.

We found we could further enhance these encouraging outcomes by limiting sugar, coffee, and alcohol intake and prescribing a physical exercise program. We emphasized the cultivation of enjoyment. We showed our patients how Norman Cousins used laughter in his own healing and encouraged them to engage in hearty laughter for five minutes twice each day. We introduced natural metabolic substances, such as L-tryptophan, L-arginine, and glutamic acid. For rapid symptom relief in severe cases, we found we could combine a brief initial course of medication with the tapping.

With this regime, we have been able to surpass the 70 percent mark. And we have gathered substantial experience indicating that stimulating selected acupoints is at the heart of the treatment and is often sufficient as the sole intervention. Over a 14-year period, our multidisciplinary team, including 36 therapists,[2] has applied tapping techniques (we also use the term "brief sensory emotional interventions") with some 31,400 patients in eleven treatment centers in Uruguay and Argentina. The most prevalent diagnosis[3] was anxiety disorder.[4] For 29,000 of these patients, our documentation included an intake history, a record of the procedures administered, clinical responses, and follow-up interviews (by phone or in person) at one month, three months, six months, and twelve months. We have also systematically conducted numerous clinical trials. Our conclusion, in brief: No reasonable clinician, regardless of school of practice, can disregard the clinical responses that tapping elicits in anxiety disorders (over 70 percent improvement in a large sample in 11 centers involving 36 therapists over 14 years).

201

Clinical Trials

The clinical trials were conducted for the purpose of internal validation of the procedures as protocols were being developed. When acupuncture stimulation methods were introduced to the clinical team, many questions were raised, and a decision was made to conduct clinical trials comparing the new methods with the CBT/medication approach that was already in place for the treatment of anxiety. These were pilot studies, viewed as possible precursors for future research, but were not themselves designed with publication in mind. Specifically, not all the variables that need to be controlled in robust research were tracked, not all criteria were defined with rigorous precision, the record-keeping was relatively informal, and source data were not always maintained. Nonetheless, the studies all used randomized samples,[5] control groups,[6] and blind assessment.[7] The findings were so striking that they are worth reporting.

Over two dozen separate studies were conducted. In the largest of these (and some of the other studies were subsets of this study), approximately 5,000 patients were randomly assigned to receive CBT and medication or tapping treatments.[8] Approximately 2,500 patients were in each group, with diagnoses including panic, agoraphobia, social phobias, specific phobias, obsessive compulsive disorders, generalized anxiety disorders, PTSD, acute stress disorders, somatoform disorders, eating disorders, ADHD, and addictive disorders.[9] The study was conducted over a 5½-year period. Patients were followed by telephone or office interviews at 1 month after treatment, 3 months, 6 months, and 12 months. At the close of therapy, "positive clinical responses" (ranging from complete relief to partial relief to short relief with relapses) were found in 63 percent of those treated with CBT and medication and in 90 percent of those treated with tapping techniques. Complete freedom from symptoms was found in 51 percent and 76 percent, respectively.[10] At one-year follow-up, the gains observed with the tapping treatments were less prone to relapse or partial relapse than those with CBT/medication, as indicated by the independent raters' assessments and corroborated by brain imaging and neurotransmitter profiles.[11]

The number of sessions required to attain the positive outcomes also varied between the two approaches. In one of the studies, 96 patients with specific phobias were treated with a conventional CBT/medication approach and 94 patients with the same diagnosis were treated using a combination of tapping techniques and an NLP method called *visual-kinesthetic dissociation* (the patient mentally plays a short "film" of the phobic reaction while watching it from a distance, and then rapidly rewinds and replays it, gradually entering the film, until a "dissociation" from the triggering event is effected). Positive results[12] were obtained with 69 percent of the patients treated with CBT/medication within 9 to 20 sessions, with a mean of 15 sessions. Positive results were obtained with 78 percent of the patients treated with the tapping and dissociation techniques within 1 to 7 sessions, with a mean of 3 sessions.[13] The course of treatment for tapping throughout all trials was generally between 2 and 4 sessions; the course of treatment for CBT/medication was generally between 12 and 18 sessions. Tapping patients were also taught simple sequences to apply at home.

Standard medications for anxiety (benzodiazepines, including diazepam, alprazolam, and clonazepan) were given to 30 patients with generalized anxiety disorder (the three drugs were randomly assigned to subgroups of 10 patients each). Outcomes were compared with 34 generalized anxiety disorder patients who received tapping treatment. The medication group had 70 percent positive responses compared with 78.5 percent for the tapping group. About half the medication patients suffered from side effects and rebounds upon discontinuing the medication. There were no side effects in the tapping group, though one patient had a paradoxical response (increase of anxiety).

Specific elements of the treatment were also investigated. The order that the points must be stimulated, for instance, was investigated by treating 60 phobic patients with a standard 5-point protocol while varying the order in which the points were stimulated with a second group of 60 phobic patients. Positive clinical responses for the two groups were 76.6 percent and 71.6 percent, respectively, showing no significant difference for the order in which the points were stimulated. In other studies, varying the number of points that were stimulated, the specific points, and the inclusion of typical auxiliary interventions such as the "Nine Gamut Procedure" did not result in significant differences between groups, although diagnosis of which energy points were involved in the problem led to treatments that had slightly more favorable outcomes. The working hypothesis of the treatment team at the time of this writing is that for many disorders, such as specific phobias, wide variations can be employed in terms of the points that are stimulated and the specifics of the protocol. For a smaller number of disorders, such as OCD and generalized social anxiety, precise protocols must be formulated and adhered to for a favorable clinical response.

In a study comparing tapping with acupuncture needles, 40 panic patients received tapping treatments on pre-selected acupuncture points. A group of 38 panic patients received acupuncture stimulation using needles on the same points. Positive responses were found for 78.5 percent from the tapping group, 50 percent from the needle group.

While it must again be emphasized that these were pilot studies, they lend corroboration to other clinical trials that have yielded promising results regarding the efficacy of energy-based psychotherapy, such as those conducted by Sakai et al. (n=714, representing a wide range of clinical conditions) and Johnson et al. (n=105, all PTSD victims of ethnic violence in Albania, Kosovo). Both of these studies were published in the October 2001 issue of the *Journal of Clinical Psychology*[14] and their full text, along with that of related studies, can be downloaded from www.tftrx. com/5ref.html. For an overview of current research in energy psychology, maintained by the Association for Comprehensive Energy Psychology, visit www.EnergyPsychResearch.org.

Indications and Contraindications

The follow-up data on the patients coming from the 11 centers in South America included subjective scores after the termination of treatment by independent raters. The ratings, based on a scale of 1 to 5, estimated the effectiveness of the energy interventions as contrasted with other methods that might have been used.[15] The numbers indicate that the rater believed that the energy interventions produced:

1. Much better results than expected with other methods.
2. Better results than expected with other methods.
3. Similar results to those expected with other methods.
4. Lesser results than expected with other methods (only use in conjunction with other therapies).
5. No clinical improvement at all or contraindicated.

It must be emphasized that the following indications and contraindications for energy therapy are tentative guidelines based largely on the initial exploratory research and these informal assessments. In addition, the outcome studies have not been precisely replicated in other settings, and the degree to which the findings can be generalized is uncertain. Nonetheless, based upon the use of tapping techniques with a large and varied clinical population in 11 settings in two countries over a 14-year period, the following impressions can serve as a preliminary guide for selecting which clients are good candidates for acupoint tapping. There is also considerable overlap between these tentative guidelines and other published reports.[16]

Rating of 1—"Much better results than with other methods." Many of the categories of anxiety disorder were rated as responding to energy interventions much better than to other modalities. Among these are panic disorders with and without agoraphobia, agoraphobia without history of panic disorder, specific phobias, separation anxiety disorders, post-traumatic stress disorders, acute stress disorders, and mixed anxiety-depressive disorders. Also in this category were a variety of other emotional problems, including fear, grief, guilt, anger, shame, jealousy, rejection, painful memories, loneliness, frustration, love pain, and procrastination. Tapping techniques also seemed particularly effective with adjustment disorders, attention deficit disorders, elimination disorders, impulse control disorders, and problems related to abuse or neglect.

Rating of 2—"Better results than with other methods." Obsessive compulsive disorders, generalized anxiety disorders, anxiety disorders due to general medical conditions, social phobias and certain other specific phobias, such as a phobia of loud noises, were judged as not responding quite as well to energy interventions as did other anxiety disorders, but they were still rated as being more responsive to an energy approach than they are to other methods. Also in this category were learning disorders, communication disorders, feeding and eating disorders of early childhood, tic disorders, selective mutism, reactive detachment disorders of infancy or early childhood, somatoform disorders, factitious disorders, sexual dysfunction, sleep disorders, and relational problems.

Rating of 3—"Similar to the results expected with other methods." Energy interventions seemed to fare about equally well as other therapies commonly used for mild to moderate reactive depression, learning skills disorders, motor skills disorders, and Tourette's syndrome. Also in this category were substance abuse–related disorders, substance-induced anxiety disorders, and eating disorders. For these conditions, a number of treatment approaches can be effectively combined to draw upon the strengths of each.

Rating of 4—"Lesser results than expected with other methods." The clinicians' post-treatment ratings suggest that for major endogenous depression, personality disorders, and dissociative disorders, other therapies are superior as the primary treatment approach. Energy interventions might still be useful when used in an adjunctive manner.

Rating of 5—"No clinical improvement or contraindicated." The clinicians' ratings of energy therapy with psychotic disorders, bipolar disorders, delirium, dementia, mental retardation, and chronic fatigue indicated no improvement. While anecdotal reports that people within these diagnostic categories have been helped with a range of life problems are numerous, and seasoned healers might find ways of adapting energy methods to treat the conditions themselves, the typical psychotherapist trained only in the rudimentary use of acupoint stimulation should have special training or understanding for working with these populations before applying energy methods.

Other Guidelines. Even though the above guidelines are preliminary and heuristic, diagnosis is clearly a key indicator of how and when to bring energy-based psychotherapy into the treatment setting. As part of the diagnostic work-up, co-morbidities should also be carefully identified. Their presence of course influences the treatment strategy. Even in cases where energy interventions are not the treatment of choice, they can be used as a complement to other psychotherapies, drugs, and medical procedures. In these cases, it is useful to orient them around well-defined emotional issues and it is critical to keep other treatment team members informed about the energy treatment and its purpose. While interventions that tap acupuncture points appear to be effective in alleviating a wide range of physical disorders, much as acupuncture with needles can be applied to illnesses ranging from allergies to cancer, strong caution must be used when addressing physical diseases or undiagnosed pain. Medical examinations and the participation of medical personnel is indicated when addressing any serious physical condition or symptoms that might prove to be the first evidence of a serious condition. One potential hazard is that tapping acupoints may bring about subjective improvement that ultimately wastes life-saving time.

Joseph Wolpe's Seminal Contribution to Energy Psychology

When Joseph Wolpe developed systematic desensitization in the 1950s, he provided the next several generations of clinicians their most potent single non-pharmacological tool for countering severe anxiety conditions. Patients were taught how to relax each of the body's major muscle groups. With the muscle groups relaxed, they would bring to mind a thought or image that evoked an item from the bottom of a hierarchy of anxiety-provoking situations they had prepared earlier. They would learn to shift the focus between *holding* the thought or image and *relaxing* the muscle groups until the thought or image was progressively associated with a relaxed response. They would then systematically move up the hierarchy, reconditioning the response to each thought or image by replacing the anxious or fearful response with a relaxed response.

This process is the closest cousin energy therapy has among traditional psychotherapeutic modalities. Both approaches bring a problematic emotion to mind and introduce a physical procedure that neutralizes the emotion. But energy therapy also has a much older relative, whose lineage substantially expands the range of problems that may be addressed and the precision with which they may be targeted. That progenitor is the practice of acupuncture.

Rather than to relax the *muscle tension* associated with anxiety or fear, energy therapy corrects for a disturbed pattern in the specific *energy path-*

ways or *meridians* that are affected when the client is mentally engaged with a problematic situation. For this reason, one of the strengths of energy-based psychotherapy is the range of emotional conditions with which it is effective. Each of the body's major energy pathways is believed to be associated with specific emotions and themes. A stimulus that brings a meridian out of harmony or balance (while this is a complex concept, terms such as *under-energy*, *over-energy*, and *stagnant energy* might each apply) also activates the emotion associated with that meridian. The treatment pairs the stimulus with an energy intervention that rebalances the meridian, bringing it back into coherence and harmony with the body's overall energy system. A disturbed meridian response is replaced by an undisturbed response. Just as deep muscle relaxation can neutralize a specific fear in systematic desensitization, calming a disturbed meridian can disengage the emotional reaction associated with that meridian.

It is because of the wide spectrum of emotions that are governed by the meridian system[17] that tapping interventions have a greater power and applicability than systematic desensitization. Systematic desensitization can neutralize anxiety-based responses by countering them with deep muscle relaxation, but that is the only key on its keyboard. Interventions capable of restoring balance to any of the major meridians can address the entire scale of human emotions, from anxiety and fear to anger, grief, guilt, jealousy, over-attachment, self-judgment, worry, sadness, and shame. Note the spectrum of problematic emotions for which the raters in the South American studies found energy interventions to produce "much better results than other methods." These impressions are corroborated by reports from practitioners in numerous other settings who have been impressed by the speed with which a wide range of problematic emotions can be overcome by using energy interventions.[18]

Possible Mechanisms

While a framework that links specific emotions with specific energy pathways requires a paradigm-leap for most Western psychotherapists, the hypothesis is central to traditional Chinese medicine, a 5,000-year-old method that is currently the most widely practiced medical approach on the planet. Its venerable though sometimes quaint concepts are now being blended with modern scientific understanding and empirical validation, and an approach is developing that holds great promise for Western medicine as well as for psychotherapy.

The most controversial idea that emerges for psychotherapy is that the body is surrounded and permeated by an *energy field which carries information.*[19] Disturbances in this energy field are said to be reflected in emotional disturbances. The concept of energy fields carrying information that impacts biological and psychological functioning is appearing independently in the writings of scientists from numerous disciplines, ranging from neurology to anesthesiology, from physics to engineering, and from physiology to medicine.[20] In energy psychology, this two-part formulation, in which biochemistry and invisible physical fields are believed to be working in tandem, has been used to explain the rapid changes that are often witnessed in long-standing emotional patterns. Changes in the energy field are understood as having the power to shift the *organization* of electrochemical processes.

Many of the electrochemical processes that are probably involved have been mapped.[21] When a person thinks about an emotional problem, activation signals can be registered by various brain-imaging techniques at the amygdala, hippocampus, orbital frontal cortex, and several other central nervous system structures. When tapping is simultaneously introduced, the receptors that are sensitive to pressure on the skin send an afferent signal, regulated by the calcium ion, through the medial lemniscus, that reaches the parietal cortex and from there is directed to other cortical and limbic regions. The interaction of these signals appears to cause a shift in the biochemical foundations of the problem.[22] One hypothesis is that the signal sent by tapping "collides" with the signal produced by thinking about the problem, introducing "noise" into the emotional process, which alters its nature and its capacity to produce symptoms. Enhanced serotonin secretion also correlates with tapping specific points.

Whether serotonin, the calcium ion, or the energy field (or some combination) is the primary player in the sequence by which tapping reconditions disturbed emotional responses to thoughts, memories, and events, early clinical trials suggest that easily replicated procedures seem to yield results that are more favorable than other therapies for a range of clinical conditions. Based on the preliminary findings in the South American treatment centers, new and more rigorous studies by the same team are planned or underway. Many are designed to corroborate the informal findings reported in this paper. Others will investigate new protocols for patients who have not responded well to more standardized energy interventions. Others will focus on the neurological correlates of energy interventions, using LORETA tomography and other brain imaging devices.

While much more investigation is still needed to understand and validate an energy approach, early indications are quite promising.

Notes

[1] "Energy psychology," "energy-based psychotherapy," and "energy therapy" all refer to the therapeutic modality represented, for instance, by the Association for Comprehensive Energy Psychology (www.energypsyche.org). Earlier therapeutic modalities within psychology and psychiatry that focus on the body's energy systems extend back at least to Wilhelm Reich and are seen in contemporary practices such as bioenergetics and Gestalt therapy.

[2] The initial group included 22 therapists. Of the 36 clinicians to eventually participate in the studies over the 14-year period, 23 were physicians (anxiety is typically treated by the primary care physician in Argentina and Uruguay; 5 of the 23 physicians were psychiatrists), 8 were "clinical psychologists" (in both countries, the use of this title requires the equivalent of a masters degree, substantial supervised clinical experience, and specialized credentials as a clinical psychologist), 3 were mental health counselors, and 2 were RNs. All of them had extended experience treating or assisting in the treatment of anxiety disorders. Their experience with energy psychology methods ranged from six months in the initial phases of the clinical trials to some who by the end had been using energy techniques for 14 years. Most were initially trained in Thought Field Therapy and later incorporated related techniques, generally customizing their approach as they gained experience. During the fourteen years, some of the 36 therapists were on staff the entire period, some on the initial team left, others came onto the team while the clinical trials were underway.

[3] Various assessment instruments were used over the course of the 14 years. However, in each clinical trial, the assessment methods were standardized. Careful clinical interviews were always taken, physical exams were given when indicated, and interview data were supplemented by scores from assessment instruments such as the Beck Anxiety Inventory, the Spielberger State-Trait Anxiety Index, SPIN for social phobias, and the Yale-Brown Obsessive-Compulsive Scale for OCD. The most objective assessment tool that was used involved pre- and post-treatment functional brain imaging (computerized EEG, evoked potentials, and topographic mapping).

[4] Anxiety disorders were defined as including panic disorders, post-traumatic stress disorders, specific phobias, social phobias, obsessive-compulsive disorders, and generalized anxiety disorders.

[5] Over the 14 years, a series of randomization methods were used for assigning patients to a treatment group or a control group. Simple randomization tables were used initially; increasingly sophisticated randomization software was subsequently introduced.

[6] Because the conventional treatment for anxiety—cognitive behavior therapy (CBT) plus medication—was already being used at the point the energy interventions were introduced to the clinical staffs, patients were randomly assigned for conventional CBT/medication treatment (which constituted the control group) or for energy-based treatment (which constituted the experimental group).

[7] The raters assessing the patient's progress at the close of therapy and in the follow-up interviews were clinicians who were not involved in the patient's treatment and were not aware of which treatment protocol had been administered. Both the patients and the raters were instructed not to discuss with one another the therapy procedures that had been used. The raters were given a close variant of the following instructions: "This patient was diagnosed with [detailed diagnosis, symptoms, and severity of the disorder as judged at intake] and a course of a given treatment was applied. Please assess if the patient is now asymptomatic, shows partial remission, or had no clinical response." Psychological testing and brain mapping were administered by still other individuals who were neither the patient's clinician nor rater.

[8] The clinicians were generally proficient in both CBT and energy methods. A team approach was used in which non-medical therapists worked with physicians who prescribed medications for the CBT patients. Patients receiving energy treatments did not receive medication. There was advance agreement among the clinical staff about the nature of CBT and about the kinds of tapping protocols that would be used with any specific subset of patients. The same clinician might provide CBT for one patient and an energy approach for another, but the two approaches were not mixed.

[9] In addition to clinical interviews and physical exams where indicated, the clinician would order specific assessment instruments that were judged as being most appropriate for measuring subsequent treatment gains based on the initial diagnosis. The Beck Anxiety Inventory was given to approximately 60 percent of these patients, but other scales, such as SPIN for social

phobias or the Yale-Brown Scale for OCD were administered instead when these diagnoses were suspected based on the intake interview.

[10] Clinical outcomes were assessed based upon interviews conducted by raters who were not involved in the therapy. These assessments were then compared with the pre- and post-treatment test scores and the pre- and post-treatment digitized brain mappings. Functional brain imaging was done with approximately 95 percent of the patients and can identify, for instance, excessive beta frequencies in the prefrontal and temporal regions, which is a typical profile of anxiety. Most recently, LORETA tomographies were introduced, allowing the identification of dysfunction in deeper structures, such as the amygdala and locus ceruleus.

While this aspect of the study could and will be the basis of future reports, in brief, the brain mapping correlated with other measures of improvement, specifically the psychological test data and the conclusions reached by the raters. The patients assessed as showing the greatest improvement also showed the largest reduction of beta frequencies.

The differences revealed by neuroimaging between the control group and the tapping group are perhaps the study's most provocative heuristic finding, and the research team is conducting further investigation into these differences. In brief, even when symptoms improved, the neurological profiles for the control group were only slightly modified from the initial pathological indicies. In the tapping group, however, the amelioration of symptoms *ran parallel* with modifications in the neurological profiles toward the normal reference range. The hypothesis now being investigated is that the tapping procedures somehow facilitate a deep, systemic homeostasis, as if the effect is not "suppression-augmentation" but rather a homeodynamic adaptation.

[11] Approximately 90 percent of the patients participated in follow-up interviews at one year. This high proportion is attributed to the relatively low mobility of the populations served, the intimate quality of the doctor-patient relationship in Uruguay and Argentina, and the persistence of the research team. Also, the follow-up interviews were most frequently conducted over the phone, with patients encouraged to come in for a more in-depth interview when relapses were reported.

Relapse or partial relapse was found more frequently in the control group than in the tapping group at each post-therapy assessment (3, 6, and 12 months). Partial relapses at one-year follow-up were 29 percent for the control group and 14 percent for the tapping group. Total relapses were 9 percent for the control group and 4 percent for the tapping group. This data is contaminated, however, by the administrative policy of inviting participants back for further treatment if the 3-month or 6-month follow-up interviews indicated relapse. Because both groups were given the opportunity for further treatment, the differences between the groups may, however, still be significant. The relapse data also varied depending on diagnosis. Disorders such as OCD and severe agoraphobia, for instance, were far more prone to relapse under either treatment condition than specific phobias, social phobias, learning disorders, or general anxiety disorder.

Differences in the stability of treatment gains between the groups were corroborated by electrical and biochemical measures. Brain mapping revealed that the tapping cases tended to be distinguished by a general pattern of wave normalization throughout the brain which, interestingly, not only persisted at 12-month follow-up but became more pronounced. An associated pattern was found in neurotransmitter profiles. With generalized anxiety disorder, for example, norepinephrine came down to normal reference values and low serotonin went up. Parallel electrical and biochemical patterns were not found in the control group.

[12] Results in this sub-study were assessed as in footnote 10. The number of sessions was determined by mutual agreement between the therapist and the patient that further treatment was not indicated.

[13] While in this particular sub-study the addition of the NLP technique may have skewed the results in favor of the tapping techniques, the overall findings with the 29,000 patients suggest that similar results are gained without the inclusion of the NLP technique.

[14] Although these articles were published along with scathing editorial critiques of the assessment techniques, case selection, data analysis, and overall design, others have found that despite these flaws, they are "fascinating preliminary reports from a clinical standpoint" (Hartung, J., and Galvin, M. *Energy Psychology and EMDR: Combining Forces to Optimize Treatment.* New York: Norton, 2003, p. 59).

[15] While subjective ratings of this nature certainly fall short of being established assessment instruments, the purpose of the ratings was to help the South American clinics generate guidelines for the use of energy interventions. The staff reports that these guidelines have proven administratively useful and clinically trustworthy, although the degree that they might generalize to other settings is unknown.

[16] Hartung & Galvin, *op. cit. 16*, pp. 31–33.

[17] See discussion beginning p. 234.

[18] This statement is based on informal interviews with over 30 practitioners of energy psychology, including many of the field's recognized pioneers and leaders, conducted by the second author while developing the *Energy Psychology Interactive* program.

[19] Feinstein, D. (2003, Summer). Subtle Energy: Psychology's Missing Link. *Noetic Sciences Review, 64*,18–23.

[20] References can be found in David Feinstein's "At Play in the Fields of the Mind," *Journal of Humanistic Psychology*, 1988, *38*(3): 71–109. The entire text of this article is on the CD.

[21] See, for instance, Kerry H. Levin and Hans O. Luder's *Comprehensive Clinical Neurophysiology* (London: W. B. Saunders, 2000).

[22] One of the unsolved puzzles within energy psychology is the observation that different tapping practitioners, using *different* techniques, points, and methodologies, get similarly strong results with most anxiety disorders. This impression was corroborated in the South America studies. What is the underlying mechanism that accounts for the positive outcomes being witnessed regardless of how the components of the approach were mixed and matched? The proponents of the various approaches tend to claim that the strong results they report are a function of the specifics of their particular technique. The common element for all of them, however, is that they stimulate *mechanoreceptors* in different parts of the body.

Mechanoreceptors are specialized receptors that respond to mechanical forces such as tapping, massaging, or holding. Among their types: Meissner corpuscles, Pacini corpuscles, Merkel discs, and Ruffini corpuscles. They are sensitive to stimulation on the surface of the skin anywhere on the body. The acupuncture points, called *hsue* in traditional Chinese medicine ("hollow" rather than "point" is actually the correct translation from the Mandarin), are loci that have a particularly high concentration of mechanoreceptors, free nerve endings, and neurovascular density. The signals that are initiated when tapping *hsue* travel as afferent stimuli that are capable of reaching the cortex, the amygdala, and the hippocampus.

So a possible explanation for the puzzle of why stimulating different points yields the same results involves the simple fact that mechanoreceptors are distributed all over the skin surface. Regardless of where you tap, you are likely to stimulate mechanoreceptors. The signal that is generated travels via large myelinated fibers, ascends ipsilaterally through the medial lemniscus, and triggers the somato-sensory cortex at the parietal lobes and the prefrontal cortex. From there, the signal reaches the amygdala, hippocampus, and other structures where the emotional problem has neurological entity, and the signal apparently disrupts established patterns. In theory, you can tap anywhere and impact emotional problems. Non-*hsue* skin areas, or "sham points," also have mechanoreceptors. But because they are not as dense as in *hsue*, the effect of tapping them is not as intense. Also, since different *hsue* send convergent signals that can release one or more neurotransmitters, the same effects may be obtained from stimulating different points.

NOTE: Phil Friedman, Ph.D., and Gary Craig provided astute critiques of an earlier version of this paper, and their contributions are gratefully acknowledged.

The Body's Energies

THE HUMAN BRAIN HAS SOME 100 BILLION NEURONS that each connect electrochemically with up to ten thousand other neurons. If you focus on the brain's electrical impulses instead of its physical matter, it is an incomprehensibly complex energy system, but it is also a natural focus for psychology. Modern brain-imaging technology is being applied to increase our understanding of almost any psychological process being seriously studied. Meanwhile, using non-intrusive and readily accessible methods for understanding and affecting the body's electrical and other energies, energy psychology provides a direct approach for working with the body's energy system.

Few concepts in the healing arts have been used more loosely than energy. While energy takes many forms, it is commonly defined as a force that produces a physical change ("the capacity of a physical system to do work"). Locomotives were propelled with the thermal energy released by burning coal. A bowling ball scatters the pins with the kinetic energy it delivers by virtue of its motion. Chemical energy, released as different substances react to one another, can be harnessed in the batteries that play a walkman or start a car. Nuclear energy, until it is released to power a submarine or devastate a city, holds together the nucleus of an atom. Whereas nuclear energy originates in the core of an atom, electrical current involves the flow of electrons that normally orbit that core.

Wherever there is an electrical current, it creates and is surrounded by an electromagnetic field. Each cell of the body functions like a miniature battery, with chemical reactions producing electrical current and an electromagnetic field. The negative polarity is outside the cell membrane; the positive polarity is inside. The human body is composed of seventy-five

215

trillion such "batteries." From the cells to the organs to the entire body, we are electromagnetic fields within fields within fields. Instruments for identifying and measuring our electrical and electromagnetic energies, from the voltmeter to the MRI, have long existed and are ever being refined.

Subtle Energies

The physical world appears through the eye of nuclear physics to be a latticework of energies; the atomic building blocks of matter vibrate dynamically and resemble waves as much as particles. The body's complex network of electrical and electromagnetic energies seems to intersect with an even more complex network of subtle energy systems that permeate the body. Subtle energy is energy that we do not know how to detect directly but which, like gravity, we know by its effects. Most basic is the "life force." When it is there, you are alive; when it is not there, even if your cells are still alive, you are dead. While an intuitively easy notion, neither the life force nor other forms of subtle energy have been registered by even our most sensitive physical instruments.

In fact, while kinetic, thermal, chemical, electrical, and nuclear energies have been well-mapped, the subtle energies that are of concern to energy psychology remain outside the Western scientific paradigm. These energies have, however, been recognized by many societies throughout history, and detailed expositions about specific kinds of subtle energy found in the literature of numerous cultures are beginning to stand up to scientific scrutiny (Collinge, 1998; Gerber, 2001; Hunt, 1995; Oschman, 2000; Radin, 1997; Tiller, 1997). Organizations such as the International Society for the Study of Subtle Energy and Energy Medicine (www.issseem.org) are producing newsletters and professional journals that scientifically investigate subtle energy.

Thought and Subtle Energy

Thought, according to recent compelling evidence, influences, and is influenced by subtle energy, difficult to measure but wielding a discernible impact on the physical world. At least 200 published studies demonstrate physical effects of visualization and prayer on people, animals, plants, organs, blood, and cells. For instance, a person can change the Galvanic skin response of another person at another location by directing calming

216

thoughts, or angry thoughts, toward that person. Cardiac patients who were prayed for had a lower chance of cardiac arrest during stressful procedures than those in a control group. Most people can be taught within a single session how to use visualization and focused intention to markedly influence the rate that blood cells in a test tube in another room will deteriorate (each of these studies, and hundreds of others, are summarized in Benor, 2001).

Energy psychology is based in part on evidence that thought affects the meridians and other energies, and also that disturbances in these energies lead to disturbances in thought and other psychological processes. This two-way effect is the domain of energy psychology. The field's promise is in its claims to have developed a set of readily accessible procedures for assessing and shifting the energies that are believed to maintain dysfunctional habits of thought, emotion, and behavior.

Principles of Energy Medicine

ENERGY MEDICINE RECOGNIZES ENERGY as a vital, living, moving force that determines much about health and happiness. In energy medicine, energy is the *medicine*, and energy is also the *patient*. You heal the body by activating its natural healing energies; you also heal the body by restoring energies that have become weak, disturbed, or out of balance. Energy medicine is both a complement to other approaches to medical care and a complete system for self-care and self-help. It can address physical illness and emotional or mental disorders, and can also promote high-level wellness and peak performance. The essential principles of energy medicine include (Eden, 1999):

1. Energies—both electromagnetic energies and more subtle energies—form the dynamic *infrastructure* of the physical body.
2. The health of those energies—in terms of flow, balance, and harmony—is reflected in the health of the body.
3. Conversely, when the body is not healthy, corresponding disturbances in its energies can be identified and treated.
4. To overcome illness and maintain vibrant health, the body needs its energies to:
   a. *Move* and have space to continue to move—energies may have become blocked due to toxins, muscular or other constriction, prolonged stress, or interference from other energies.

b. *Move in specific patterns*—generally in harmony with the physical structures and functions that the energies animate and support. "Flow follows function."

c. *Cross over*—at all levels, from the microlevel of the double helix of DNA, extending to the macrolevel where the left side of the brain controls the right side of the body and the right side controls the left.

d. *Maintain a balance with other energies*—the energies may lose their natural balance due to prolonged stress or other conditions that keep specific energy systems in a survival mode.

5. Flow, balance, and harmony can be non-invasively restored and maintained within an energy system by:

a. *tapping, massaging, pinching, twisting,* or *connecting* specific energy points on the skin;

b. *tracing* or *swirling* the hand over the skin along specific energy pathways;

c. *exercises* or *postures* designed for specific energetic effects;

d. focused *use of the mind* to move specific energies;

e. *surrounding an area* with healing energies (one person's energies impact another's).

219

Orienting a New Client to an Energy-Based Approach

YOUR CHOICE OF LANGUAGE IN DESCRIBING strange-looking procedures whose mechanisms are not understood invites careful consideration. The growing acceptance of acupuncture within medical care provides one bridge into established methods. The mapping of the role of amygdala hyper- or hypo-arousal in many emotional problems provides a bridge into established explanations. The approach used within energy psychology has, for instance, been described to other professionals as a way of teaching clients the "self-modulation of arousal through acupressure."[1]

When introducing an energy-based approach to a client, it is of course necessary to orient your comments according to the person's familiarity with and receptiveness to alternative treatments and your own familiarity with clinical and research support for using energy-based techniques with the client's specific problems (see discussion of indications and contraindications, p. 204). Some practitioners pointedly avoid introducing concepts early on that are not well understood or accepted, such as "energy" or "meridians." They might be more likely to simply say something along the

---

[1] Comment by Maarten Aalberse at the Third Annual Conference of the U. S. Association for Body Psychotherapy, the Johns Hopkins University, Baltimore, June, 2002.

lines of, "Here is a simple procedure that is proving itself to be surprisingly effective" and then demonstrate it on an issue where the client will be able to quickly feel a difference. Energy methods lend themselves well to such a "show me" approach. Further explanation can come later. Other practitioners, however, prefer to bring the client right into the energy paradigm. The following sample transcripts[2] provide generic examples of how one might begin.

Introducing an Energy-Based Approach

"You are probably aware that chemical imbalances are involved in psychological problems such as anxiety and depression. Evidence is mounting that the body's energies are also involved in emotional disturbances, and that interventions into the body's energy system can shift the brain chemistry in a way that helps overcome many psychological problems. The interventions you will be learning have been effective in a wide range of situations, including helping people during major disasters and the aftermath of trauma. They make use of a simple process you already know: comforting yourself using your own hands and your own words.

"Your hands carry an electromagnetic charge, and your body's energies include the electrical charge in every cell and organ, the electrical pathways in the nervous system, the electromagnetic fields surrounding every organ as well as the entire body, and also more subtle energies, such as the chi spoken of by acupuncturists and the prana spoken of by yoga practitioners. With psychological problems, an experience you regularly encounter causes your brain to send out electrical signals that lead to an emotion (perhaps anxiety, depression, or anger), a perception, or a behavior that is not appropriate for the current situation. The triggering experience may be one you encounter with some frequency, such as being in situations where you feel tested, but it also may be internal, a recurring memory, image, or thought. One way to approach the problem is to work directly with the energies that maintain the pattern in your brain's response to the triggering experience. That is the approach used in energy psychology.

"After gathering information about how the energies in your body are involved in your problem, any energy disturbances that are identified can be corrected through a variety of procedures I will be showing you. For instance, if every time you think about a particular situation, certain parts of your brain become overstimulated, leading to emotions that get in your

221

---

[2] Formulated in collaboration with Fred P. Gallo, Ph.D.

way, we can have you think about the situation while you touch or tap or massage trigger points that alter the dysfunctional response in your brain. This retrains your body and brain so that the thought or situation no longer causes the overreaction. The trigger points, incidentally, are often the same points that are used in acupuncture, though needles are not necessary to achieve the desired effect. This process alone can overcome many emotional and psychological problems, but we will be using it within the context of other treatments as appropriate.

Introducing Energy Checking

"Information about how your body's energies are involved in your problem can be gathered using a simple procedure where I apply some pressure to your outstretched arm. In this way, we can gauge the relative firmness of your muscle while you are thinking about your problem vs. when you are thinking about something else. Your muscles and your nerves work together, so when you have an upsetting emotion, it causes a change in your muscles as well. The muscles tend to become firmer with positive thoughts or emotions and somewhat weaker with negative thoughts or emotions. It isn't that the muscles are really weak at such times, just that the electricity moving through the nerves gets interrupted so that the muscle momentarily cannot operate at its best.

"The method involves checking the firmness in a shoulder muscle while you hold your arm out straight. I'll ask you to think about the problem that you want help with to see how this affects the muscle. I'll also have you touch certain places on your body that are like circuit breakers and check the muscle in response to certain statements. I may ask you to do some other things, like moving your eyes in different directions, humming, and counting. We will be working together to learn how your body's energies are responding to various aspects of your problems and to their treatment. Would this all be okay with you?"

Informed Consent

OBTAINING "INFORMED CONSENT" is one of the most fundamental procedures for protecting a client's rights. Informed consent means that the potential client has been provided enough information to make a reasonable determination about whether to accept the recommended treatment. This information includes the procedures and goals of the psychotherapy; the qualifications of and approach used by the therapist; warnings about possible side effects; information about fees, length and frequency of sessions, and likely duration of treatment; alternative therapeutic approaches; and potential sources of help besides psychotherapy. Essential for informed consent are that the client be able to understand this information and be able to freely choose whether to proceed with the treatment. Having the client sign a statement early in (or prior to) the treatment is one of the ways that informed consent can be obtained.

Some practitioners of energy psychology take the position that since details about specific procedures are not usually included in the written informed consent statements used by most clinicians, they are not necessary or appropriate within energy psychology. Because the treatment techniques are often complex and unfamiliar, they do not always lend themselves well to a brief written statement. These practitioners obtain informed consent verbally, often while providing hands-on demonstrations of the methods. Other practitioners do incorporate descriptions of their approach to energy psychology into their written statements.

The following paragraphs may be revised and included in a more comprehensive informed consent statement designed to be signed by the client. The sample provided here may or may not be applicable within your state and local jurisdiction. The final wording you use should be reviewed by an attorney.

Excerpts from a Comprehensive Informed Consent Statement

I have been advised and understand that a component of the treatment I will receive may utilize a technique called "energy checking" and involve work with energy treatment points.

Energy checking is an assessment tool for determining how energy patterns affecting my body and mind may be related to the problems I wish to address in pursuing treatment with my psychotherapist. The technique involves my therapist applying physical pressure that will determine if a specific muscle stays firm or loses strength when I bring to mind a particular thought, emotion, or problem state and resist the pressure. The outcome, as indicated by the relative firmness maintained by the muscle, provides information to both my therapist and myself about emotional dimensions of my problems that may not be available to me through introspection. Based partially on this information, my therapist will advise me on which energy points may best be used in helping me achieve my treatment goals.

Energy treatment points, adapted from the practice of acupressure, are located on the surface of the skin throughout the body and can be stimulated for the purpose of correcting disturbed energy patterns that might underlie emotional and psychological problems. Stimulation may include touching, rubbing, or tapping the point. In most instances, I will be instructed on how to stimulate the appropriate points myself. In some instances, my therapist may ask my consent to directly work with specific treatment points.

I understand that the use of energy checking and energy treatment points within the field of psychotherapy is a new development and that at this time there is very little published research in established scientific journals investigating these methods. While clinical reports of successful outcomes using these methods do exist in the published literature of the field known as energy psychology, and the methods are being developed and refined under the auspices of organizations such as the Association for Comprehensive Energy Psychology, I understand that clinical reports do not constitute conclusive scientific evidence. I further understand that

even if the clinical effectiveness of these methods is scientifically established, results will vary from person to person.

I have thoroughly considered all of the above and have obtained whatever additional input and/or professional advice I deemed necessary or
appropriate about commencing treatment that utilizes energy checking
and energy treatment points. By my signature below, given freely and
without pressure from any person, I consent to the use of these methods
in my treatment.

Opening Phases Task Sequence

Begin building rapport.

↓

Gather information about client's background and treatment goals.

↓

Explain an energy-based approach and obtain informed consent.

↓

Establish a familiarity and some success with energy checking.

↓

Check for and correct neurological disorganization.

↓

Check for and resolve global psychological reversals.

↓

Formulate an appropriate target problem.

↓

Check for and resolve single-context psychological reversals
involved with the problem.

↓

Access the problem state, rate it, and lock it in.

↓

Specific energy interventions can now be focused directly
on the target problem.

Tapping Instruction Sheet

Donna Eden and David Feinstein

Why does tapping work? The most fundamental rhythm in your body is the beating of your heart. Your arteries and capillaries carry its pulse throughout your body. Your body's energy system carries other pulses as well. Acupuncturists "read" some of these energy pulses when they perform a diagnosis. The body is accustomed to the type of rhythm that is created when you tap. Tapping at an energy point uses the body's own language to stimulate that energy. Receptors that are highly sensitive to mechanical stimulation are also found in higher concentrations at the acupuncture points.

Four Non-invasive Energy Interventions. Tapping, holding, tracing, and massaging are four primary interventions in energy medicine. Like tapping, holding energy points and tracing meridians also speak to the body in its own language, using the electromagnet charge of one's hands and fingers to influence the body's electromagnetic system. Massaging specific points is particularly effective for stimulating the neurolymphatic system, which can pump the energies through clogged pathways. But the body tends to respond to tapping where it might resist deep massage on an overcharged point.

Send Deep Impulses. Two kinds of impulses move through the nerve cells and the energy system. One is more rapid; the other, which is slower, penetrates more deeply. If you "just tap," you often engage the first kind of impulse but not the second. To activate both pulses, tap ten times, pause as you take a deep breath, and resume with five to ten taps. The pause triggers the second impulse. A way to pace your tapping without counting is to tap during a deep inhalation and exhalation, pause during a deep inhalation and exhalation, and again tap the same point on a third inhalation and exhalation.

Tap the Torso. Tapping the acupoints on the hands and feet will activate the meridians, but if you tap the other end of the meridian, closer to or on the torso, the effects will be deeper and more lasting. Tapping acupoints on or near the torso simultaneously tends to engage the chakras, the neurolymphatics, and the nerves connected to the spinal system. Acupoints on the elbows, wrists, knees, and ankles are in "zones" that are also particularly responsive to tapping, sending strong impulses into the nervous system.

Tap and Breathe. Breath moves energy. Whatever other methods you are using to intervene with the body's energies, deep, conscious breathing enhances them.

Tap for Special Effects. Tapping an acupoint supports the functions governed by its meridian (e.g., tapping a spleen point helps you assimilate information). Tapping on the lymphatic points assists in the removal of toxins. Tapping on a chakra can spin the information held in a thought or affirmation into the energy of the chakra and down through its layers to your deepest core. Tapping over the thymus makes you more robust and better able to handle stress.

Tap to Your Own Element. Because we are each physiological and energetically unique, the speed and strength of the tap should be adjusted by what "feels right." Remedies also need to be attuned to the person's "element" (see *Energy Medicine*, Chapter 7). This includes the meridian that might be the focus of the treatment, the words used in an affirmation, and the experiences sought to balance one's life. A "metal element" person will get more balance from activities within metal's control cycle, fire (e.g., wild parties and out-of-control dancing), while a "wood element" person will get more balance from activities within wood's control cycle, earth (e.g., immersion in nature).

Tap to Reverse Habit Patterns. First tap out the negative, then tap in the positive. Use an insistent, consistent tap, timed to your own rhythm. Example presenting problem: "I dread being criticized about my acting. I'm terrified of tomorrow's performance. I feel it in the middle of my chest, just above the thymus, at my heart chakra." Treatment: Tap there stating the problem you are "tapping out," saying perhaps, "I dread being criticized about my acting." Tap a few seconds, take a deep breath, begin tapping again. Follow with a positive statement, e.g., "I know it will be a great performance," tapping as feels right, perhaps, for instance, shifting now to an open hand and a slower pace.

Tap, Rub, or Imagine. Treatment points can be stimulated by tapping them, touching and rubbing them, "breathing into" the points (in John Diepold's Touch and Breathe method, TAB, the acupoint is lightly touched as the client takes one full respiration—a more complete description of TAB is on the CD), or imagining the energy at the point flowing naturally. Some practitioners, such as Lee Pulos, Ph.D., routinely have new clients try each method to gauge the client's sensitivities and preferences.

Tap with Several Fingers. It may be difficult to determine the exact treatment point from the charts. In addition, everyone's energy points matches their anatomy somewhat uniquely. One person's spleen point may be a bit higher in relationship to the ribs than another's. If you form a three-finger notch (thumb, index, and middle) and tap in the general area you understand the point to be, you will probably reach it or sufficiently stimulate adjacent areas.

A Basic Tapping Sequence

Preliminaries: Three Thumps/Three Navel Touch, Select Problem, Rate Problem from 1 to 10, Word the "Reminder Phrase."

Part 1: Rub chest sore spot while saying three times, "Even though [name problem], I deeply love and accept myself."

Part 2: Tap the points (see below) while saying out loud your reminder phrase.

Part 3: Tap the point between the little and fourth finger, beneath the knuckle as you: look down to the right, down to the left, circle eyes, circle in opposite direction, hum a bar of a song, count to five, hum again, sweep out and up.

Part 4: Repeat Part 2.

Part 5: Rate problem again. If above 0, return to Part 1 and repeat sequence. If at 0 or near 0, imagine having an ideal response in the situation, rate it on how plausible this seems (0 to 10), and repeat Parts 1–4, this time using a reminder phrase that represents your ideal response and visualizing your ideal response as you tap. Repeat sequence until believability is up to 8 or higher. Then you are ready to test the gains in a "real life" setting.

The tapping points:
  Inside of eyebrows
  Outside of eyes
  Under eyes
  Under nose
  Under lower lip
  K-27 points
  Over thymus
  Spleen points (4 inches below underarms)
  Side of legs between hip and knee
  Karate chop points
  Point between the little and fourth finger, beneath the knuckle

Neurological Disorganization Summary

Triggers, Checks, and Corrections Chart

ENERGY TRIGGER	ENERGY CHECK	CORRECTION
1. Meridians Running Backward (p. 64)	Reverse Walk Check	K-27/Cross Crawl
2. Triple Warmer in Overwhelm (p. 66)	Palm-around-Ear Check	Smoothing behind the Ears, Wayne Cook Posture, Triple Warmer/Spleen Hug
3. Polarity Reversal (p. 68)	Hand-over-Head Check	Crown Pull, Navel/Third-Eye Hook-Up
4. Ocular Lock (p. 69)	Left/Right Eye Rotation	Palming Eyes, K-27, Navel Massage
5. Homolateral Patterning (p. 69)	X & 11 Check	Homolateral Crossover
Stabilizing (p. 70)		Eights, Polarity Unswitching
Homework (p. 72)		5-Min Routine, Collarbone Breathing, Lymphs

Two Generic Neurological Disorganization Correction Sequences

The Three Thumps/Three Navel Touch (pp. 19–21)
  1. Tap or massage the K-27 points
  2. Tarzan Thump
  3. Tap or massage the spleen points (4 inches under armpits)
  4. Navel/Skull-Base Hold (about 12 seconds)
  5. Navel/Tailbone Massage (about 12 seconds)
  6. Navel/Third-Eye Hook-Up (about 12 seconds)

The Three-Part/Three-Minute Routine (p. 59)
  1. Crown Pull
  2. Separating Heaven and Earth
  3. Wayne Cook Posture

Psychological Reversal Summary

Standard Affirmation

Even though I [describe problem], *I deeply love and accept myself.*

(For a valuable alternative to the standard wordings in working with a psychological reversal, see the "Choices Method," accessed from the Embedded Topics Index of the CD.)

Types of Psychological Reversal

1. Global ("I want to be happy.")
2. Specific-Context ("I want to be over this problem.")
3. Intervening ("I want to be *completely* over this problem.")
4. Criteria-Related:
    - "deserve to"
    - "safe to/safe for others"
    - "possible"
    - "deprived"
    - "good for me/good for others"
    - "will get over"
    - "role"
    - "permission"
    - "identity" (etc.)

Treatment Points for Psychological Reversals (p. 90)

1. Vigorously massage the chest sore spots.
2. Tap the gamut spot.
3. Tap spleen points, about 4 inches below each armpit.
4. Hook up third eye and navel with middle fingers, gently pushing in and pulling up.
5. Tap the karate chop points.

Bridging and Anchoring Techniques

Bridging Techniques

The Nine Gamut (p. 130)
Blow-Out/Zip-Up/Hook-In (p. 131)
Elaborated Cross Crawl (p. 131)
Separating Heaven and Earth (p. 132)

Anchoring Techniques

Eye Roll (p. 135)
Third Eye Tap (p. 155)
Auric Weave (p. 155)

The Meridians and
the Emotions

IN THE TIME-HONORED and strikingly sophisticated "five element theory" of traditional Chinese medicine (known as *wu zing* and probably conceived around 400 B.C.), each of five basic "elements" is associated with a primary impulse or rhythm found in nature (represented by the metaphors of water, wood, fire, earth, and metal). These impulses (a more precise translation than elements is "phases in dynamic motion") have two distinct varieties, one being more active and outwardly focused (yang), the other being more passive and inwardly focused (yin). Each of twelve major energy pathways or meridians is associated with one of these primary impulses in its more active or more passive state.

The characteristics of each meridian and its functions reflect the characteristics of its element. When an imbalance arises in the energies of a meridian, this may be a precursor to physical illness related to the meridian's element and function, but it is also often expressed more immediately through the activation of a specific emotion. For instance, the "water element" meridians, not surprisingly, are kidney and bladder. The emotions that are associated with water element fall along the continuum from fear to intelligent caution. Imbalances in the kidney meridian, which is the yin aspect of water element, lead to an internal fearful state. Imbalances in the bladder meridian, which is the yang aspect of water element, lead more to reactive fears as events unfold.

Each meridian governs a specific emotion derived from its element and energetic (active or passive). While the form and expression of that emotional impulse may vary considerably as it interacts with the many other factors making up a human personality, the basic relationship that is of concern within energy psychology is that a disturbance in a meridian's energies tends to evoke a specific emotion. Treating the energy disturbance deactivates the emotion. For further discussion of "five element" theory, see Chapter 7 of *Energy Medicine* (Eden, 1999).

Meridian Emotions[1] and Affirmations[2]

These emotions and affirmations are also listed on the individual meridian charts. The meridians are listed here in alphabetical order.

Bladder Meridian
Reactive emotions/themes: Fear, anxiety, futility
Balancing emotion/theme: Hope
Sample affirmations: *I am hopeful. I am hopeful about [solving this problem].*

> Why:[3] *Bladder meridian governs the nervous system. The nervous system transports millions of pieces of information every second. When the energies that support it are in their flow, the capacity to fulfill every potential is activated, the future is bright, hope abounds. When its energies are disturbed, problems cannot be solved, the world becomes fearful, aspirations futile.*

---

[1] Because emotions are determined by many factors, and because each person is psychologically and energetically unique, the meridians and corresponding emotions, as listed, must be understood as generalizations rather than unvarying cause-effect relationships. However, you may be surprised by how well these generalizations hold in your clinical practice. While earlier formulations have been used within energy psychology, this list represents a conciliation of previous lists, the "five element theory" from Chinese medicine, and consultations with medical clairvoyant Donna Eden about how she "sees" meridian imbalances and the resulting emotional consequences.

[2] The affirmations must also be understood as generalizations, starting points in crafting a statement that is attuned to the presenting problem and the energies and emotions that underlie it.

[3] While based more on analogy than empirical findings about a meridian's functions and its associated emotions, these "whys" attempt to provide a beginning rationale for understanding these relationships.

Central Meridian

Reactive emotion/theme: Feeling vulnerable

Balancing emotion/theme: Feeling centered and secure

Sample Affirmations: *I am clear, centered, and secure. I am confident about how I will [meet this challenge].*

> Why: *Central meridian runs up through five of the body's seven chakras, or energy centers. When central is in its flow, the major energy bases are nourished and the sense of being "centered and secure" is prominent. When central is disturbed, you cannot access the strength that comes from your major energy centers, leaving you feeling vulnerable and actually being vulnerable.*

Gall Bladder Meridian

Reactive emotions/themes: Rage, judgmentalness

Balancing emotions/themes: Tolerance, kindness

Sample affirmations: *I feel kindly toward . . . , I release my judgment and forgive.*

> Why: *The bile produced by the liver to break down fats, toxins, and stomach acid is stored in the gall bladder, ready at a moment's notice to do its nasty work on complex foods. The gall bladder meridian goes through the gall bladder, surfaces at the outer eye, and is associated with looking outward. The combination of this surveillance and propensity to rip things apart, when the gall bladder's energies are disturbed, can escalate from a tendency to pass judgment to a monolithic rage toward whoever or whatever crosses its path. When gall bladder meridian is in its flow and its power to destroy toxins secure, it can look toward the world with kindness and mercy.*

236

Governing Meridian

Reactive emotion/theme: Lacking courage to move forward, "no backbone"

Balancing emotion/theme: Sense of strength, "standing tall"

Sample Affirmations: *YES, I can. YES, I can [overcome this problem].*

> Why: *Governing meridian runs up the spine. It is the energy behind you. When this energy is in its flow, it makes your posture straight. You stand tall. You have power. When it is disturbed,*

*what appears as a lack of courage is actually a lack of energy trav-
eling up the spine that would give you the power to be brave.*

Heart Meridian

Reactive emotion/theme: Heartache or heartbreak
Balancing emotion/theme: Love for self or others
Sample affirmations: *I breathe love into myself. I can [do what is required]
with love.*

> Why: *Intense feelings go straight to the heart. It sets the mood for
> all the organs. When the heart's energies are in their flow, love and
> joy flourish. When overwhelmed with pain or grief, the heart aches
> and can literally break.*

Kidney Meridian

Reactive emotions/themes: Fearful isolation, shame
Balancing emotions/theme: Gentleness with self
Sample affirmations: *I step out gently. I move forward courageously.*

> Why: *The kidneys are a phenomenal disposal system, filtering
> toxins from the blood and urine and ridding them from the body.
> If the energies of kidney meridian are disturbed, this critical, life-
> sustaining task is disrupted. No other organ can accomplish what
> needs to be done, and a disturbed kidney meridian labors in
> fearful isolation. The shame of failing to keep you alive hangs in
> the outcome. When kidney meridian is in its flow, this isolation
> and shame, looming as potentials, are countered by gentleness and
> understanding, as if speaking to a frightened child.*

Large Intestine Meridian

Reactive emotions/themes: Controlling, holding on
Balancing emotion/theme: Releasing
Sample affirmations: *I surrender (or let go). I let go of the hooks keeping me
attached to [this problem].*

> Why: *Some of what was taken in for the purposes of nutrition
> cannot be used and must be expelled. After the body's multi-
> system process of sorting through what to keep, the critical job of
> the large intestine is to make a final determination about what is
> not needed and to let it go. When the energies of the large intestine
> meridian are in their flow, the waste is easily and naturally sorted*

from what needs to be reabsorbed. It is released back into the world. When the energies are disturbed, waste and sustenance are not clearly distinguished and the urge is to hold on, to retain what is toxic because it has not been differentiated from what is needed.

Liver Meridian
Reactive emotions/themes: Rage against self, guilt
Balancing emotion/theme: Kindness toward self
Sample affirmations: *I like myself. I no longer feel guilty angry at myself.*

> Why: *The liver is the largest organ in the body, with hundreds of functions. Removing toxins is among the most important. Liver meridian also governs the eyes and is associated with an inner seeing, as if the eyes are turning back to look at oneself. When the propensity to break down poisons combines with sight turning inward, rage directed toward the self is the disease of a disturbed liver meridian. When liver meridian is in its flow, poisons of body and mind are comfortably removed and a kind eye turns within.*

Lung Meridian
Reactive emotions/themes: Grief, detachment
Balancing emotions/themes: Inspiration (in-breath), letting go (out-breath), faith
Sample affirmations: *I have faith [this problem will be resolved]. I embrace love and release [this problem].*

> Why: *Lung meridian breathes in the energy of life, bathes every cell in that energy, and releases the residue back to the world. Each outbreath is based on faith that an in-breath will follow. When lung meridian is in its flow, faith is easy as each release is followed by new inspiration. When this energy is disturbed, the release seems a threat, the desire is to hold on, letting go means loss, grief follows, detachment is the reflexive defense.*

Pericardium Meridian
Reactive emotions/themes: Bewildered by choices and demands, neglecting heart's needs
Balancing emotion/theme: Discernment, prioritizing heart's needs
Sample affirmations: *I am discerning. I support my heart's needs.*

> Why: *The pericardium is the buffer between the beating heart and the other organs. Like a good secretary, it must make clear choices*

238

about how the boss's energy and resources are managed. When the pericardium meridian is in its flow, discernment thrives and decisions support the heart's needs, which reflect the soul's longing. When the pericardium meridian is disturbed, the demands from without and within become overwhelming, and the heart and soul's needs become lost in the confusion.

Small Intestine Meridian

Reactive emotion/theme: Feeling divided, pulled in more than one direction

Balancing emotion/theme: Decisiveness

Sample affirmations: *I know what I want (or will do). I feel decisive about [overcoming this problem].*

> Why: *The job of the small intestine is to decide what to do with the food. Sorting through chemical complexity that is sobering to imagine, the small intestine must make instant decisions about what will become you and what will be eliminated. When the energy of small intestine meridian is in its flow, decisiveness prevails, choices are easy. When this energy is disturbed, even the simplest decision will divide you.*

239

Spleen-Pancreas Meridian

Reactive emotions/themes: Over-compassionate, inability to assimilate input

Balancing emotions/themes: Fairness toward self, metabolizes input into self

Sample affirmations: *I feel compassion for myself. I keep my balance as I assimilate [the situation].*

> Why: *The spleen and the pancreas are the body's great metabolizers. The useful life of a red blood cell is but a month, and the spleen (along with the liver) is involved in the breakdown of 10 million worn-out blood cells a second so their materials can be used in the creation of 10 million new blood cells the next second. The pancreas secretes insulin that converts sugar to energy, and it secretes other hormones and enzymes that metabolize other foods, converting it from what was outside of you into what is you. The spleen-pancreas meridian is involved in metabolism of all forms, from food to emotions to experience. It is oriented to recognizing possibility in the other, the other's value (whether a sugar molecule*

or a rival colleague) as a potential resource toward the greater good. When this meridian is disturbed, it works even harder to find what is right in the other, with compassionate perception overwhelming even its own needs and interests. Fairness toward the self as well as to others is the mark of a spleen-pancreas meridian in a balanced flow.

Stomach Meridian

Reactive emotions/themes: Obsessive worry
Balancing emotion/theme: Trust in the larger picture
Sample affirmations: *I let go of worry. I trust the process (or the Universe).*

> Why: *The stomach stores the source of the body's energies. When all is well and its energies are in their flow, there is trust that the next meal will come. When stomach meridian is disturbed, the body's source of energy is threatened, and worry, gloom, and fear may become obsessive.*

Triple Warmer Meridian

Reactive emotions/themes: Fight, flight, or freeze
Balancing emotion/theme: Feeling safe
Sample affirmations: *I am safe. I am [we are both] safe as I [overcome this problem].*

> Why: *Triple warmer governs the fight-or-flight response out in the world, the immune response to internal invaders, and the survival habits that are induced by threat. When this meridian is in its flow, we are cradled in a sense of safety within its protective hands. When it is disturbed, all systems go on alert and defense is elevated above any other purpose.*

240

Advanced Meridian Intervention Flow Chart

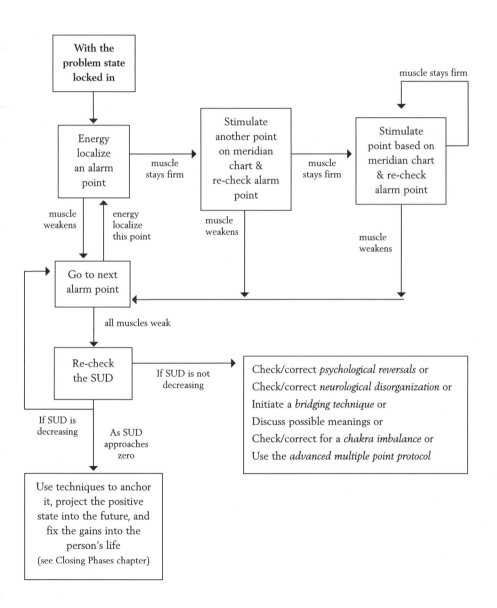

Meridian Treatment Checklist [1]

Apply treatment daily or whenever problem begins to reoccur.

MERIDIAN	1. REACTIVE EMOTIONS/THEMES 2. BALANCING EMOTIONS/THEMES 3. AFFIRMATIONS	TREATMENT POINTS
GOVERNING	1. Lacking courage to move forward, "no backbone" 2. Sense of strength, "standing tall" 3. Yes I can! Yes, I can [overcome this problem].	Under nose (GV-26) Center of forehead (GV-24.5) Top of head (GV-21) Head/tailbone hold (GV-15 & 2)
CENTRAL	1. Feeling vulnerable 2. Feeling centered and secure 3. I am clear, centered, and secure. I am confident about how I will [meet this challenge].	Navel (CV-8)/3rd Eye (GV-24.5) Under lower lip (CV-24) Breast bone (CV-20)
STOMACH	1. Obsessive worry 2. Trust in the larger picture 3. I let go of worry. I trust the process [or the Universe].	Below eyes (ST-1) Betw collarbone/nipples (ST-14/15) Betw ankle crease/2nd toe (ST-43)
SPLEEN/PANCREAS	1. Over-compassionate, anxiety about other's welfare 2. Fairness toward self 3. I feel compassion for myself.	4" under arms (SP-21) Beneath nipples (Neurolymphatic) Inside bottom of knee (SP-9) Outside corner big toenail (SP-1)
HEART	1. Heartache or heartbreak 2. Love for self or others 3. I breathe love into myself. I can [do what is required] with love.	Wrist crease (HT-7) Twist little finger (HT-9) Little fingernail (HT-9) Thymus (Heart Chakra) Arm wrap (HT-2)
SMALL INTESTINE	1. Feeling divided, pulled in more than one direction 2. Decisiveness, discernment 3. I know what I want [or will do]. I feel decisive about [overcoming this problem].	Elbow groove (SI-8) Bottom of cheekbone (SI-18) Karate chop points (SI-3, 4, 5)
BLADDER	1. Fear, suspicion, futility 2. Courage, trust, hope 3. I move forward with courage and trust. I am hopeful about [solving this problem].	Inner edges of eyebrows (BL-2) Inside corners of eyes (BL-1) Neck/head meeting (BL-10)

KIDNEY	1. Fearful isolation, shame 2. Movement toward others, gentleness with self 3. I am gentle with myself. I move forward courageously.	Under collarbone (K-27) 4-5" Above inner ankle (K-8) Behind ankle (K-3) Bottom of foot (K-1)
PERICARDIUM	1. Bewildered by choices and demands, neglecting heart's needs 2. Definitive, prioritizing heart's needs 3. I am clear about my desires. I support my heart's needs.	Middle fingernail (PC-9) Palm crease (PC-8) Middle of wrist (PC-7) Center of elbow crease (PC3)
TRIPLE WARMER	1. Fight, flight, or freeze 2. Feeling safe 3. I am safe. I am [we are both] safe as I [overcome this problem].	Outside of eyebrows (TW-23) Gamut point (TW-3) Smooth behind ears (TW-23 to 16) Hold temples (TW neurovasculars)
GALL BLADDER	1. Rage, judgmentalness 2. Tolerance, kindness 3. I will be kind and forgiving.	Middle of leg (GB-31) Middle of eyebrows (GB-14) Outside of eyes (GB-1) TMJ (GB-2)
LIVER	1. Rage against self, guilt 2. Kindness toward self 3. I like myself. I am no longer angry at myself.	Temple points (Neurovasculars) Bottom of ribcage (LR-14) Knee indents (LR-8) Inside Center of Upper Leg (LR-9)
LUNG	1. Grief, detachment 2. Inspiration (in-breath), letting go (out-breath), faith 3. I have faith [this problem will be resolved]. I am letting go of [this problem].	Arm attachment (LU-1) Inside wrist (LU-9) Thumb pad (LU-10) Outside thumbnail corner (LU-11)
LARGE INTESTINE	1. Controlling, holding on 2. Releasing 3. I surrender. I let go of the hooks keeping me attached to [this problem].	Sides of nose (LI-20) 1" beneath elbow crease (LI-10) Thumb/index web (LI-4) Index finger nail (LI-1)

[1] Gary Peterson, M.D., provided the model on which this chart is based. This checklist can be printed from the CD in a single-page format.

Common Elements of Energy Sessions

MANY ENERGY-BASED APPROACHES for the rapid relief of psychological problems, after basic preliminaries (see Chapter 5, Opening Phases), have the client:

1. Access and lock in a problem state.
2. Rate the amount of distress it causes (SUD and MUD ratings).
3. Address neurological disorganization.
4. Correct psychological reversals before and during the treatment sequence.
5. Shift the energies related to the problem state using appropriate energy treatments.
6. Introduce additional procedures to lower the SUD level (e.g., The Nine Gamut, Separating Heaven and Earth, Eye Roll), anchor it in when it has reached zero, and bridge the gains into back-home situations.

This sequence can be used whether point 5 involves work with the meridians, chakras, or the radiant circuits.

Taking Energy Psychology Another Step

(Adopted from the *Energy Psychology Interactive Self-Help Guide.*)

WHEN YOU ARE ABLE TO PRECISELY IDENTIFY an isolated emotional response that does not serve you well (e.g., irrational fear, irrational guilt, irrational hatred, irrational jealousy) and you apply the basic protocol, the early clinical indications emerging from energy psychology suggests that the pattern will shift in a surprising proportion of situations. The tapping protocol is, for instance, probably a far more effective intervention than if (suppose the irrational fear were around spiders) you were simply to state an affirmation such as, "I will stay calm and relaxed whenever I see a spider." In addition to reprogramming unwanted emotional responses, reports are accumulating that the same methods can be applied with reasonable success for attaining goals. Using the tapping protocol to increase the believability when you envision an ideal response in a given situation appears to translate into greater personal effectiveness with enough frequency that it is probably worth experimenting with it.

Some practitioners go so far as to recommend applying the basic protocol to all aspects of one's life. Steve Wells, a psychologist in Australia, suggests using the tapping procedure with every problem you have, and he further advises that you continue with the process until all remaining intensity about each problem is completely cleared. He recommends using the methods not only in a remedial fashion to eradicate existing problems, but also to change basic life patterns, to help create a "new future." He believes that even people who know the technique underestimate its potential for attaining greater emotional freedom and supporting their most fundamental goals and potentials.

It is too early in the field's development to know whether this optimistic assessment about the power of energy psychology is rooted mostly in an early adherent's enthusiasm or is a harbinger of a new paradigm that can endow each citizen with greater emotional freedom and control. Until research and other evidence is available, you will get the best answers from the laboratory of your own personal experimentation with the methods. Their popularity seems to be growing as increasing numbers of individuals are finding them empowering.

But what if the methods are not working? Assuming you are applying them precisely as they are presented and that you are not attempting to apply them in areas where the services of a qualified mental health professional are indicated (e.g., in the treatment of such conditions as major depression, severe anxiety, personality disorders, bipolar disorders, dissociative disorders, the aftermath of severe trauma, substance abuse, or psychotic disorders), you would next look to physical factors and psychological factors.

Physical Factors. When stress or fatigue interfere with the flow and balance of the energies that support brain function, energy interventions for bringing about psychological change are less effective (as discussed in Chapter 3). The most obvious first steps are to be sure you are getting enough rest and exercise and a nutritious diet. With that in place, the basic Energy Routine (see the CD's Embedded Topics Index) presents a set of procedures that have been found to be quite effective for optimizing the body's energies and enhancing the functioning of the nervous system to promote clear thinking, ease of learning, and overall vitality. These can be applied just prior to the tapping protocol or can be used as a daily routine or "energy vitamin" for establishing optimal energy patterns. A health professional who works directly with the body's energies can further guide you in this area.

Another factor that some practitioners feel interfere with the effectiveness of the tapping protocol in some proportion of cases involves sensitivities or subtle allergic reactions to foods (it has been estimated that over 10,000 chemical toxins have entered the food supply), medications, perfumes, specific clothing, or other environmental substances. While this is a controversial area, some people seem particularly susceptible to the effects of ingested substances and environmental conditions. These concerns are discussed further at: www.allergyantidotes.com, www.naet.com, and www.alternativementalhealth.com/articles.

A third set of physical considerations involves the choice of which acupuncture points are stimulated. Many practitioners believe that for some individuals and some conditions, basic standardized protocols are not adequate. Different and often more elaborate protocols are applied. While a health professional capable of using more advanced methods may indeed be useful, many practitioners also believe that most people can attain at least some promising results with at least some of their issues using the basic protocol.

Psychological Factors. The most common reason that the standardized protocols will not lead to the desired effects when properly applied is that the target problem is a component of or an *aspect* of a larger complex of emotional issues. This may indicate that work with a mental health professional is needed to overcome the problem, but often simply neutralizing the aspects of the problem is all that is necessary.

As mentioned at the close of Chapter 7, Gary Craig, the founder of EFT, uses the metaphor of a table to describe the way he approaches a problem such as generalized anxiety or incessant feelings of shame. If the presenting problem is the top of the table, the legs are the *aspects* of the problem, particularly specific events in the client's life that produced similar feelings. By chipping away at the legs, the table top often falls away spontaneously or with minimal further intervention. So rather than beginning with the "table top" or global problem, such as "I feel shame," Craig works with the "legs," addressing the problem's history—specific event by specific event—until every memory involving shame is cleared (after addressing several specific events—Craig estimates the typical range as being between 5 and 20—there is a "generalization effect" so the remainder become emotionally resolved).

Sometimes, to clear a memory, it is necessary to separate it into smaller aspects still ("the feeling of ice in my heart," "the look in her eye when she discovered me," "the sound of his voice," etc.) and treat them one at a time. Craig reports not only an extremely high success rate when focusing on these micro-aspects of a problem, but also that the gains are far more durable than when only using a global (table top) formulation of the

247

problem. Craig's website, www.emofree.com, has a powerful search engine where you can find discussions of EFT with hundreds of specific issues.

When Professional Help Is Needed. The psychotherapy community has become increasingly sophisticated and able in addressing a wide range of emotional problems. If you have taken this program as far as you can and the problems of concern persist, seriously consider seeking outside help. Or if after simply bringing focus to an issue you find yourself emotionally overwhelmed, this may indicate that a problem has been brewing and is begging for your attention. Effective resources are available. Finding the *right* therapist is an important choice. Both competence and compatibility are critical factors. Talk with friends and local professionals about possible referrals. Any of many websites may also be of value in helping you find the right therapist, such as:

> www.psych.org/public_info/PDF/psythera.pdf
> www.therapistlocator.net
> http://helping.apa.org/find.html
> www.find-a-therapist.com

248   Also, see the Links page (p. 273) for lists of therapists who specifically utilize an energy perspective.

Energy Interventions and Other Forms of Psychotherapy

THE SYSTEM PRESENTED IN THIS PROGRAM IS, for the most part, *psychodynamically atheoretical*. It is not rooted in any particular assumptions about the relative roles of childhood experience, genetics, or environment in the genesis of psychological problems. Again, as with traditional Chinese medicine, its most venerable ancestor, the theoretical core of energy psychology is:

> *Whatever the presenting problem, it has a counterpart in the client's energy system and can be treated at that level.*

This psychologically streamlined theoretical base allows energy approaches to be readily integrated with virtually any other form of psychological treatment, including psychodynamic therapies, cognitive-behavioral therapies, narrative therapies, Transactional Analysis, Gestalt, bioenergetics, art therapy, addictions counseling, and therapies that use hypnosis, guided imagery, or meditation. Energy interventions also weave well into couples, family, and group psychotherapy, other personal development approaches, and into organizational contexts. Energy interventions have also been successfully used with special populations, such as those suffering with dissociative disorders, addictions, PTSD, and eating disorders (several such applications are detailed in Fred Gallo's anthology, *Energy Psychology and Psychotherapy*, 2002, one of the first titles in the authoritative *Energy Psychology Series* by W. W. Norton Professional Books).

Although energy interventions themselves are psychodynamically atheoretical, they can serve as a powerful adjunct for facilitating deep psychodynamic change. In addition to reflecting on early experiences that shaped the client, and analyzing here-and-now transference dynamics, if deeply ingrained patterns are targeted for energy interventions, change can often be induced with greater speed and precision.

DSM Axis II personality disorders are a good example. The South America study (p. 197) found tapping methods to be only marginally indicated with personality disorders, judging them as less effective than other therapies (grouping them in its fourth category of five). But other practitioners are finding ways to "tap away" at aspects of the personality structure, going ever deeper with energy methods that work with core beliefs, early decisions, dissociated parts of the personality, trauma-based coping strategies, and transference/counter-transference issues.

Combining an energy approach with established systems that target specific populations or that possess other clinical strengths can increase the potency of the energy approach as well as of the more conventional treatment. *Energy Psychology Interactive* provides a knowledge base from which you can experiment in incorporating an energy perspective with other clinical approaches you have already mastered. For instance, while meridian-based treatments in themselves have not been particularly effective with major depression, they have been effectively combined with cognitive behavior therapy (see discussion of depression accessed from the Embedded Topics Index of CD). Preliminary formulations for integrating energy psychology with other forms of psychotherapy are also presented in several chapters of the Norton anthology (Gallo, 2002), with a particular focus on hypnosis, EMDR, Adlerian psychotherapy, and spiritual approaches to therapeutic change.

Representative Approaches within Energy Psychology

NOTE: MANY SYSTEMS WITHIN ENERGY PSYCHOLOGY are referred to by their acronyms, leading to more than one quip from the platform at the major conferences about the field's "alphabet soup." These acronyms are nonetheless used in the following list.

BSFF (Be Set Free Fast) www.besetfreefast.com

EDxTM (Energy Diagnostic and Treatment Methods) www.energypsych.com

EFT (Emotional Freedom Techniques) www.emofree.com

ESM (Emotional Self-Management) www.gem-systems.com

EvTFT (Evolving Thought Field Therapy) www.tftworldwide.com

FFFF (Freedom from Fear Forever) www.freedomfromfearforever.com

HBLU (Healing from the Body Level Up) www.jaswack.com

HSE (Human Software Engineering) www.innerhumansoftware.com

NET (Neuro Emotional Technique) www.netmindbody.com/index_ie.htm

PEAT (Psycho Energetic Auro Technology) www.spiritual-technology.com/eng/ index1.php?_link=techniques/peat.php

SEEMORG MATRIX WORK www.seemorgmatrix.com

TAAP (TAAP Training Institute) www.energypsychotherapy.com

TAT (Tapas Acupressure Technique) www.tat-intl.com

TEST (Thought Energy Synchronization Therapies) www.thoughtenergy.com

TFT (Thought Field Therapy) www.tftrx.com

3 in 1 (Three-in-One Concepts) www.3in1concepts.net

The Future of Energy Psychology

IT IS NEVER EASY TO PREDICT just how an adolescent will turn out. But the indications are that this young field will go far and influence many. "How will energy psychology impact the average person's inner life, emotional mastery, and personal development? How will it transform the treatment of minor and major psychiatric conditions? What are its implications for business . . . education . . . government . . . family life? How will it influence our relationship with our spirituality? How can it best be harnessed and distributed? All these questions are challenges for the field in the coming years, and this presentation will begin to explore them." From this description in the Conference Program[1], the following theses and implications were explored in the talk:

Thesis: Empirical investigation will demonstrate that the methods of energy psychology provide a neurologically potent intervention for strengthening the mental habits and attitudes that promote psychological well being and for weakening the mental habits and attitudes that interfere with it. Specifically:

> The mechanical stimulation of selected acupuncture points or other energy centers while mentally activating memories that are at the root of negative patterns reduces the neural connec-

---

[1]Based on the closing plenary address, delivered by David Feinstein, Ph.D., at the Fifth Annual Energy Psychology Conference in Toronto, November 1, 2003.

tions in the amygdala and other brain centers that trigger problematic emotions.

Stimulating other acupuncture points or energy centers
while simultaneously activating positive images or affirmations
facilitates the formation of neural connections that strengthen
those images and affirmations.

Thesis: This second finding, in particular, will result in laypersons and
professionals experimenting with energy interventions in all walks of life.
The experience that will be gathered will refine the procedures, demonstrate the necessary and sufficient conditions for effective interventions,
and identify the powers and limitations of the approach.

Thesis: Related cutting edge areas in mental health will utilize energy
interventions to further their impact. For instance, energy interventions for
increasing empathy can be used to enhance *emotional intelligence*, energy
interventions for increasing optimism can be used within *positive
psychology*, and energy interventions for decreasing self-negating thoughts
can be used within *cognitive psychology*.

Implications:

253

- Children will be taught energy interventions as routinely as they are
  taught the basic principles of first aid.
- Individuals will be expected to have a reasonable degree of competence in managing problematic emotions such as irrational anger,
  anxiety, jealousy, and self-hatred.
- Couples will be able to reduce reactiveness toward one another, heal
  past hurts and resentments, and change family-of-origin patterns that
  interfere with the current relationship.
- Therapists, counselors, life coaches, educators, clergy, and human
  resources personnel will routinely utilize energy methods to help
  people overcome dysfunctional emotional and psychological patterns,
  increase health, and enhance peak performance.
- Ethical concerns will emerge both in terms of the practitioner's
  competence and scope of practice issues as well as blatantly manipu-
  lative applications, such as the military using energy interventions to
  make soldiers less conscience-bound in their ability to hurt others.
- Although still outside established Western paradigms, the value of
  energy interventions will come to be recognized within the broader

culture, much like meditation and yoga, but the path to this acceptance will be somewhat jagged. At this time, the close of 2003, the field has been largely ignored by the allied health care professions. As research begins to establish its efficacy, there will be a large backlash, particularly within the psychotherapeutic and pharmaceutical establishments, attempting to discredit even robust research findings. Meanwhile, insurance carriers, with an eye toward efficient treatment rather than the vested interests of any particular method or ideology, will be more readily persuaded. Eventually, like the 5,000-year-old practice of its ancestor, acupuncture, the field's methods will prevail.

The CD's Embedded Topics List

IN ADDITION TO SEVEN MODULES with no corresponding chapter in this book (covering Core Beliefs, Protocols & Shortcuts, Chakras, Radiant Energies, Clinical Illustrations, Other Energy Approaches, and Integrating Energy Approaches with Other Forms of Psychotherapy), the CD also contains a file on each of the following topics, some of which are included in this Appendix:

Attuning Clinical Intuition to Energy Fields
Brain Images before and after Treatment
Biochemistry of Fight-or-Flight
Bridging and Anchoring Techniques
Clinical Evidence for Energy Therapy
Common Elements of Energy Sessions
Choices Method
Depression
Energy Medicine Newsletter
EP/EMDR Hybrid Technique
EFT Cases
EFT Eight-Point Treatment Chart
Ethical Considerations
"Fields of Information" Paper
Five-Minute Daily Routine
Healing from the Body Level Up (HBLU)
Indications and Contraindications
Informed Consent
Keys to Successful Treatment
Meridian Assessment Chart
Meridian Emotions & Affirmations Table
Meridian Single Point Chart
Meridian Treatment Charts (Index)
Meridian Treatment Checklist
Meridian Intervention Flow Chart
Negative Affect Erasing Method (NAEM)

Neurobiology of Trauma and Treatment
Neurovascular Holding Points
Neurological Disorganization Treatments
Opening Phases Task Sequence
Orienting a New Client
Peak Performance Protocol
Practice Sessions
Principles of Energy Medicine
Protocols for Specific Problems
Psychotherapy Networker Case Study
Psychological Reversal Checklist
Seemorg Matrix Work
Simple Basic Sequence
Radiant Circuit Charts (Index)
Readings in Energy Psychology
References
Research on Energy Checking
Surrogate Treatments
Tapas Acupressure Technique (TAT)
Tapping Instruction Sheet
Touch-and-Breath Technique (TAB)
Temporal Tap
The Body's Energies
Theoretical Considerations
Trauma Debriefing
Triple Warmer & Psychological Problem

APPENDIX II

Meridian Charts

General Charts

The EFT Eight-Point Treatment Chart   259

One-Point-per-Meridian Treatment Chart   260

Meridian Assessment Chart   261

Treatment Charts for Specific Meridians (listed alphabetically)

Bladder Meridian   262

Central Meridian   263

Gall Bladder Meridian   264

Governing Meridian   265

Heart Meridian   266

Kidney Meridian   267

Large Intestine Meridian   268

Liver Meridian   269

Lung Meridian   270

Pericardium Meridian   271

Small Intestine Meridian   272

Spleen-Pancreas Meridian   273

Stomach Meridian   274

Triple Warmer Meridian   275

Note: For color versions of these charts, print directly from the CD using a color printer.

THE EFT EIGHT-POINT TREATMENT CHART

**TAP EACH
POINT ABOUT
7 TIMES
(either side
or both
simultaneously)**

KC: Karate
Chop Points

EB: Beginning
of Eyebrow

SE: Side of Eye

UE: Under Eye

UN: Under Nose

Ch: Above Chin

CB: Collarbone
(indent
beneath CB)

UA: 4" Under
Arm

Bacchus by Michelangelo (detail)

Two Additional Useful Points:
   Thymus Thump ("Tarzan Spot")
   Outside of Leg (midway between hip and knee)

259

ONE-POINT-PER-MERIDIAN TREATMENT CHART

EB: Beginning of Eyebrow (BL-2, Bladder)

SE: Side of Eyes (GB-1, Gall Bladder)

UE: Under Eyes at top of cheekbones (ST-1, Stomach)

CB: CollarBone (K-27, Kidney)

TT: Tarzan Thump, center of chest (Lung Neurolymphatic Point)

BN: Below Nipple 1 inch below either breast (LR-14, Liver)

UA: 4" below Under-Arms (SP-21, Spleen)

EC: An inch beneath inside Elbow Crease in line with pointer finger (LI-10, Large Intestine)

Bacchus by Michelangelo (detail)

Finish with

G: Gamut Spot, below knuckle and between ring and little fingers (TW-3, Triple Warmer)

KC: Karate Chop points, fingers of one hand tapping side of other. (SI-3, Small Intestine & HT-8, Heart)

H
O
O
K
I
U
P

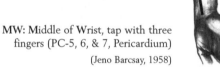

MW: Middle of Wrist, tap with three fingers (PC-5, 6, & 7, Pericardium)

(Jeno Barcsay, 1958)

Follow the 12 TAPS with a HOOK-UP of Central (CV–8) and Governing (GV–24.5):

Middle finger of one hand in belly button.
Middle finger of other hand at third eye.
Press in and pull the skin gently upward.
Hold about 30 seconds, or until there is a spontaneous deep breath.

MERIDIAN ASSESSMENT CHART
(The Alarm Points)

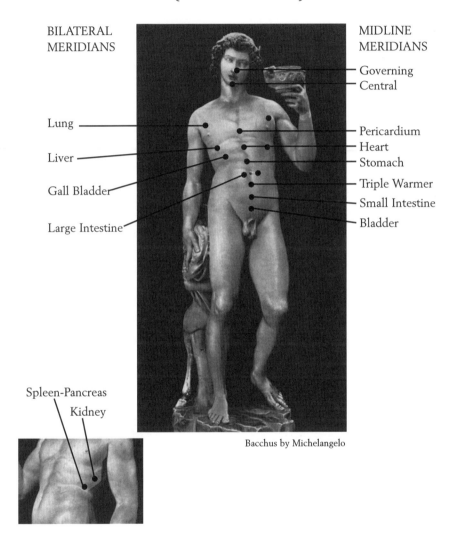

BILATERAL
MERIDIANS

MIDLINE
MERIDIANS

Governing

Central

Lung

Pericardium

Liver

Heart

Stomach

Gall Bladder

Triple Warmer

Large Intestine

Small Intestine

Bladder

Spleen-Pancreas

Kidney

Bacchus by Michelangelo

Note: The points shown for central and governing in Gallo's *Energy Diagnostic and Treatment Methods* are somewhat different from those shown here. Both sets work; some practitioners believe these to be somewhat more reliable. This chart is first used in conjunction with the Advanced Meridian Treatments chapter.

261

THE BLADDER MERIDIAN

Reactive emotions/themes: Fear, suspicion, futility
Balancing emotion/theme: Courage, trust, hope

Sample affirmations:
*I move forward with courage and trust. I am hopeful about
[solving this problem].*

Hold third eye point
Tap in *only* with posi-
tive thoughts or feelings
(Between BL–2
Points)

Tap inner edges of
eyebrows (BL–2)

Hold inside corners of
eyes (BL–1) and
push up

Tap indent where top
of neck meets bottom
of head (BL–10)

Hold middle indent
where top of neck
meets bottom of
head (BL–10)
Hold along with third
eye point for at least 30
seconds

Nude Youth by Michelangelo (detail)

THE CENTRAL MERIDIAN

Reactive emotion/theme: Feeling vulnerable
Balancing emotion/theme: Feeling centered and secure
Sample affirmations:
*I am clear, centered, and secure. I am confident about
how I will [meet this challenge].*

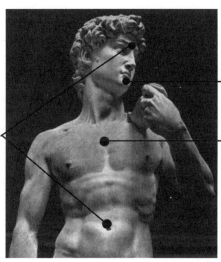

Place middle finger
of one hand in navel
(CV–8), other at
third eye (GV–24.5)
Push in, lift up, hold
for about 30 seconds

Tap indent under
lower lip (CV–24)

Tap point about
an inch below the
top of the breast
bone (CV–20)

David by Michelangelo (detail)

THE GALL BLADDER MERIDIAN

Reactive emotions/themes: Rage, judgmentalness
Balancing emotions/themes: Tolerance, kindness
Sample affirmations:
I feel kindly toward . . . , I release my judgement and forgive.

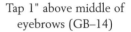

Tap 1" above middle of
eyebrows (GB–14)

David by Michelangelo (detail)

Zechariah by Michelangelo
(detail)

Tap at outside
middle of leg
(GB–1)

Tap TMJ points at
the hinge of the "V"
when mouth is open
(GB–2)

Tap outside
of eyes
(GB–1)

THE GOVERNING MERIDIAN

Reactive emotions/themes: Lacking courage to
move forward (no backbone)
Balancing emotion/theme: Sense of strength
(standing tall)
Sample affirmations:
YES, I can. YES, I can [overcome this problem].

Tap under nose
(GV–26)

Place finger at middle
indent where bottom
of head meets top
of neck
(GV–15)

Simultaneously tap
or hold bottom of
tailbone
(GV–2)

David by Michelangelo (detail)

Touch top of head (GV–24.5)

Tap center of
forehead
(GV–24.5)

Place thumb, index, and
middle fingers at center of
forehead (GV–24.5)

Place thumb, index, and
middle fingers of other hand
at indent where bottom of
head meets top of neck
(GV–15)

Zechariah by Michelangelo
(detail)

Hold 30 to 60 seconds

265

THE HEART MERIDIAN

Reactive emotion/theme: Heartache or heartbreak
Balancing emotion/theme: Love of self or others
Sample affirmations:
I breathe love into myself. I can [do what is required] with love.

Nude Youth by Michelangelo (detail)

Bacchus by Michelangelo
(detail)

Tap thymus
(middle of chest)
(Heart Chakra)

Twist ends of little
fingers or wrap hand
around little finger
and hold (HT–9)

Tap inside of
nails of little
fingers (HT–9)

Wrap hand around
side of arm so fingers
are in line with point
of elbow. Pump
fingers, massaging
deeply (HT–2)

Tap little finger sides
of wrist (HT–7)

(Jeno Barcsay, 1958)

THE KIDNEY MERIDIAN

Reactive emotions/themes: Fearful, isolation, shame
Balancing emotions/theme: Gentleness with self,
movement toward others
Sample affirmations:
I step out gently. I move forward courageously.

Cross hands and tap
or massage under
collarbone (K–27)

(Jeno Barcsay, 1958)

Tap hand's width
above ankles
(K–8)

Tap center bottom
of ball of foot
(Wellspring of Life
points, K–1)

Bacchus by Michelangelo
(detail)

Tap behind ankle (K–3)

267

THE LARGE INTESTINE MERIDIAN

Reactive emotions/themes: Controlling, holding on
Balancing emotion/theme: Releasing
Sample affirmations:
*I surrender (or let go). I let go of the hooks keeping me
attached to [this problem].*

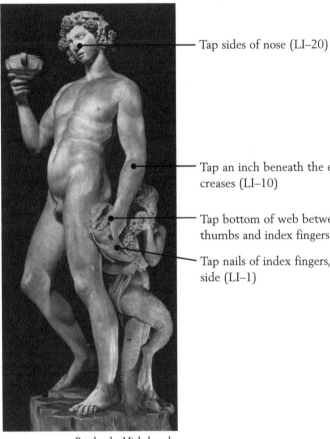

Tap sides of nose (LI–20)

Tap an inch beneath the elbow
creases (LI–10)

Tap bottom of web between
thumbs and index fingers (LI–4)

Tap nails of index fingers, thumb
side (LI–1)

Bacchus by Michelangelo

268

THE LIVER MERIDIAN

Reactive emotions/themes: Rage against self, guilt
Balancing emotion/theme: Kindness toward self
Sample affirmations:
I like myself. I no longer feel guilty or angry at myself.

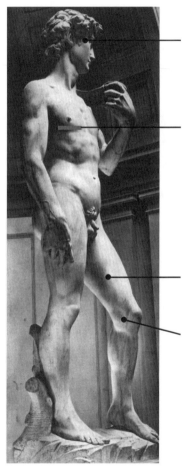

Thumbs rest on temple points as
fingers rest at hairline
(these are all neurovascular
points)

Tap liver alarm point (LR–14)

Inside center of upper legs
(LR–9), crossing hands and
tapping simultaneously

Tap points in indent on inside of
knees (LR–8)

David by Michelangelo

THE LUNG MERIDIAN

Reactive emotions/themes: Grief, detachment
Balancing emotions/themes: Inspiration (in-breath),
letting go (out breath), faith
Sample affirmations:
I have faith [this problem will be resolved].
I embrace love and release [this problem].

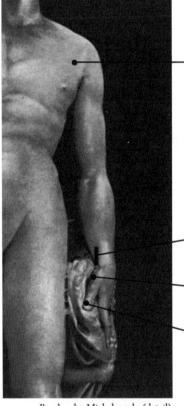

Cross arms and tap points about 1½"
from where arms attach to torso
(LU–1)

Tap with 3 fingers on the INSIDE of
the wrist, below the thumb (LU–9)

Tap fatty part of thumb pad, palm side
(LU–10)

Tap outside corner of thumbnail
(LU–11)

Bacchus by Michelangelo (detail)

THE PERICARDIUM MERIDIAN CHART

Reactive emotions/themes: Bewildered by choices and demands,
neglecting heart's need
Balancing emotion/theme: Definitive, prioritizing heart's needs
Sample affirmations:
I am clear about my desire to . . .
I support my heart's needs.

Tap nail of middle finger,
index finger side (PC–9)

Tap elbow crease—
inside, center (PC–3)

Bacchus by Michelangelo (detail)

Tap points of center
creases of palms between
second and third fingers
(PC–8)

Tap points directly
below middle of wrist
with three fingers

(Jeno Barcsay, 1958)

271

THE SMALL INTESTINE MERIDIAN

Reactive emotion/theme: feeling divided, pulled in more
than one direction
Balancing emotion/themes: Decisiveness, discernment
Sample affirmations:
I know what I want (or will do).
I feel decisive about [overcoming this problem].

Tap at bottom of cheek-
bone (SI–18)

Nude Youth by Michelangelo (detail)

Tap in elbow groove (SI–8)

Tap karate chop points
along side of hand
(SI–3, 4, and 5)

Nude Youth by Michelangelo (detail)

THE SPLEEN-PANCREAS MERIDIAN

Reactive emotions/themes: Over-compassionate, inability
to assimilate input
Balancing emotions/themes: Fairness toward self,
metabolizes input into self
Sample affirmation:
*I feel compassion for myself. I keep my balance as I
assimilate [the situation].*

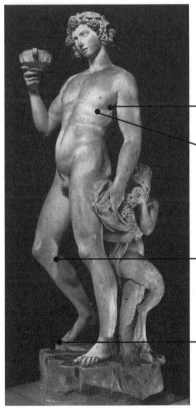

Bacchus by Michelangelo

Tap points 4" under armpits
(SP–21)

Tap points beneath nipple, two ribs
beneath bra line (Spleen
Neurolymphatic)

Tap bottom of knee at edge of bone
on inside of leg (SP–9)

Tap outside corners of big toe
toenails (SP–1)

THE STOMACH MERIDIAN

Reactive emotion/theme: Obsessive worry
Balancing emotion/theme: Trust in the larger picture
Sample affirmations:
*I let go of worry. I trust the process (or the Universe or
the larger picture).*

Tap points on cheek-
bones directly below
eyes (ST–1)

Cross hands and simultaneously
tap points halfway between the
collarbone and the nipples
(ST–14/15)

David by Michelangelo (detail)

David by Michelangelo (detail)

Tap points halfway
between the ankle
crease and second toe
(ST–43)

THE TRIPLE WARMER

Reactive emotions/themes: Fight, flight, or freeze
Balancing emotion/theme: Feeling safe
Sample affirmations:
I am safe. I am [we are both] safe as I [overcome this problem].

With 4 fingers of each hand, smooth or tap points surrounding outside of ears from front to back. Make 4 or 5 passes (Temporal Tap) (covers TW–16–22)

Tap in hollow at outside of eyes (TW–23)

Hold TW Neurovascular Points with thumbs and place pads of fingers on forehead while breathing deeply for 15 to 20 seconds

Zechariah by Michelangelo (detail)

Tap gamut spot (TW–3)

Nude Youth by Michelangelo (detail)

Links

(For instant hyperlink access, find the Links Page in the CD's Embedded Topics Index.)

Discussion Groups and Support Sites:

http://es.onelist.com/group/energym (EnerGym Discussion Group: "a forum for those with an interest in the application of Energy Psychology in its various shapes and forms")

http://groups.yahoo.com/group/meridiantherapy (Meridian Therapy Professional Support List)

www.emofree.com/email.htm (Emotional Freedom Techniques E-Mail Support List)

www.eftsupport.com (Emotional Freedom Techniques Support Website)

www.eftsupport.com/practstatelist.htm (Emotional Freedom Techniques)

www.unstressforsuccess.com (Tapas Acupressure Technique Support Site)

Free Newsletters/Reports (to subscribe, go to the website):

www.eft-innovations.com (*Emotional Freedom Techniques Innovations*)
www.energypsychresearch.org (Reports Research Findings in Energy Psychology)
www.ijhc.org/ (*International Journal of Healing and Caring*)

Practitioner Referral Lists:

www.energypsych.com (Energy Diagnostic and Treatment Methods)

www.emofree.com/Practitioners/referralMain.asp (Emotional Freedom Techniques)

www.matrixwork.org/directory.htm (Seemorg Matrix Work)

Nonprofit Organizations Concerned with Energy Psychology:

www.energypsych.org (Association for Comprehensive Energy Psychology—ACEP)

www.theamt.com (Association for Meridian Therapies)

www.energymed.org (Energy Medicine Institute)

www.issseem.org (International Society for the Study of Subtle Energies and Energy Medicine—ISSSEEM)

(To send comments about *Energy Psychology Interactive:* epi@innersource.net).

278

Energy Psychology Interactive Forum:

For psychotherapists, graduate students, and other health care professionals who are studying or applying the *Energy Psychology Interactive* CD and/or companion book—to share your experiences, ideas, questions, and research findings.

To join, visit: **http://groups.yahoo.com/group/EnergyPsychology**

References

Amen, D. G. (2002). *Images into human behavior: A brain SPECT atlas.* Newport Beach, CA: Mindwords.

Becker, R. O. (1990). *Cross currents: The promise of electromedicine; the perils of electropollution.* New York: Tarcher/Penguin Putnam.

Benor, D. (2001). *Spiritual healing: Scientific validation of a healing revolution.* Southfield, MI: Vision Publications.

Bessant, A. W., and Leadbeater, C. W. (1969). *Thought forms.* Wheaton, IL: Quest (originally published 1905).

Callahan, R. (2001). The impact of Thought Field Therapy on heart rate variability. *Journal of Clinical Psychology. 57*: 1153–1170.

Carrington, P. (2001, November). Interview with Deborah Mitnick. *EFT News and Innovations, 1*(4): 3–8.

Cho, Z. H. (1998). New findings of the correlation between acupoints and corresponding brain cortices using functional MRI. *Proceedings of National Academy of Science, 95,* 2670–2673.

Collinge, W. (1998). *Subtle energy: Awakening to the unseen forces in our lives.* New York: Warner Books.

Cory, G., Cory, M. S., and Callanan, P. (1997). *Issues and ethics in the helping professions* (5th ed.). Belmont, CA: Wadsworth.

Craig, G. (1999). *Emotional freedom techniques: The manual* (3rd ed.). El Paso: Mediacopy.

Currey, K. (2002). *EFT for parents* [E-book]. Sedona, AZ: Joyful Mission. http://www.joyfulmission.com/joyful_mission_00000b.htm.

Dossey, L. (1993). *Healing words: The power of prayer and the practice of medicine.* San Francisco: Harper.

Dumitrescu, I., and Kenyon, J. (1983). *Electrographic imaging in medicine and biology.* Suffolk, England: Neville Spearman.

Eden, D. (with Feinstein, D.). (1999). *Energy medicine.* New York: Tarcher/Penguin Putnam.

Feinstein, D. (1998). At play in the fields of the mind. *Journal of Humanistic Psychology, 38*(3): 71–109. (The entire text of this article can be found on the CD.)

Fowler, R. (2002). Neal Miller: A giant in American psychology. *Monitor on Psychology, 33*(5), 9.

Gach, M. R. (1990). *Acupressure's potent points: A guide to self-care for common ailments.* New York: Bantam.

Gallo, F. P. (1999). *Energy psychology: Explorations at the interface of energy, cognition, behavior, and health.* New York: CRC Press.

Gallo, F. P. (2000). *Energy diagnostic and treatment methods.* New York: Norton.

Gallo, F. P. (Ed.) (2002). *Energy psychology in psychotherapy.* New York: Norton.

Gerber, R. (2001). *Vibrational medicine* (3rd ed.). Santa Fe, NM: Bear & Co.

Grudermeyer, D., and Grudermeyer, R. (2000). *The energy psychology desktop companion.* Del Mar, CA: Willingness Works.

Harris, W. S. et al. (1999). A randomized, controlled trial of the effects of remote, intercessory prayer on outcomes in patients admitted to the coronary care unit. *Archives of Internal Medicine, 159*: 2273–2278.

Hartmann, S. (2003). *The advanced patterns of EFT.* Eastbourne, England: Dragon Rising.

Hartung, J., and Galvin, M. (2003). *Energy psychology and EMDR: Combining forces to optimize treatment.* New York: Norton.

Hover-Kramer, D. (2001). *Healing touch: A guide book for practitioners* (2nd ed.). Albany: Delmar.

Hui, K. K. S., Liu, J., Makris, N., Gollub, R. W., Chen, A. J. W., Moore, C. I., Kennedy, D .N., Rosen, B. R., and Kwong, K. K. (2000). Acupuncture modulates the limbic system and subcortical gray structures of the human brain: Evidence from fMRI studies in normal subjects. *Human Brain Mapping, 9*(1): 13–25.

Hunt, V. (1995). *Infinite mind: The science of human vibrations.* Malibu, CA: Malibu Publishing.

Hurt, D. (2000). *Character is the ultimate currency: The role of ethics in energy therapies.* Ashland, OR: Siskiyou Essence.

Kendall, F. M. P., and McCreary, E. K. (1993). *Muscles: Testing and function* (4th ed.). Baltimore: Williams and Wilkins.

McAdams, D. P. (1996). Personality, modernity, and the storied self: A contemporary framework for studying persons. *Psychological Inquiry, 7,* 295–321.

McCraty, R. (in press). The energetic heart: Bioelectromagnetic communication within and between people. In *Clinical applications of bioelectromagnetic medicine,* P. Rosch & M. Markov (eds). New York: Marcel Dekker.

Mildad, M. R., and Quirk, G. J. (2002). Neurons in medical prefrontal cortex signal memory for fear extinction. *Nature, 420,* 70–74.

Monti, D., Sinnott, J., Marchese, M., Kunkel, E., and Greeson, J. (1999). Muscle test comparisons of congruent and incongruent self-referential statements. *Perceptual and Motor Skills, 88,* 1019–1028.

Motoyama, H. (1998). *Measurements of ki energy, diagnosis and treatments.* Tokyo: Human Science Press.

Nader, K., Schafe, G. E., and LeDoux, J. E. (2000). Fear memories require protein synthesis in the amygdala for reconsolidation after retrieval. *Nature,* 406:722–6.

Oschman, J. L. (2000). *Energy medicine: The scientific basis.* New York: Harcourt.

Pearsall, P. (1998). *The heart's code.* New York: Broadway.

Pert, C. B. (1997). *Molecules of emotion: The science behind mind-body medicine.* New York: Simon & Schuster.

Porges, S. (1997). Emotion: An evolutionary by-product of the neural regulation of the autonomic nervous system. *Annals of the New York Academy of Sciences, 807,* 62–77.

Pulos, L. (2002). The integration of energy psychology with hypnosis. In F. P. Gallo (Ed.), *Energy psychology in psychotherapy.* New York: Norton.

Radin, D. (1997). *The conscious universe: The scientific truth of psychic phenomena.* San Francisco: HarperCollins.

Radomski, S. (2001). *A manual for the energy psychology treatment of allergies.* Jenkintown, PA: Author.

Rose-Neil, S. (1967). The work of Professor Kim Bong Han. *The Acupuncturist*, 1,15.

Russek, L. G. E., and Schwartz, G. E. (1996). Energy cardiology: A dynamical energy systems approach for integrating conventional and alternative medicine. *Advances: The Journal of Mind-Body Health, 12*(4), 12–24.

Shealy, C. N. (1988). Clairvoyant diagnosis. In T. M. Srinivasan (Ed.), *Energy Medicine around the World* (pp. 291–303). Phoenix: Gabriel Press.

Tiller, W. A. (1997). *Science and human transformation: Subtle energies, intentionality and consciousness.* Walnut Creek, CA: Pavior.

Van der Kolk, B. (1999). The body keeps the score: Memory and the evolving psychobiology of posttraumatic stress. In M. J. Horowitz (Ed.), *Essential papers on posttraumatic stress disorder.* New York: New York University Press.

de Vernejoul, P. (1985). Study of the acupuncture meridians with radioactive traces. *The Bulletin of the Academy of National Medicine* (Paris), 169, 1071–1075.

Voll, R., & Sarkisyanz, H. (1993). *The 850 EAV measurement points of the meridians and vessels including secondary vessels* (A. J. Scott-Morley, Trans.). Milan, Italy: Medicina Biologica.

Wang, P., Hu, X., and Wu, B. (1993). [Displaying of the infrared radiant track long meridians on the back of the human body], *Chen Tzu Yen Chiu Acupuncture Research, 18*(2), 90–93.

Wells, S., Polglase, K., Andrews, H. B., Carrington, P., and Baker, A. H. Evaluation of a meridian-based intervention, Emotional Freedom Techniques (EFT), for reducing specific phobias of small animals. *Journal of Clinical Psychology* (in press).

Wolpe, J. (1958). *Psychotherapy by reciprocal inhibition.* Stanford, CA: Stanford University Press.

Also see the more comprehensive "Readings in Energy Psychology and Related Areas," accessed from the CD's Embedded Topics Index.

Index

Aalberse, M., 220
acupoints
    choice of, 247
    distribution of, among meridians, 137
    effective and ineffective, survey
        outcomes, 168–69
    electrical resistance of, 5, 116–17
    imagining a fear-provoking situation,
        1–2
    interrupting emergency response
        through, 154
    mechanoreceptors concentrated at, 5,
        213
    selecting for treatment, 120–22
    stimulating, 117–23
        in treatment of anxiety, 4
        sequence in a clinical study, 203
    tapping, 122–23
        and verbal treatment, 145
    for treatment, clinical trial of, 198
acupuncture
    for anesthesia, 9, 194
    clinical research on, 166
    eight tapping points based on, 27
    as energy psychology's progenitor,
        206–7
    law of opposites in, 138
    meridians of, defined, 38, 110
    needles versus tapping treatments, 203
    validation of, through scientific
        research, 112
acupuncture points, see acupoints
acute distress disorders, energy
        psychology treatment for, 15–16

adaptive mechanism, psychological
        reversal as, 76–77
addictive disorders
    energy-based approach to, 16
    energy intervention response versus
        other modalities, 205
Advanced Multipoint Protocol, 150
affirmations
    in Emotional Freedom Techniques,
        23–25
    and meridian emotions, 235–40
    for projecting successful treatment into
        the future, 157
    for psychological reversals, 84, 87–89
    set-up, for psychological reversals, 78
    in treatment of a problematic thought
        field, 144–45
alarm points
    checking, during outcome projection,
        158
    from Chinese medicine, 139–41
    re-checking with indicator muscle, 142
Amen, D.G., 4
American Professional Agency
    Insight newsletter of, 184
    Newsletter on Risk Management for
        Psychologists, 97
American Psychological Association, code
    of ethics of, 9, 107
amygdala
    acupoint stimulation transmitted to,
        213–14
    imaging of, and registration of
        emotional problems, 208

mapping the role of, in emotional problems, 220

anatomy, of the body's energy system, 109

anchoring techniques
practice session, 155–57
summary chart, 233

Andrade, J., 4, 112–13, 198

Andrews, H.B., 167

anecdotal evidence, 15–17

anesthesia, through acupuncture, 9

anxiety
energy intervention response compared with other modalities, 204–5
treatment of, 199–201
by energy psychology, 15–16, 181

Applied Kinesiology
assessing meridian energy flow and, 41
for diagnosing the flow of meridian energies, 183
psychological methods drawn from, 169
tools from, use in energy psychology, 104

art, energy checking as an, 171–72

assessment, of energy psychology techniques, survey outcomes, 170–72

Association for Comprehensive Energy Psychology, 203, 209
code of ethics of, 97
research web site of, 185

attitudes
changing with energy psychology treatment, 187
during an energy check, 51

attorney, review of informed consent instruments by, 224

aura, 150
defined, 110
importance of, compared with other energy systems, 182
relationship with the biofield, 155–56

Auric Weave, anchoring with, 155–56

autoimmune illnesses, meridian energies in, 114

backlash, to energy interventions from the professional community, 254

Baker, A.H., 167

balanced energetic state, association with a trigger of a psychological problem, 120

balancing procedures, for improving the Positive Belief Scale (PBS), 158–59

baraka, defined, 6

basic concepts, of energy psychology, 15–36

basic grid, 150
compared with other energy systems, 182–83

basic protocol, variations in clinical practice, 35–36

basic sequence, of set-up affirmations, 33–34

Beck Anxiety Inventory, for assessing energy interventions, 210–11

Becker, R.O., 9, 117

Benor, D.J., 7, 163, 217

benzodiazepines versus tapping treatments, 202–3

Be Set Free Fast (BSFF), 17

Bessant, A.W., 118

beta frequencies, change in, after therapy, 211

biochemical/electrical basis of energy psychology, survey outcomes, 167–68

biochemistry
of awareness, xiii
changes in, due to energy point stimulation, 187–88
of mental activity, 173

bioenergetics, 209

biofield
properties of, 6
relationship with the aura, 155–56
see also aura

biological cycles, energies that control, 109

bipolar disorders
caution in treating with energy psychology, 96
contraindication of energy psychology for, clinical trials, 205
meridian-oriented approach contraindicated for, 16

bladder meridian, 234–35, 262
fear as the reactive emotion of, 145

blow-out/zip-up/hook-in bridging technique, 131

body, the energies of, 215–17

brain
chemistry of, electrochemical shifts in, 4
electrochemical impulses of, 215

brain balancing procedures, efficacy of,
   survey outcomes, 169–70
brain imaging, clinical assessment using,
   209–11
brain mapping
   of acupoint stimulation effects, 198
   after acupoint tapping, 212
brain waves
   of client and therapist, relationship
     between, 175
   normalization of ratios, after acupoint
     tapping, 168
   patterns of, and acupuncture point
     stimulation, principles of, 4
bridging techniques, 130–32
   balancing procedures with, 158
   to project successful treatment into the
     future, 158
   summary chart, 233
   with tapping, 29–30
Burr, H., 9

calcium ion regulation, through tapping,
   208
calibration of an indicator muscle, 46–48.
   see also indicator muscles, qualifying
Callahan, R., 18, 29, 72, 75, 103, 117–20,
   169, 172, 183
Carbonell, J., 120
Carrington, P., 24–25, 160, 167
case examples
   claustrophobia, 2–3
   phobias, fear of snakes, 151–52
   post-traumatic stress disorder, 1–2
cells, as miniature batteries, 215
centers, of the body's energy system, 109
central meridian, 236, 263
cerebral hemispheres, conflict between,
   77
chakras, 149–50
   compared with other energy systems,
     182–83
   as energy centers, 110
checking
   of an alarm point, 140–41
   for psychological reversals, 80–82
   see also energy checking
chi (ki)
   defined, 6
   the meridian system as a transport
     mechanism for, 110–11

children, teaching energy interventions
   to, 253
Chinese medicine
   acupoint definitions in, 213
   alarm points in, 139
   eight-point tapping system based on, 27
   energy psychology methods traced to,
     18
   five element theory in, 234
   maps of the meridian system, 112
   mechanisms of energy intervention in,
     207
   meridians described in, 38
   pulses revealing condition of the
     energy system, 41
   on treatment of the presenting
     problem, 180
Cho, Z.H., 4–5, 112
choice points, in the multipoint
   approach, 146–47
Choices Method, 24–25
chronic fatigue, contraindication to
   energy psychology for, from clinical
   trials, 205
clairvoyance
   and energy checking, 42
   and energy systems, 183
   for reading the body's energies, 43–44
   systematic investigation of, 118
claustrophobia, case example, 2–3
client
   bridging treatment to the home
     setting, 162–64
   emotionally blocked, encouraging in
     therapy, 102
   energetic exchange with therapist, 175
   history in relation to treatment goals,
     89
   home setting, supporting success in,
     147–49
   introducing energy psychology to,
     51–52, 98
   orienting to an energy-based approach,
     220–22
   psychosocial history of, 95
   retraumatizing while accessing the
     problem, 102
*Clinical Acupuncture and Oriental
   Medicine* (journal), 9
clinical intuition
   in energy checking, 172

sources of, 175
see also clairvoyance
clinical practice, energy system approach
    incorporated into, 18
clinical procedures, differences among
    energy psychology practitioners,
    165–86
clinical reports, CD demonstrations of
    "single-session phobia cures", 16
clinical strategy, for acupoint selection,
    120–22
clinical studies, 201–3
    of acupoint validity, 120
    of appropriate issues for energy
        psychology, 181–82
    of energy checking, 171
    of energy psychology, preliminary,
        197–98
    of energy psychology techniques,
        166–68
    of energy psychology treatments, 9–10
        South America, 15–16
    of prayer in prognosis of cardiac
        patients, 174
clinical training, for managing clients
    with psychological difficulties, 95–96
closing phases of treatment, 151–64
Cognitive Behavior Therapy/medication
    compared to energy psychology treat-
        ment, 10
    as a control for clinical testing
        of energy intervention, 197–98,
        210
        of tapping treatments, 202
cognitive dimension, of a psychological
    reversal, 84–85
cognitive dissonance, psychological
    reversal as a form of, 76–78
cognitive psychology, energy interven-
    tions within, 253
Collinge, W., 9, 216
compact disk (CD) cross-reference
    acupoint selection, 121
    advanced meridian treatments, 150
    brain scan images after stimulation of
        acupuncture points, 4
    central and governing meridians, 111
    chakras, 130
    of the Choices Method, 24
    controlled studies of energy checking,
        171

core beliefs, 163
EEG brain scans following tapping and
    acupuncture, 167
embedded topics list, 255–56
energy checking, research on, 42
energy routine, 246
energy systems and benefits of working
    with each, 110
Five Keys to Successful Energy
    Psychology Treatment, 100
five-minute energy routine, 133
home routines, 72
Meridian Assessment Chart, 143
post-traumatic stress disorder treat-
    ment, 2
radiant circuits, 61, 130
radiant energies, 71
relationship of the book to, 12–13
of single-session phobia cures, 16
surrogate treatment, clinical examples,
    168
Temporal Tap used at home, 162
transcripts of EFT sessions by Gary
    Craig, 35
Trauma Debriefing, 160
components, of energy-based psychother-
    apies, 10
concepts of energy psychology, 178–79
conditioned response
    altering, in the meridian system, 40
    to emergencies, energy intervention for
        interrupting, 153–54
connecting heaven and earth
    as a correction for neurological disor-
        ganization, 60–61
    use in bridging techniques, 132
connections, among energy systems of
    the body, 109
consent, informed, 223–25
conventional therapies, energy
    psychology treatments adjunct to, 16
convergent signals, from acupoint stimu-
    lation, 215
corrections for neurological disorgan-
    ization
    generic, 59–64
    stabilizing, 70–71
counterindications, for energy interven-
    tions, 204–6
counter-transference, as an aspect of
    interpersonal influence, 174–75

couples' relationships, use of energy
  interventions to maintain well-being
  in, 253
Cousins, N., 200
Craig, G., 2, 18, 28, 35, 102, 120, 136,
  159, 184, 214, 247
crime victims, rapid symptomatic relief
  from energy treatments, 16
criteria-related psychological reversals,
  79–81
  self-suggestion to resolve, 87–88
cross-crawl
  correction for meridians running back-
    ward, 65–66
  elaborated, for bridging techniques, 131
crown pull, as a correction for neurological disorganization, 60

dancing to the eights, 71
deep impulses, sending, 227
deep-seated survival strategies principle,
  154–55
  and duration of an energy correction,
    152
delirium
  contraindication of energy psychology
    for, clinical trials, 205
  meridian-oriented approach contraindi-
    cated for, 16
deltoid indicator muscle, assessment
  methods, 53–54
dementia
  energy psychology contraindicated for,
    from clinical trials, 205
  meridian-oriented approach contraindi-
    cated for, 16
depression
  energy-based approach adjunctive to,
    16
  major endogenous, energy intervention
    response versus other modalities,
    205
  reactive, energy intervention response
    versus other modalities, 205
  severe, caution in treating with energy
    psychology, 96
detection, of neurological disorder, 57–58
de Vernejoul, P., 112
diagnosis
  categories for energy intervention,
    181–82
  in energy psychology, 139

as an indicator for energy-based
    psychotherapy, 205–6
Diamond, J., 169, 183
dissociation from the object of a phobia,
  151–52
dissociative disorders
  caution in treating with energy
    psychology, 96
  energy intervention adjunctive to, 16
  energy intervention response versus
    other modalities, 205
Dossey, L., 7
Dumitrescu, I., 39

eating disorders, energy intervention
    adjunctive to, 16
Eden, D., xv, 42–43, 59, 110, 112,
  191–92, 218, 235
efficacy of energy psychology, survey
    outcomes, 166–67
eight-point treatment chart, 259
eight tapping points, 26–28
electrical patterns, on the skin, meridians
    corresponding to, 38
electrical resistance of acupoints, 5
electrocardiogram (ECG), as an example
    of biofield measurement, 6
electrochemical impulses
  and acupuncture points, 5
  in the brain, 215
  tapping of meridian points to affect, 19
electrochemical shifts
  in brain chemistry, and acupuncture
    points, 4
  correlation with fear reduction, 5
electroencephalograph (EEG), and treat-
    ment effects using energy
    psychology, 167–68
electrolytic fluid, in the tubule system,
  112
electromagnetic energy, and neurological
    disorganization, 58–59
electromagnetic fields in the human
    body, 215–16
electromagnetic radiation, from merid-
    ians, 111
electromagnetic receptiveness, 35–36
emotion, molecules of, xiii-xiv
emotional disorders, special skills for
    treatment of, 96–97
Emotional Freedom Techniques (EFT),
  17–18

chart, 260
for client self-help, 163
for home study, 16–17
for neutralizing different aspects of a
    problem, 247
overview of, 22–35
selecting acupoints for treatment with,
    120–23
emotional intelligence, increase with
    energy interventions, 253
emotional problems
    delimited, energy psychology treat-
        ments for, 15–16
    individual management of, 253
emotional responses
    reproducing, to test treatment results,
        161–62
    undesired, 100
emotions
    constructive role of, 178
    and meridians, 113
Emoto, M., 7, 119
empathy, energy interventions for
    increasing, 253
empirical evidence
    as the basis of energy intervention, 192
    of energy fields, 9–10
    future demonstration of strengthening
        mental habits and attitudes
        promoting well-being, 252
    of meridian energy flow, tenuous
        nature of, 112–13
    of meridians, 111–13
    of thought fields, 6
    see also clinical studies
energy, defined, 215
energy-based psychotherapy. see energy
    psychology
energy checking, 37–55
    assessing the usefulness of, 170–72
    for assessing treatment, 142
    to confirm SUD ratings, 103
    for homolateral patterning, 70
    introducing to a client, 222
    overview of, 41–42
    procedure for, 41–42
    wording for, 89
Energy Diagnostic and Treatment
    Methods (EDxTM), 17
Energy Diagnostic and Treatment Methods
    (Gallo), 43

energy dimension of psychological
    reversals, 85–86
energy field
    activation of, by energy point stimula-
        tion, 187
    impact on physical matter, 8
    information carried by, 208
energy gateway points, 17
energy interventions
    formulating, 127–36
    neurological and electromagnetic
        receptiveness for, 35–36
    for neurological disorganization, 58–59
    psychological reversals and, 78–79
    purpose of, 109
    to resolve psychological reversals,
        90–91
    in the set-up affirmation, 25–26
energy medicine, principles of, 218–19
Energy Medicine (Eden), 43, 59, 110
energy pathways, see meridians
energy points, stimulating, in psycholog-
    ical reversal treatment, 87
energy psychology, approaches within,
    251
Energy Psychology Desktop Companion,
    The (Grudermeyer & Grudermeyer),
    161
Energy Psychology Interactive
    Advisory Board of, clinical records on
        successful treatment, 9–10
    principles and practice of, 14
Energy Routine, 246
energy sessions, common elements of,
    244
energy system
    involved in the problem, identifying,
        149–50
    psychological reversals and, 78–79
energy therapy, see energy psychology
energy triggers, and corrections, 64
ethics
    concerns about, in future applications
        of energy interventions, 253–54
    of disclosure of personal information,
        107
    of energy intervention, 97–98
evidence of the efficacy of energy
    psychology, 199–214
exercise, as cure for neurological disor-
    ganization, 58

expectations, the client's, exploring in initial interviews, 94
experiences, identifying for treatment, 159
experiment with energy interventions, 253
eye contact, during an energy check, 50
Eye Movement Desensitization and Reprocessing (EMDR), 200
for client self-help, 163
Eye Roll Technique
as an anchoring technique, 155
as a bridging technique, 135

fears
extinguishing a response to, 153
neutralizing early in therapy, 102
Feinstein, D., 118
field of information, as a component of thought, 118
Fifth International Energy Psychology Conference, 165–66
fight-or-flight response
meridian energies in, 114–15
and neurological disorganization, 66
and psychological reversal, 86
as rapid adaptability example, 153
first correction, assessment after, 146
five element theory (*wu zing*), 150, 177, 234
"Five Keys to Successful Energy Psychology Treatment", 100
five-minute energy routine, between rounds of acupoint stimulation, 133
flow chart, for the opening phases of treatment, 105–6
follow-up, relapse rate in control and energy intervention groups, study, 211–12
formative events, and energy intervention, survey outcomes, 179–81
formula, for addressing psychological reversal, 90
formulation, of energy interventions, 127–36
Fowler, R., 39
Friedman, P., 214
future developments in energy psychology, 252–54

Gach, M.R., 27
gall bladder meridian, 236, 264
issues governed by, 114–15

Gallo, F.P., xv, 43, 79, 93, 95, 137, 150, 157, 221
Galvanic skin response, change in, by visualization or prayer, 216
Galvin, M., 212–13
gamut point, 30
balancing procedures with, 158
in the bridging technique, 135
tapping to resolve psychological reversals, 90
general indicator muscle, 43–46
Gerber, R., 9, 216
Gestalt therapy, 209
getting started, in the CD and the book, 12–13
global psychological reversals, 79
self-suggestion to resolve, 87–88
goals for energy psychology, 245–48
governing meridian, 236–37, 265
functions of, 113
group psychotherapy, integrating energy psychology with, 249–50
Grudermeyer, D., 100, 161
Grudermeyer, R., 100, 161

hand-over-head check, for polarity reversal, 68–69
hands-on training, in energy checking, 43
Harris, W.S., 7
Hartung, J., 212–13
healing forces, channeling, survey outcomes, 173–74
health care specialist, for conditions underlying neurological imbalance, 73
heartbreak, healing of, 193
heart meridian, 237, 266
functions of, 113
heart rate variability, correlation with subjective units of distress, 103
heart signals, of client and therapist, relationship between, 175
hippocampus
acupoint stimulation transmitted to, 213–14
imaging of, and registration of emotional problems, 208
home setting
anchoring treatment success in, 147–49
ethical considerations in assigning self-- treatment, 97–98
routines for neurological disorganization, 72

supporting successful outcome of treatment, 162–64
homolateral crossover, as a correction for meridians running backwards, 66
homolateral patterning, 69–71
hooking up, to resolve psychological reversals, 90
Hover-Kramer, D., 9
hsue (acupuncture points), 213–14
Hu, X., 111–12
Hui, K.K.S., 4
Human Energy Systems Laboratory, 175
Hunt, V., 43, 216

immune response
    and psychological reversal, 86
    as rapid adaptability example, 153
immune system, and the triple warmer, 66
indications for energy interventions, 204–6
indicator muscle
    accessing the problem state with, 102
    assessment methods using, 53–54
    balancing procedures with, 158
    for checking ocular lock, 69
    Positive Belief Scale corroborated by testing, 157
    problem signaled by, 141–43
    qualifying
        at the beginning of therapy, 98–99
        with a new client, 54–55
information, transmission by structures outside the brain, 6
informational substances, biochemical, xiii
informed consent, 223–25
infrared photography, meridians revealed by, 111–12
inhalation and exhalation, for tapping rhythm, 143
initial interviews, exploring client expectations in, 94
insight
    in energy psychology, 177–78
    place of, 188
Institute of HeartMath, 175
intention
    failure to conform to, psychological reversal as a form of, 76–78
    role of, in energy psychology, 173–74

International Society for the Study of Subtle Energy and Energy Medicine, 216
interpersonal influences on treatment outcomes, 174–76
intervening psychological reversals, 80, 82–84
issues, appropriate, for energy psychology, survey outcomes, 181–82

Johnson, 203
Journal of Clinical Psychology, 167, 203

K-27 points, 19–20
    for correcting ocular lock, 69
    for correcting meridians running backward, 65
karate chop points, tapping to resolve psychological reversals, 90
Kendall, F.M.P., 43
Kenyon, J., 39
ki, defined, 6
kidney meridian, 234, 237, 267

laboratory studies
    of energy checking, 42–43
    of meridian energies and neurons, 39
language, for describing energy intervention, 220–21
large intestine meridian, 237–38, 268
    issues governed by, 114
Larson, V., 175–76
latissimus dorsi indicator muscle, 45
    assessment methods, 53–54
law of opposites, in acupuncture, 138
Leadbeater, C.W., 118
learning disorders, energy intervention response versus other modalities, 205
LeDoux, J.E., 4
left/right eye rotation, as a check for ocular lock, 69
Leg Lock
    for locking in the problem state, 104
    in treatment of a problematic thought field, 144
licensing of energy-based psychotherapists, 184–86
life force as a subtle energy, 216
life lessons, paradoxical response to relieving symptoms, 96–97

limitations of energy-based therapy, 95–97
links to web sites, 277–78
liver meridian, 238, 269
localization of energy, for determining treatment points, 142–43
locking in the problem state, 103–5
longevity of energy corrections, 152–55
LORETA tomography for brain imaging, 208–11
lung meridian, 238, 270
lymphatic congestion, 72
lymphatic points, as sore spots, 25

McAdams, D.P., 77
McCraty, R., 6
McCreary, E.K., 43
magnetic field of the heart, detecting, 175
magnetic resonance imaging (MRI), acupuncture treatment results studied by, 112
May, Rollo, 175
mechanical/energetic component, of energy system treatment, 17–18
mechanical mechanisms of energy intervention, 167–68
mechanical stimulation of acupuncture points, 252–53
mechanisms of energy intervention, 167–68, 207–9
mechanoreceptors, stimulation of, 213–14
medial lemniscus
    acupoint stimulation transmitted to, 213–14
    signals from acupoint tapping mediated through, 208
medications for anxiety, versus tapping treatments, 202–3
megbe, defined, 6
memory, clearing, 247–48
mental activity, impact on physical matter, 7–8
mental movie, 33
mental retardation, contraindication of energy psychology for, clinical trials, 205
meridian assessment chart, 140–43
meridian diagnostic points, *see* alarm points
meridian energy response to enclosed places, 2

meridians
    advanced treatments using, 137–50
    assessing the state of, by energy checking, 170–72
    assessment chart, 261
    basics of use in treatment, 109–25
    central, 111
    charts of, table of contents, 257–76
    compared with other energy systems, 182–83
    conflict in, and psychological reversal, 86
    correction for a disturbed pattern in, 206–7
    disruption of, in psychological reversal, 78
    emotional themes of, self-suggestions attuned to, 144–46
    and the emotions, 234–43
        survey outcomes, 176–77
    energy checking of, 37–41
    energy psychology treatment focused on, 15–16
    governing, 111
    intervention flow chart, 241
    intervention into, 116–25
    isolating and treating, 136
    nature of the, 110–11
    reasons for inadequate response to stimulation of, 149
    running backward, 64–66
    survival response disruptive to, 154
    tapping, 26, 129–30
    thought's effects upon, 217
    treatment checklist, 242–43
    working with, 150
Meridian Treatment Checklist, 148
Messages from Water (Emoto), 7, 119
metabolic substances, natural, prescribing for rapid relief of panic and anxiety, 201
metaphor, thought field as, survey outcomes, 172–73
micro-focus, on the aspects of the problem, 136
Mildad, M.R., 153
Miller, N., 38
motor skills disorders, energy intervention response versus other modalities, 205
Motoyama, H., 112
Moyers, B., 9

multiple energy systems, relative importance of, survey outcomes, 182–83
multipoint approach, 137–39
Muscles: Testing and Function (Kendall and McCreary), 43
muscle testing, 41. *see also* energy checking
muscular units of distress (MUD)
and choice point selection, 146–47
energy checks to corroborate SUD rating, 103
between rounds of acupoint stimulation, 134–35
Myss, C., 43

Nader, K., 4
navel/K-27 massage, for ocular lock correction, 69
navel/skull base hold, 21
navel/tailbone massage, 21
navel/third-eye hook-up, 21
neural connections of brain centers triggering problematic emotions, 253
neuroimaging, in a clinical study of energy intervention, 211
neurological changes, from energy point stimulation, 187–88
neurological coding, of mental and behavioral processes, 173
neurological correlates
of energy intervention, 208
of treatment effects, 167–68
neurological disorganization, 47, 57–73
checking in outcome projection, 158
identifying in the opening phases of treatment, 99
procedures correcting for other energy disruptions, 149–50
rating the importance of, survey outcomes, 178–79
between rounds of acupoint stimulation, 133
summary chart, 231
neurological receptiveness of energy intervention, 35–36
neurological sequence, clinical phenomena not explained by, 168
neurolymphatic massage, for dislodging toxins, 72

neurons
brain functions of, 215
firing of, link to meridian energies, 39
neurotransmitter profiles
of acupoint stimulation effects, 198
anxiety patterns in, clinical study of energy intervention, 212
neurotransmitters, release by tapping of meridian points, 19
neutralization, of debilitating memories, 2
Nine Gamut Procedure, 29–30
as a bridging technique, 130–31
clinical testing of, 203
efficacy of, survey outcomes, 169–70
see also gamut point
non-invasive energy interventions, 227
norepinephrine, change in levels of, with energy intervention, 212
normalization, in treating anxiety, 4–5

obsessive compulsive disorders
energy intervention response of, clinical study, 205
relapse after treatment, 212
ocular lock, 69
one-point-per-meridian protocol, 123–25
treatment chart, 260
opening phases
task sequence in, 226
of treatment, practicing, 128
orbital frontal cortex, imaging of, and registration of emotional problems, 208
O-Ring Test, for energy checking, 46
Oschman, J.L., 9, 155, 216
Outcome Projection Procedure, 157
over-energy, 207
overview of *Energy Psychology Interactive*, 11–12

palm-around-ear check, for the triple warmer in overwhelm, 67
panic disorders, energy psychology treatments for, 15–16
success of, 181
parietal lobes, acupoint stimulation transmitted to, 214
pathways of the body's energy system, 109

patient, energy as the, 218
Pearsall, P., 6
pericardium meridian, 238–39, 271
personal issues, Emotional Freedom Techniques (EFT) applied to, 32–34
personality disorders
  energy-based approach versus primary treatment for, 16
  energy intervention response versus other modalities, 205
  special skills for treatment of, 95–96
Pert, C.B., 6
phobias
  energy psychology treatment for, 15–16, 151–52
  height, energy psychology treatment of, 1–2
  relieving with energy treatment, 16–17
    success of, 181
  uncomplicated, 3–4
    energy treatment of, 17
physical considerations, prior to an energy check, 49–50
physical factors, effects on energy interventions, 246
physical illness, meridian functions in relation to, 234
placebo effect versus energy psychology, 169–70
polarity reversal, 68–69
polarity unswitching, correction for neurological disorganization, 71
Polglase, K., 167
Porges, S., 115
Positive Belief Scale (PBS), 157
positive psychology, energy interventions for increasing optimism within, 253
positive thinking in psychology, 187
post-traumatic stress disorder (PTSD), energy psychology treatment of, 1–2, 15–16, 181
practice sessions
  anchoring techniques, 155–57
  balancing the meridians, 124–25
  complete, 148–49
  for neurological disorganization, 73
  for resolving psychological reversal, 91
  for verbal treatments, 145–46
prana, defined, 6

prayer
  effect of, on prognosis of cardiac patients, 174
  healing by use of, 168
  physical effects of, 7–8, 216
prefrontal cortex, acupoint stimulation transmitted to, 214
principle of highest leverage, 100
principles of energy medicine, 218–19
problems
  locking energetically to the body, 93
  suppressing, as a hazard of energy intervention, 180
problem state
  accessing, 101–2
  activating, 28
  assessing distress associated with, 103
  locking in, 103–5
procedural issues, in energy psychology, 168–70
professional affiliations, of Energy Psychology Codnference attendees, 166
professional mental health services, indications for, 248
professionals
  energy psychology in relation to, 184
  future use of energy interventions by, 253
  training of, for energy psychology practice, 97
projective identification, as an aspect of interpersonal influence, 174–75
protection of the body, energy system for, 109
protocols, defining for clinical trials, 203
psychodynamics, and energy psychology, 180
psychological cycles, energies that control, 109
psychological equilibrium, disruption of by intervention, 96
psychological factors
  effects of, on energy interventions, 247–48
  in energy system treatment, 17–18
psychological problems
  aspects of, 34–35
  balancing meridians involved in, 116

complex aspects of, and duration of treatment, 159
meridian relationship to, 39–40
psychological reversals, 31, 75–91
checking in outcome projection, 158
effect on energy techniques for treatment, 57
identifying in the opening phases of treatment, 99
rating importance of, survey outcomes, 178–79
resolving internal conflict about change in, 23
between rounds of acupoint stimulation, 133–34
summary chart, 232
psychological stress, response to, in the meridian system, 115
psychological structures, conflict among, 77
psychopathology, latent conditions of, and ethical considerations for energy psychology, 98
psychosis, caution in treating with energy psychology, 96
psychosocial history
benefits from taking, 95–96
identifying target problem through, 100
psychotherapeutic resonance, 175–76
psychotherapists, energy-based, licensing of, 184–86
psychotherapy
energy intervention and, 249–50
integrating energy psychology methods into practice, 184–85
psychotic disorders
contraindication of a meridian-oriented approach for, 16
contraindication of energy psychology for, clinical trials, 205
public domain, energy based methods in the, 184
Pulos, L., 42, 117
punishments, shaping the young with, 85

Quirk, G.J., 153

radiant circuits, 150
activating as a correction for neurological disorganization, 61–62
compared with other energy systems, 182–83

radiant energies, 110
and dancing to the eights, 71
Radin, D., 6–7, 216
radioactive phosphorous isotopes, injecting into acupuncture points to identify meridians, 112
Radomski, S., 73
randomized studies, pilot, of success rates with energy psychology treatments, 10
rape victims, rapid symptomatic relief from energy treatments, 16
rapid adaptability principle, and duration of an energy correction, 152–54
rapport, with the client, 94
receptors, of acupuncture points, 5
reframing, of psychological reversal, 84–85
Reich, W., 209
reinforcements, for shaping the young, 85
rejection, energy intervention response versus other modalities, 204
reminder phrase
adjustment of, 32
for keeping a problem state active, 104
in a tapping sequence, 28–29
see also affirmations
research, on energy field's claims, 10
resolution, of psychological reversals, 87–89
resonance locking, techniques for, 104–5
retraumatization, while accessing the problem state, 102
reverse walk check, for meridians running backward, 65
Rose-Neil, S., 112

Sakai, 203
sandwich treatment sequence, 128–32
Sarkisyanz, H., 38, 116
Schafe, G.E., 4
scientific scrutiny of subtle energies, 216
self-affirmation, in client home techniques, 163–64
self-esteem, targeting in shaping behavior, 85
self-judgment, and psychological reversal, 85
self-negation, and psychological reversal, 85
self-sabotage, psychological reversal as, 76–77

self-suggestions
  based on the properties of the
    meridian being treated, 144–45
  pairing with an energy point, to resolve
    psychological reversals, 87–88
separation anxiety disorders, energy
  psychology treatments for, 15–16
serotonin
  change in levels of, with energy inter-
    vention, 212
  secretion of, correlation with tapping
    points, 208
setbacks, addressing, 162–63
set-up affirmation, 23–26, 31
  for psychological reversal, 78
  see also affirmations
Shealy, C.N., 43
"signal and brain wave" hypothesis, 5–6
signals, during an energy check, 51
single-point-per-meridian treatment, 138
  protocol for, basic, 128–29
skepticism
  about energy psychology, 191–94
  replies to, 3–4
sleep, as a cure for neurological disorder,
    58
small intestine meridian, 239, 272
smoothing behind the ears, correction for
    the triple warmer in overwhelm, 67
somatic counterparts of psychological
    states, 39
somato-sensory cortex, acupoint stimula-
    tion transmission to, 214
sore spots
  chest, for neurolymphatic massage, 72
  massaging to resolve psychological
    reversals, 90
  and set-up affirmation, 25
specific-context psychological reversals,
    79–80
  checking for, 101
  self-suggestion to resolve, 88
SPIN, for assessing energy interventions,
    210–11
spindle cell releasing maneuver, 53
  practice for, 55
spindle cell strengthening maneuver, 55
spirituality, of energy psychology, survey
    outcomes, 173–74
spleen hug, as a correction for triple
    warmer in overwhelm, 68
spleen-pancreas meridian, 239–40, 273

spleen points, 19–20
  tapping to resolve psychological rever-
    sals, 90
SQUID-based magnetometer, for
    measurement of a biofield, 6
stagnant energy, 207
stomach meridian, 240, 274
  affirmation for, example, 144–45
  functions of, 113
stress-related illnesses, meridian energies
    in, 114
subjective units of distress (SUD)
  assessing in the opening phase of treat-
    ment, 93
  and choice point selection, 146–47
  for evaluating choice of meridians, 129
  for evaluating treatment success, 132
  lowering in the opening phases of
    treatment, 109
  lowering with the Eye Roll, 155
  in the opening phase of treatment, 93,
    103
  between rounds of acupoint stimula-
    tion, 134–36
subtle energy, xiv, 7–9, 216–17
  as a missing link in psychology, 187–89
supervised practice, in energy checking,
    43
surrogate treatments, healing by use of,
    168
survival mechanism
  and psychological reversal, 86
  and the triple warmer, 66
symptoms, purposes of, 96
synesthesia, 41
systematic desensitization, 40–41, 206–7

Tapas Acupressure Technique, 17
tapping
  clinical study of treatment results, 202
  versus examination of the source of the
    problem, survey outcomes, 177–78
  instructions for, 227–30
  interventions using, versus systematic
    desensitization, 207
  method for, 122–23
  points for, bilateral, 123
  signals from, to the parietal cortex, 208
  techniques for, 210
    in the client's home, 163–64
    defined, 17–18
  verbalization with, 145

tapping sequence, 26–29
    for anxiety and panic patients, 200
    basic, 230
    to project successful treatment into the
        future, 158
    repeating, 30–31
target problem, identification of, 22–23,
        100
Tearless Trauma technique, 102
technetium, acupoint injection of, for
        mapping, 112
Temporal Tap, home use of, 162
theory of energy psychology, 199–214
Therapeutic Touch, clinical research on,
        166
Therapeutic Touch (Hover-Kramer), 9
therapist, energetic exchange with the
        client, 175
Third Eye Tap, anchoring with, 155
Third Eye Up technique
    for locking in the problem state, 104
    in treatment of a problematic thought
        field, 144
thought
    impact of, on the physical world,
        118–20
    as subtle energy, 216–17
Thought Energy Synchronization
        Therapies (TEST), 17
thought field
    for accessing the problem state, 101–2
    acupoints for altering, 117–22
    disturbance of, association with
        meridian energies, 119
    efficacy of, 172–73
    empirical evidence of, 6
    problematic
        accessing, 154
        in advanced meridian treatments,
            144
Thought Field Therapy (TFT), 17–18,
        118, 209
    selecting acupoints for treatment,
        120–23
three energy checks, postures for, 43–48
three-finger notch, in finger tapping, 28
three-part/three-minute sequence, for
        correcting neurological disorganiza-
        tion, 59–64

Three Thumps/Three Navel Touch,
        18–22
    as a correction for neurological disor-
        ganization, 59
thymus points, 19–20
Tiller, W.A., 6, 9, 216
touch, in energy-based psychotherapy,
        51–52
Touch and Breathe method, 122
Tourette's syndrome, energy intervention
        response versus other modalities,
        205
toxins
    accumulation at lymphatic points, 25
    neurolymphatic massage for dislodging,
        72
    rating the importance of, survey
        outcomes, 178–79
transference, as an aspect of interpersonal
        influence, 174–75
trauma
    caution in treating with energy
        psychology, 96
    relationship with earlier traumas,
        159–60
traumatization, as a hazard of energy
        intervention, 180
treatment
    from assessment to, 142–46
    in energy psychology, 139
    opening phases of, 93–107
    outcome of
        challenging, 161–62
        projecting into the future, 157–59
    strategies for
        defined, 40
        generic, offered by Emotional
            Freedom Techniques (EFT), 23
treatment point, stimulation of, 143–44
    to treat a problematic thought field,
        144–45
"treatment sandwich", 30
trigger event, in activation of a problem,
        120
triple warmer meridian, 111, 240, 275
    conscripting energy from other merid-
        ians, 114
    defined, 66
    emergency response and, 161

in overwhelm, 66–68
and psychological reversal, 86
and rapid adaptability, 153–54
tubule system, parallel to the meridian
pathways, identifying, 112

under-energy, 207

verbal treatments, practice session,
145–46
videotaped treatment sessions from
websites, 16
Vietnam veteran, energy psychology
treatment of post-traumatic stress
disorder of, 1–2
visualization, physical impact of, 7, 216
Voll, R., 38, 116

wakan, defined, 6
Wang, P., 111–12
water crystals, modification of, by
thought, 8, 118–19

Wayne Cook posture
as a correction for neurological disorganization, 62–63
for the triple warmer in overwhelm, 67
websites for bringing energy systems to
the public, 184–85
Wells, S., 167, 245
will, place of, 188
Wolpe, J., 40, 206–7
Wu, B., 111–12
wu zing, 234

X and parallel line test, for homolateral
patterning, 70

Yale-Brown Scale, for assessing energy
interventions, 211
yang, 234
yesod, defined, 6
yin, 234
yoga, energy centers in, 110

OTHER PROGRAMS FROM INNERSOURCE

Energy Medicine
Energy Psychology
Energies of Love

Books

Videos

CDs/DVDs

Seminars

e-Groups

Home Study CE

www.innersource.net

24-hour Order Line
(or request product list)
1-800-835-8332